John Lonergan was born in Bansha, County Tipperary, in 1947. When he retired in June 2010 he was Ireland's longest-serving prison officer. For twenty-two of his forty-two years in the prison service he ran Mountjoy Prison.

The Governor

JOHN LONERGAN

PENGUIN BOOKS

PENGUIN BOOKS

Published by the Penguin Group
Penguin Books Ltd, 80 Strand, London WC2R ORL, England
Penguin Group (USA) Inc., 375 Hudson Street, New York, New York 10014, USA
Penguin Group (Canada), 90 Eglinton Avenue East, Suite 700, Toronto, Ontario, Canada M4P 2Y3
(a division of Pearson Penguin Canada Inc.)
Penguin Ireland, 25 St Stephen's Green, Dublin 2, Ireland (a division of Penguin Books Ltd)
Penguin Group (Australia), 250 Camberwell Road, Camberwell, Victoria 3124, Australia
(a division of Pearson Australia Group Pty Ltd)
Penguin Books India Pvt Ltd, 11 Community Centre, Panchsheel Park, New Delhi – 110 017, India
Penguin Group (NZ), 67 Apollo Drive, Rosedale, Auckland 0632, New Zealand
(a division of Pearson New Zealand Ltd)
Penguin Books (South Africa) (Pty) Ltd, 24 Sturdee Avenue, Rosebank,
Johannesburg 2196, South Africa

Penguin Books Ltd, Registered Offices: 80 Strand, London WC2R ORL, England

www.penguin.com

First published by Penguin Ireland 2010
Published in Penguin Books 2011

1

Copyright © John Lonergan, 2010
All rights reserved

The moral right of the author has been asserted

Typeset by Palimpsest Book Production Limited, Falkirk, Stirlingshire
Printed in England by Clays Ltd, St Ives plc

ISBN: 978-0-718-19147-4

www.greenpenguin.co.uk

MIX
Paper from
responsible sources
FSC
www.fsc.org   FSC™ C018179

Penguin Books is committed to a sustainable
future for our business, our readers and our
planet. This book is made from paper certified
by the Forest Stewardship Council.

To those in our society who never got a chance in life,
and still don't . . .

Apart from those prisoners and personnel clearly identified in the text by being given their full names, all other prisoners and personnel mentioned have been given pseudonyms to protect their privacy.

Contents

On 27 March 1850, immediately following the famine when hundreds of thousands of Irish people died of starvation, Mountjoy Prison opened for business. The building is exactly the same today as the day it opened 160 years ago.

On 2 June 1984, I became governor of Mountjoy, serving for twenty-two years. My name is John Lonergan. This is my story. It's also the previously untold story of why prison is such a costly, destructive and brutal system.

My First Day in Prison

I'll never know for sure what made me answer the advert. Perhaps it was just destiny. Now here I was going into the unknown. I knew nothing whatsoever about the job. I knew nobody who worked in a prison and I knew nothing about prisoners. I left Dublin on the evening of Friday, 7 March 1968, travelling by train to Limerick City, with all my worldly goods in a suitcase and a letter from the Department of Justice:

> Report to the Governor,
> Limerick Prison,
> Mulgrave Street, Limerick
> 10 a.m. on Saturday 8th March 1968

The letter instructed me to bring two white shirts, a dark blue or black tie, and to present the letter at the gate on arrival.

Saturday was a nice dry morning. The B&B where I'd spent the night was a short walk to the jail. In my suitcase was an alarm clock, a razor, a toothbrush, a pair of shoes, my few clothes and a pair of football boots. I also carried my hurley, since hurling had been a big part of my life in Tipperary.

As a boy attending hurling matches in the famous Gaelic Grounds on the Ennis Road in Limerick City, I'd often passed the jail on my way to and from home, because Mulgrave Street linked Limerick City with the Tipperary Road. Halfway up on the right was Shaw's Meat Factory, then Gerry O'Dea's pub. And just before St Joseph's Mental Hospital was the jail.

The jail stuck out. It looked old and depressing. Beyond the silver railings and well-kept lawns were the high walls. As I made my way to the imposing wooden doors in the high wall facing Mulgrave Street, I thought to myself, *What's behind them? What'll it be like? Am I going to survive in there?* Later I learned that this entrance to the prison was called the main gate. It comprised two huge heavy wooden doors, and the left-hand door had a smaller door of normal size integrated into it to allow people to pass through without the big doors having to be opened. It was called a wicket door. I gave the huge black metal knocker on the small door such a belt that the noise could've wakened the dead.

A small slide opened and a man peered out at me. He opened the wicket door and I could see he was in his twenties, just a few years older than me, and was dressed in a dark blue uniform, a white shirt, blue tie and uniform cap. After I presented him with the letter from the Department of Justice he introduced himself as Frank McCarthy and said, 'They're expecting you', which put me at ease. We were in a small enclosed space. About five yards in front, opposite the door I had come through, was a huge steel gate painted silver. To the left and the right of where we were standing were wooden doors. He brought me through the door on the right into a small office full of books and journals of all shapes and sizes. I later discovered that they were the records of everyone coming into and going out of Limerick Prison. I watched Frank writing the time and my name into a big ledger. Then he said, 'We'll go to the general office. There's a welcoming party there to meet you.'

We passed through the big steel gate, which had a massive lock that needed a huge key to open it. He led me towards an old three-storey building where I was introduced to two men. One was the chief officer, Patrick Crowley, who wore a dark blue uniform like Frank's. Frank had to return to his post at the main gate but said he'd see me later. His friendliness had given me a boost. I felt if he'd survived the job, I would too. Though I knew nothing about ranks, I noticed that Patrick Crowley had two gold stripes on each epaulette and a gold cloth harp on the front of his cap. On a long, leather strap hanging from his arm was a huge bunch of the biggest keys I'd ever seen. He was friendly and very energetic, and seemed the complete opposite to the other man, who was behind a counter. He was wearing glasses, civilian clothes and had a professorial air. He was the clerk, P. M. Kelly, and little did I know that this low-key, quiet man would be one of the most influential people in my life.

He produced a bundle of forms for me to sign, and it seemed to take ages. They dealt with such issues as the use of political influence, which was forbidden, and circulars about pensions, but the one that really stood out was the Bankruptcy Act. I could be sacked if I was declared bankrupt. So I knew I'd have to be careful; my gross wage was twelve pounds and I'd signed a form to authorize a one-pound-a-week wage deduction for official accommodation.

Then Patrick Crowley announced, 'You'll need a uniform', and rushed me over to the stores at such a pace, I was almost running. The General Stores was a small two-storey building close to the main gate where all the supplies were stored for the prison. Behind a wooden counter was a stocky older man who had a big head of white hair and wore glasses. This was Mick Ryan, the storekeeper. He was quick to tell me that he was a Limerick man, and when I told him I was from Tipperary, he slagged me about Tipperary people being tight with money and thinking they could play hurling.

Mick Ryan did his best to find a uniform to fit me, but everything he had in stock was too big. I was of medium height and build: five foot eight and eleven stone.

'Waist?' he asked.

'Thirty-two,' I said.

'And,' he muttered, 'short leg.'

He went into a small room at the back and soon came out with dark blue trousers, threw them on the counter and said, with a smirk on his face 'You'll grow into them. Jacket?'

'Size 40,' I said.

'Doubt that I have anything that small. All the fellows here have big bellies.' When he returned he announced, 'This is the smallest I have.'

I had no problem with the tunic. It looked okay. It had two rows of silver buttons at the front and a belt with a big silver buckle.

He threw me a cap for size. It was so big, it fell down over my eyes. 'I thought all Tipperary men had big heads,' he said. I knew he was joking, and joined in the banter. I had expected it all to be very formal and militaristic, so I was relieved that those in charge were quite relaxed and normal. When he eventually found a suitable cap, he gave me a silver badge for it. It was round, about two inches in diameter, and had a harp engraved in the centre.

'It has two purposes,' said Mick. 'One's to fix it on the front of the cap and the other is that when you're lodging your money in the Post Office you can stamp the lodgement forms with the harp. Coming from Tipperary, you'll be using it often!' Then he rooted through a box under the counter and handed me a silver whistle. He told me it was so that I could raise the alarm if I was in trouble or to prevent an escape. 'Keep this safe and put it in your breast pocket. Keep it there until you're drawing your last breath, then blow out through it and help will arrive, hopefully. But I wouldn't bet my life on it, knowing the energetic lot working here.'

I said, 'They obviously need more Tipperary men in Limerick.'

In a big journal I signed for the uniform, and a young officer came to show me my living quarters. He introduced himself as Pat Carroll from County Westmeath. He led me across the grounds to an old tower located in the very centre of the jail. Its main function was to form a link between the four wings of the prison. In the basement was the furnace for heating the prison. It burned coal and the cinders were used to make dry pathways around the outside of the boundary wall. Following Pat into the tower and up the dark stone stairs, I entered a big, cold-looking room. It had three wardrobes and three iron beds. He pointed to the bed on the right. It had a neat pile of white sheets, three woollen blankets and a white bedspread. 'The others are taken,' he said.

Then it struck me: I'd be sharing a room with two strangers. It was a bit of a shock and totally unexpected. I'd be undressing with no privacy, an experience I was not looking forward to.

While Pat helped me make the bed, we chatted about the jail, Dublin and of course Tipperary. Again, I was meeting someone who would become a lifelong friend. He fixed the badge on the cap for me and I tried it on. I found it uncomfortable and didn't like it. Indeed, I never got used to it and thought it was a nuisance.

'Put on your uniform,' he said, 'and I'll be back to take you to the mess for lunch.'

Everything had happened quickly from the moment I knocked on the gate. There was no time for reflection, but all the officers I had met were friendly and helpful and that was a good beginning. I was ready to start training.

The officers' mess was a new building at the front of the prison near the General Stores. It had a kitchen, a dining room and rooms for about fourteen single officers. A cook came in every morning to make breakfast and dinner. Married officers went home for lunch at 12.45 and returned at 2 p.m., but most of the officers were in their twenties and single men.

After lunch, all the staff lined up in the small hallway leading to a gate in the curved wall of the old tower – the circle gate – which led into the prison proper. I joined the line-up. My name was called out by the chief, Pat Crowley, who was holding a huge book. He shouted, 'Lonergan!'

'*Anseo!*'

Then he began reading out duties. 'Ryan: kitchen. Burke: wood yard. O'Keeffe: reception. Lonergan: laundry.'

I didn't have time to ask what being given laundry meant. The chief left at full speed, telling me to report to his office. Following him, I went through the circle gate, into the circular ground floor of the tower and then down three steps into one of the wings. The chief's desk was in the first cell on the left. When he sat down, he reeled off numerous instructions, handed me two rulebooks and said, 'Read the Governor's Orders as soon as possible. They are in the drawer in the desk in the circle.'

Suddenly he was up from his desk again.

'Follow me.'

To keep up with him I was almost running again. He sped ahead, down one of the wings, out a steel gate and into what he called the wood yard, where some prisoners were sawing wood with cross-cut saws. Others were splitting blocks with axes. Their shirts were a sort of orange brown and made of heavy cotton.

I followed the chief into a shed where there were six big, white enamel sinks with an old wooden washboard in each. Five prisoners were washing, one was rinsing and another operated the dryers. With prisoners being issued a clean shirt and socks once a week, there was a lot of washing, and it was hard labour. I will never forget the shrivelled-up skin on the men's hands as they scrubbed clothes on the wooden washing boards, using white carbolic soap to soften the dirt.

'Take charge of them,' said the chief.

Standing inside the door that opened onto the wood yard, as the prisoners worked away, I looked on. This was training on the job, but the prisoners knew I hadn't a clue. At that stage, my future was irrelevant. I had no ambition and certainly no idea that I was starting on a journey that would lead to me governing Ireland's largest prison for almost a quarter of a century.

1. Early Life Lessons in Bansha

I was born on 3 September 1947 at our home in the townland of Toureen in the parish of Bansha and Kilmoyler in County Tipperary. I was the third of eight children: four boys – Ned, Paddy, me and Jim – and four girls – Cait, Chrissie, Philomena and Agnes; Agnes and Jim were twins. My father, Ned, was a native of Toureen and was born, reared and lived all his life in the same house, a thatched cottage on a small farm of bogs and rushes and hills and furze bushes. He worked as a handyman-cum-gardener in Toureen Wood House, a big place at the front of Toureen Woods, first for a retired army doctor, Dr Heffernan, and later for the American who bought it, Mr Roderick. When we were small he was working for four old Irish pounds and nine shillings a week. As well as being a handyman and a gardener he was also a bit of a craftsman.

My parents married in October 1943. My mother, Brigid Peters, came from Ballydrehid, the townland next to Toureen on the Cahir side. They met at a 'platform' on 'the green', a small open space on the side of the road leading from Cahir to Kilmoyler Church. Platforms were big wooden floors set up at a crossroads or on open ground that acted as open-air dancehalls. A few local musicians provided the music, and people danced until the early hours. My father was much older than my mother: when they got married he was forty-four and she was twenty-nine. They were married at 8 a.m. in Kilmoyler Church and went back to her family's house for the wedding breakfast. We used to ask her, 'Where did you go on your honeymoon?' and she would say, 'Honeymoon, never heard of a honeymoon, the only honeymoon I got was that we drove around the roads in the pony and trap for an hour or so.'

My mother was one of nine. Her aunt, Kate Peters, had drowned when the *Titanic* sank in 1912. She had been on her way back to America, where she worked in a boarding house on the lower eastside of

Manhattan. Her third-class fare cost her seven pounds and fifteen shillings. Her father, my great-grandfather, later got forty pounds and six shillings in compensation for her death. Three of my mother's brothers emigrated to America in the 1930s and two of her sisters emigrated to England. My mother lived in Chester herself for two years. After coming back from England she worked for a family called Strappes in Clonmel until marrying my father.

One of our great thrills as children was getting a parcel from America. My mother's brother Pattie had a shop in New York, and he used to send home food and clothes, a box or two of biscuits and a few bags of sweets. I can still see the blue and red stripy airmail envelopes that arrived regularly. There was always a few dollars in them, and dollars were worth a lot of money in those days. They were a godsend and she was always delighted to get them.

One of my early memories of my father is of watching him up on a ladder thatching the roof of our house. Thatching was an art, but also a big drawn-out job. First up was getting the straw or the rushes. He used to pull the straw from a big reek, because not all straw was suitable and it had to be hand-picked for thatching. When he used rushes, he used to cut them himself in the bogs with a scythe. Then he had to get what were called scallops. Scallops were made out of sally bushes, and they grew in bogs beside ponds. He used to cut them with a slash hook and bring them home in big bundles on his back. He was a small man, but he had powerful shoulders and didn't know his own strength. Then, with the pointing of the scallops, the real skilled work began. He would bring a bundle of the sally sticks into the kitchen and sit near the open fire, cutting the sticks into lengths of about two feet and splitting them down the middle. Then he'd pare both ends until they had sharp points like arrows. The sally was very flexible, and he would bend the scallops into hook shapes and drive them down through the old straw with his fist to hold the new straw in place. It was a wonderful craft, placing the straw vertically upwards along the roof in fistfuls and then securing it by pushing the scallops down into the roof.

My father was also a part-time butcher, and used to kill pigs and cure the bacon for many people in our locality. Regularly on a Saturday afternoon, he would take off on his bike with a .22 rifle tied to the crossbar and a bag of razor-sharp knives hanging on the handlebars. He used to shoot the pig in the forehead and then bleed it. With the help of others, he would then throw it into a big steel tub of boiling water. The water would soften the hair on the pig, and he would shave it using one of the sharp knives. When all the hair was removed he would roll the pig onto a wooden ladder, tie its back feet to the top of the ladder, lift it up and put it against the side of the house or the wall of a shed. Then he would cut the pig open and remove all its insides. The pig's guts, along with the liver, heart and kidneys, were used to make black puddings.

The pig would be left on the ladder overnight in a shed or outhouse, and on Sunday afternoon he would go back and cut it up. He would rub salt into the sides of bacon and put them in a big wooden barrel called a stan, where they would be left for three weeks. The salt would melt into liquid form and soak its way into the bacon. Then it would be taken out and hung around the house and often up the chimney. In those days there were open fires in most houses in the country, and after a few weeks in the smoke the bacon would get as black as soot. It would take two or three days of steeping to clean it and get a lot of the salt out of it before it could be cooked.

The women always made the black puddings. They used the blood from the pig, minced up the pig's liver and fat meat, and threw in a big lump of lard along with chopped onions, oatmeal and some spices. It would all be mixed in a big steel basin or bucket. Then they would stuff the mixture into two feet or so of the pig's gut, tie it up and make a figure of eight shape out of it. They would boil it in a big pot for hours, holding it in place by putting the handle of a sweeping brush through one end of the figure eight and across the pot and then changing the ends around when the first half was cooked.

A great old tradition was for whoever killed a pig to send bits of pork steak and black puddings to their neighbours around the countryside. It was a wonderful custom, and many times every year we would get a bag of pork steak and black puddings from our neighbours. If we got a big bag my mother would say, 'I knew they were always decent people', and if we only got a small amount she would say, 'Miserable crowd, a hungry lot, never lost it, they should have kept it.' My father always brought home a bag of pork steak on Sunday evenings after he finished cutting up the pig, and many's the Sunday night we had a lovely big feed of fresh pork steaks with onions.

We had three or four cows at times, and we sent milk to the creamery, usually in the spring and summer. Going to the creamery was a social event as much as a business trip. I used to go when I was on holiday from school. The stainless steel milk churn would be tied with a rope in the middle of the cart, and away I went with the trotting pony, feeling like the squire. Tankardstown Creamery, which was a mile and a half from our home in Toureen, was my destination. When you got to the creamery there could be eight to ten horses and carts waiting in a line to deliver their milk. And when it was my turn I drove the pony and cart up alongside the platform and lifted the churn up, throwing the milk into a big container that measured the amount of milk I had. The creamery manager, Jimmy Lonergan – no relation – took a sample of the milk to see how much cream was in it; we only got paid for the cream. Then I drove around to the back and waited to collect the skim milk, which I brought home to feed the calves.

Going to the fair was also as much a social event as a business trip. Fair days were totally different from the open markets held around the country nowadays. The old fair days were for buying and selling cattle, horses, sheep and pigs. Bringing animals to the fair meant getting up at the crack of dawn to drive them on foot along the roads into the square in Cahir. The horse and cattle dealers would be there bright and early, some of them rough and tough men, and the battles between the farmers and the dealers were intense, the deals sealed by spitting on their hands. However, many a deal broke down over a disagreement about 'the luck penny', which the buyer always demanded. 'I'll give you ten pounds for him, with ten shillings for luck,' the buyer would shout, sticking out his hand and spitting on it. This really meant that the person selling was only getting nine pounds and ten shillings. It was all part of the psychology of bargaining. But the farmers in those days were very shrewd and every bit as tough as the best of the dealers; they knew almost to the penny what a beast was worth and, by eye, what it weighed.

Trying to keep your cattle or sheep together was impossible, and it was havoc when one herd of cattle ran into another; attempting to identify which were which was a nightmare. If you didn't sell your animals it was so disappointing to have to bring them home again. Then it was a case of waiting for better luck at the next fair.

The big annual job in rural Ireland was saving the hay. Back then – in the 1950s – it was a lengthy exercise. With no balers or big machinery, the hay was saved by hand. It was cut with a machine, often drawn by horses. After a day or so it had to be turned by hand with hay forks, so that each swart would get the sun on it and dry. Then we used to cock it – put it into cocks, which were about the size of one good forkful of hay. When it had dried out in the little cocks, it was piked (the Tipperary term for putting hay in very large cocks was 'piking'). The best part of saving the hay was having tea out in the fields – it tasted much nicer than in the house – and there was also the chance of getting a drink of Bulmer's Cidona.

My father grew our own spuds and cabbage. There are no spuds today like the spuds of my youth: big snow-white ones would burst out of the clay when my father stuck his fork down into the drills, and we used to eat them skins and all. 'Balls of flour,' he called them.

My father was very active in Muintir na Tíre and he was a member of the local parish council for years. He took a great interest in local activities, especially in St Pecaun's annual pattern, which was held on 1 August every year, and the annual Sports Day, which was held on the first Sunday in August every year. He also loved to play cards, mainly Forty-Fives, and he would cross the fields once or twice a week to visit a family called Bourkes and play cards with them into the early hours of the morning.

He was a heavy smoker all his life, and smoked thirty Woodbines, the strongest cigarettes of all, every day. Not surprisingly, they eventually killed him. He died in April 1977 after about ten heart attacks. He tried several times to give them up – always after a heart attack, when he was highly motivated – but he never really succeeded. He tried the pipe and tobacco too for a while, but eventually concluded, 'Ah filling the pipe is a bloody nuisance.'

My mother also had a number of neighbours she called to regularly. Visiting neighbours was a great custom when I was a child. We loved going visiting because we always got tea and cake or lemonade.

We got our first wireless in 1952. An electric wireless. In 1947, as part of the Rural Electrification Scheme, our little parish of Bansha and Kilmoyler had been selected by the ESB (Electricity Supply Board) to be the first rural parish in Ireland to get electricity. Bansha and Kilmoyler was selected, over Cahir, our neighbouring parish and main competitor, because it was the parish of Canon Hayes, the founder of Muintir na Tíre, and the ESB knew that he would have the organization to deliver the scheme. As I was born in 1947 I have always claimed that I brought the light to Bansha.

Compared with today's radios the wireless was huge, with a big glass front and four big knobs. It was dark brown, and my father made a shelf for it, screwed it to the wall in the kitchen just inside the door and plugged it in. The electric wireless was a mighty invention compared to the old wet-battery radios. It's long forgotten now, but the wireless was the biggest breakthrough in the 1930s and '40s for rural Ireland. If it wasn't for the wireless the people of rural Ireland wouldn't have known what was going on in the rest of the country or the world. We always listened to the news in stony silence.

Both my father and mother were staunch De Valera supporters. They came down very much on his side in the Civil War and both their families voted Fianna Fáil, so they were carrying on a family tradition. They took politics very seriously, and they knew the politics of every family for miles around, or thought they did. They would never miss voting in an election. In my youth Dan Breen, the freedom fighter from the old IRA, was their man, and he was still seen as a hero in the '50s and '60s. The other Fianna Fáil fellow they used to vote for was Mick Davern from Cashel, a South Tipperary TD for many years.

Apart from the news of what was going on in the country and further afield, the wireless provided all kinds of entertainment. But for me it was all about Michael O'Hehir and his commentaries on hurling and football matches. We used to sit in front of the radio and listen to his every word, especially when Tipperary teams were playing. We knew all the great hurlers of that era without ever seeing them – too many legends to start naming here. Michael O'Hehir was a one-off, and he had the gift of making you feel that you were actually at the match.

And when the big match ended, we would go out to O'Heney's field in front of our house and replay the match ourselves. I was Christy Ring most days, and when I played against my brother Ned I always scored the winning goal, no bother whatsoever. I'm sure that Michael O'Hehir inspired thousands of young boys to play hurling and football all over Ireland and beyond. He was a legend, and when I met him in person in the late '60s I was not disappointed: he was an absolute gentleman. On Sunday nights we listened to Seán Óg Ó Ceallacháin for the GAA results, another legend and lovely man.

The travelling roadshows were also a source of entertainment in my youth. These would be called variety shows now: a combination of one-act plays, comedy sketches, singing and dancing. Just beyond Tankardstown there was a little hall owned by Biddy O'Brien where the shows came during winter. Sometimes films were shown – that's if the projector didn't break down or the film roll snap. I remember seeing John Wayne there for the first time. Admission was a shilling, and Biddy also had a little sweet shop beside the hall, where we would buy sweets if we were in the money.

In the late '50s I saw my first ever television. A neighbour of ours, Michael Regan, got one from England, and although the picture was poor we used to sit looking at it for hours. I remember going over once to see a fight between Sonny Liston and Cassius Clay and seeing nothing except a lot of snow, and now and then the shadow of a boxer flickering across the screen. By the mid 1960s most people had televisions, and they dramatically changed lifestyles in rural Ireland. Out went the visitor, the cards and the chatting, and in came *Tolka Row*, *The Riordans*, *The Late Late Show*, *Radharc*, *Seven Days* and, of course, Charles Mitchell reading the news.

Like all mothers of her era, mine was a great worker and did absolutely everything around the house. She did all the cooking, washed and darned all the clothes by hand, knitted socks, carried the water from the stream (we had no running water): everything. The cooking was done over the open fire, and a big black kettle hanging over the fire provided all our hot water. If you looked up the chimney over the fire you could see the bright blue sky during daylight and the moon and the stars at night. There was a big bar that was pulled over the fire called 'a crane', and all the pots and the kettle were hung from it.

Baking bread on the open fire was an art, and my mother was a great old-fashioned baker. She mixed the flour with bread soda and a pinch of salt in a basin – it was all in her hands how she mixed it; it was a skill – and then she wet the mixture with sour milk, kneaded it, made it into a round and, very importantly, made a sign of the cross on the top, before putting it into a big black metal pot. Then she put on the lid and it was hung over the fire. She would take a shovel or two of red hot cinders, or *spreis* as we call them, and put them on top of the pot. The spreis helped to cook the bread on the top while the fire cooked it on the bottom. When it was cooked it would be three inches deep, a huge big cake of bread divided into quarters by the cross. The odd time she would throw a fist of currants into the white dough and we would have currant cake. Other times she would make brown bread. When we had apples in the haggard she would bake an apple tart.

I never remember my mother being sick or out of the house overnight, not once. She used to say to us, 'I'm a slave here for you all', and she was. She never went on a holiday and her only outing was to go on the bus to Cahir, which was three miles from our house. She was scrupulously honest, and no way would she owe anybody anything or wrong anybody. If I arrived home from the shops with extra change she would send me back to return it. Or if they gave me something extra by mistake, like an extra pound of sugar or an extra pound of butter, she would make certain to tell them next time she was in the shop. Every night she said the rosary. She knew all the mysteries and she had prayers all off by heart; it went on for what seemed like hours and was an education in itself just to listen to her.

But she was also witty. I was at a wedding with her in later years when a neighbour Paddy Hoare, a great guy and a great character, said to me, 'Are they your own teeth you have yet?' Before I replied she nipped in and said, 'Why wouldn't they be his own? Sure when he was a child he got very little use for them!'

When anyone came to visit the house they always got whatever was going – even down to the last bit of bread. Though there mightn't be much, it was always put on the table and shared. We would say, 'We will have nothing for our supper tonight', and she always said, 'There's fear of you, ye won't die with the hunger.'

My mother died in St Joseph's Hospital in Clonmel in February 1991. She was a great woman and a survivor, living through tough times, when most of her work was absolute drudgery. I have often said that if she was alive today and I went home and told her that we were in a bad recession she would laugh at me, because she knew what real recession was and so did all the other mothers of her time.

Women like my mother and her contemporaries were the backbone of the community and of parish life. And the parish was central to our lives. We were blessed in Bansha in having the famous Canon Hayes from Murroe, County Limerick, as our parish priest from 1946 until he died in January 1957. Even in those days, way before television, he was internationally known.

While he was a curate in Tipperary town in 1937, Father Hayes had founded the first guild of Muintir na Tíre. The new organization was all about developing communities in rural Ireland. He believed in self-sufficiency, and said that communities should share and care and provide for one another. In the late 1940s he started up a number of small factories in Bansha – a jam factory and a glove factory – finding ways to create employment in the parish.

Canon Hayes was born into a poor family and he never forgot it; indeed, he was one of the few people in authority who identified with the poor, and this was his greatest strength. He stood for everything that was Christian, and was in many ways totally against what the Catholic Church practised. It had the gospels, the Bible, the theology, but it identified with the rich, and the more money you had the more you were liked. Canon Hayes was a revolutionary. When he came to Bansha and Kilmoyler as parish priest in 1946, the first thing he did was to get rid of the custom of rich families buying pews in the church, saying, 'Everyone is equal in God's house.' That was a landmark statement, and better still he put it into practice.

Listening to Canon Hayes as a child I didn't understand much of what he was saying, but he had charisma and a force of personality. He was a wonderful motivator and organizer and in many ways ahead of his time. He would say, 'There are more sides to life than merely the economic side; and we must realize the dangers of having men classified as producing-machines.' And my favourite: 'There are two kinds of people, the ones who do the work and the ones who take the credit, and there is much more competition amongst the latter.' He said that materialism led to nothing but greed, competition and jealousy, and he warned that there was a real danger that as a people we were inclined to think that bigness is greatness. We now know how right he was.

In contrast to Canon Hayes's enlightened approach, every year we had a mission that went on for two weeks. The Redemptorists or the Passionists normally gave the missions, with Mass every morning and a sermon every evening, and they were packed. The whole parish used to go, young and old, rich and poor. Sometimes the sermons were quite mad. The missioner would be roaring on and on about sinning, talking down to people, putting the fear of God in them and threatening them. They were amazing occasions, but it's hard to know what they ever achieved. Not surprisingly the good preacher was the guy who had a bit of humour and could connect with the ordinary people, but most preachers were boring and completely out of touch.

In those days travel was at a minimum – we went into Cahir on the bus and that was about it, and that wasn't very often – so when we were growing up the annual Sports Day was huge: having athletes and cyclists coming to Toureen from all over Munster was big stuff. The standards were pretty high, and only a few locals ever got a look in. The prizes were glass bowls, lamps and household goods. We thought that they were lovely, but looking back now they were probably auld rubbish. There were a few novelty events too, like an egg and spoon race, a three-legged race and a sack race. I won the sack race one year and got a biro in a lovely box – I thought I was Ronnie Delaney. There was also a stall selling lemonade, chocolate and ice cream. Ice cream was a novelty, and if you could afford a six-penny wafer ice cream, it was like winning the lottery.

Shortly before the Sports we had the pattern, which was held every year in a field beside the ruined monastery and church of St Pecaun, our local saint. On pattern evening, families gathered in the field and older men collected money for the prizes in their hats. Most people would throw in a few bob, usually two shillings or a half-crown. Then they would run races for all age groups, starting with the under-fours. If you won a race you got two shillings or sometimes a half-crown. You would kill yourself to win, because two shillings in those days was a lot of money. And of course the Sports would be coming up in a few days, so you needed the money for that. The pattern was a very special occasion and continues to this day.

There was also an annual gymkhana in Bansha. People brought horses and ponies from miles around to compete. I so much wanted to be jumping in it one day, but I never got the chance. Bansha Agricultural Show eventually took over the horse-jumping events, and the old gymkhanas are no more.

When I was a child we always had a pony and trap. This was a great thrill for us as children – going to Mass on a Sunday in the pony and trap. And as I got a little bit bigger, the highlight for me was when my father gave me the reins to drive the pony. The pony could have gone to Mass and back on his own, but I thought it was great, having the reins in my hands.

My father had a great interest in horses. Our neighbour Jimmy O'Heney did too, and he was very gifted with them. My father used to say that if Jimmy O'Heney couldn't break in or handle a horse, then nobody could. Jimmy told me when I was a young lad that the secret with a horse was to show him kindness, to treat him with sensitivity and to have a light, tender touch with your hands. He said, 'Communication with horses is done mainly by your hands through the bit in the horse's mouth.' And he showed me how to get a horse to relax, the way to communicate through the reins. 'Always be kind to a horse and he will never forget it,' he said. He told me never to be cruel or vicious, never to lose your temper with a horse, and always respond with tenderness and kindness. I learned in later life the same principles applied to human beings as well. Tenderness, kindness and humanity are all sure winners with people too.

2. A Sense of Identity to Last a Lifetime

My first memory of home is of the day my sister Philomena was born: 22 February 1951. I clearly remember going up to the room and seeing her for the first time, lying on the bed beside my mother. I can still picture her little black head sticking out from under the clothes in the bed with a white shawl wrapped around her. I was a little over three years old.

I started national school in Ballydrehid in early September 1951, when I was four. We lived up a boreen about a half mile off the main road, and I can still remember walking down it that first day with my mother, my older brother Ned and my sister Cait, who had both already started school.

My mother always said that I was wild. She said that I used to throw stones at people and do all sorts of mad things. To control me she used to tie me with a rope to the electricity pole in the yard. First thing that morning at school I had to sit on a long stool up at the front of the room and was given a blue slate and a bit of white chalk; trying to scribble on the slate was hard. I hated not being free to walk around the room and out into the schoolyard. It was a two-teacher primary school, and when I started there was no divide between the classrooms; it was just one big room with about fifty children sitting in it. The bigger boys and girls, from third class up, sat at one side of the room with the master, Denis McGrath; and the smaller children – the infants and first and second class – were on the other side with the mistress, Mrs Ennis.

In the summer we used to have bread and jam and a bottle of cold milk for our lunch; we all brought a bottle of milk in our school bags with a cork to stop it spilling. In the winter all the families would bring in a box with mugs, cocoa and sugar in it. The fifth- and sixth-class children used to mix the cocoa in the morning, and at lunchtime Mrs Ennis would pour boiling water from the kettle into the mugs and we all had hot cocoa.

As a little fellow I used to spend a lot of time with our neighbour Jimmy O'Heney. I spent every hour I could with him, just walking along behind him or sitting in the horse's cart. One evening when I came home from school, I went up to a field Jimmy was ploughing with two horses and a single board plough. When I got to the field, he was lying at the headland having a little snooze. But the horses were standing there ready to go. This was my chance to plough with the horses, so I picked up the reins and grabbed hold of the plough handles, even though they were way above my head and I could hardly reach them. The horses knew exactly what to do and walked off in a straight line; the only problem was that I couldn't hold the plough in place because we were on a bit of a slope. The plough jumped in and out of the furrow, increasingly out of control, the sod breaking up every few feet. I had only gone fifty or sixty yards when Jimmy woke up. I can still hear him running after me, roaring at the horses, 'Whoa! Whoa!'

I was mad about cattle as well. One day on the way home from school I wandered into one of Jimmy's fields to admire the cattle. But I forgot to close the gate and they all walked out onto the boreen, not taking one bit of notice of a little lad like me trying to get them back in again. I got into a lot of bother at home over things like that.

Still, whatever scrapes I got into, I always managed to make it to Christmas with the promise of something in my sock. As little children, we used to be glued to the wireless at around 6.30 p.m. on Christmas Eve, listening to the 'live' Raidió Éireann broadcast from Santa and his helper in the North Pole, where he was about to set out on his big journey. Every single year the same thing would happen: Santa would promise his helper that he would take him with him on the sleigh, but just before take-off there was a crisis and to make room for the helper Santa would have to take off a big bag of toys, which would mean some boys and girls wouldn't get their presents. In the end, Santa always decided that the presents would have to stay on board and the poor old helper would have to stay behind. It was an early lesson in naked self-interest: *What if our toys were in the bag that was going to be taken off?* Though we felt sorry for the helper, we always agreed with Santa's decision.

In those days life was simple, poverty wasn't far around the corner and we were very lucky to get anything at all on Christmas morning. Small things like oranges were a real treat. One year I got a little silver cap gun and six rolls of caps, and thought I was Roy Rogers without the horse. I rapid-fired all the caps, used them up in less than ten minutes and that was it: the gun was of little use without caps.

The biggest milestones in primary school were making my First Holy Communion and my first confession. Mrs Ennis used to go to great efforts to prepare us for both ceremonies, beginning with Holy Communion. She would cut up white paper in the shape of hosts and go through the whole thing as if she was giving us Holy Communion herself, but always with a warning: 'Don't swallow that paper!' Of course I did swallow it once, and she was raging with me.

Then it was time to learn about confession. We would have to make our first confession before we could make our first communion. I think there were only six of us in the class that year, and one day Mrs Ennis loaded us all into her car and drove us to Kilmoyler Church. Taking the part of the priest, she went into the centre compartment of the confessional box. I went into the box as the person making their confession, and knelt down on a cushion. I felt like a midget. It was pitch dark and I couldn't see a thing. After what seemed like ages she pulled back the shutter, and, looking up, I could see her head behind the screen. I said, 'Bless me, Father, for I have sinned. This is my first confession.' Then I told her a pile of made-up sins, sins that had no meaning for me. I remember that I said one of them was 'impure thoughts' – although what impure thoughts I had back then beats me. She went through this routine with all of us two or three times until we knew it well.

My First Holy Communion suit was my first ever suit. I went with my mother on the bus into Cahir one Saturday afternoon after dinner. Cahir was only three miles from our house, but I could have been going to New York I was so excited. As far as my mother was concerned there was only one drapery shop in Cahir, and that was Sheehan's on the square; she always got our communion outfits there. I got a lovely grey suit with short pants, a new white shirt, a red tie, white ankle socks and brown crêpe-soled sandals. On the day, Mrs Ennis gave us all a white rosette to pin on our suit. I was walking on air for days afterwards, I was so happy.

I was an altar boy for many years and served Mass in Kilmoyler Church for three years. I think we used to start serving Mass in third class. With all the scandals of child abuse that have emerged, I must note that all the priests I met during that period were kind and nice, and always completely above board.

The highlight of serving at Mass was the weddings. The real interest we had in weddings was the money we got – sometimes a pound, which was a fortune at that time. Of course, when I brought it home I would give it to my mother and she'd give me back two shillings. Handing over the money we got for working on Saturdays or during our holidays was what all children did in my youth.

Funerals were another big ceremony for us altar boys, but before the funeral came the wake, and wakes were big events. It is amazing that in the last few years, even in urban Ireland, the wake is returning. It's the old tradition coming back, and it is a lovely one. Back then the dead person remained in the house for at least one night and perhaps, in some cases, two or three nights, and all the neighbours came and sat around, chatted and drank whiskey or porter and stayed up all night to show respect to the dead person and to support the family.

I went to my first wake in 1960, for a man called Mickey Nolan. My mother brought me with her to the house. He was laid out on the bed in one of the bedrooms, and because I knew him well when he was alive it was a huge shock to see him dead. His wife and daughters sat close to the head of the bed, with other women around them. After paying our respects – it was the first time I heard the expression 'I am very sorry for your troubles' – we went out to the kitchen, where the men were drinking bottles of porter and the women were drinking tea. I got a cup of red lemonade and a biscuit, and that helped take my mind off the shock of seeing a corpse for the first time.

Generally speaking I enjoyed primary school, and I remember Mrs Ennis and Denis McGrath as decent people. But, of course, corporal punishment was around in my school days and I got plenty of wallops of the bamboo cane. It was about three foot long with a crooked handle, and hung at the front of the master's desk. We always got slapped on the palms of our hands and it would sting for ages afterwards. The knack was to let your hand drop a bit just before the cane connected with it, which took a lot of the sting out of it; holding your hand rigid was a disaster.

In those days, primary school finished with the primary certificate exam – a test in Irish, English and Arithmetic. It was a big thing to pass your primary. I got 100 per cent in Arithmetic, my strongest subject.

The year I left primary school – 1959 – was also the year I got my first bicycle. From her time in Clonmel my mother knew a man who owned a bicycle shop, Bill Purcell. She bought the bicycle from him on hire purchase. I went down to the main road one evening to meet Bill at the crossroads near us, where he was going to drop it off. Neither Seán Kelly nor Stephen Roche in their prime would have felt as proud as I did when I got that little bike. It was a blue and cream Raleigh, and I had it for years and rode it the three miles to and from secondary school.

There were two secondary schools in Cahir: St Joseph's, a fee-paying private college, and the vocational school, which also charged a small fee. I went to the vocational school, where Ned and Cait had gone before me. Though its fees were small, with three of us going it was a struggle for my parents to pay them.

I joined the youth club Macra na Tuaithe, nowadays Foróige, and I had a great time in it. They had a scheme where members could borrow from the Bank of Ireland to invest in some project. I borrowed twenty pounds, bought two piglets for ten pounds and sold them six months later, as fat pigs, for thirty pounds, but it had cost me much more than ten pounds to feed them for six months, and this ended my entrepreneurial ambitions. In Macra na Tuaithe we did a lot of public speaking, which gave me great confidence and was a skill that proved very useful in later life.

From the late 1950s onwards I cycled up to Bansha to play hurling and football in the parish leagues. John Moloney, who later became famous as an All Ireland referee, used to organize the leagues for lads of about

ten years of age and upwards. The leagues were great: we learned how
to play both football and hurling, and because John Moloney stood
for no nonsense, we also learned to be disciplined, to have manners
and to respect others.

I saw my first ever football match on a Sunday afternoon in the mid
1950s when a great man and a local football legend, Larry Maher,
packed us into his big old blue van and drove us up to Bansha to see
Galtee Rovers/St Pecaun's playing a football match against Rockwell
Rovers, a team from the little village of New Inn. When he picked us
up, we were playing on the green, the open space on the road leading
from Cahir to Kilmoyler Church, near Killaldriffe Cemetery. For
years and years, up to twenty young, and not-so-young, men played
hurling and football on that tiny piece of ground. When I hear all the
talk nowadays about facilities and playing conditions for the youth, I
marvel at the wonderful entertainment and enjoyment so many people
got from playing on that simple pitch.

As I grew up, hurling and football became a massive part of my life.
I'm sure it's the same today, but certainly in my time, playing senior
hurling or football for the club was the ultimate achievement. Putting
on that red and white jersey of Galtee Rovers/St Pecaun's was such an
honour, and I felt I had truly made it when I played at senior level.

We don't always recognize the value and importance of having a
sense of identity. Playing for Galtee Rovers/St Pecaun's provided me
with just that. In Charles Kickham's great book *Knocknagow*, Matt the
Thrasher summarizes the sentiment very well when, during a hammer-
throwing competition and with his back to the wall, he said, 'for the
sake of the little village'. And our little parish meant so much to us: it
was where we belonged and continues to be where our roots are.

Of course, growing up in Tipperary in the 1950s and '60s we were
spoilt in regard to hurling, as it was without doubt the greatest era for
the sport in the county. Tipperary appeared in All Ireland Finals in
1960, '61, '62, '64, '65, '67, '68 and '71, and they won five – in 1961, '62,
'64, '65 and '71. We had some outstanding hurlers who left us with
memories to last a lifetime.

I went to my first ever Munster Senior Hurling Final in 1960 in
Thurles. The match was between Cork and Tipperary. Matt Nugent,

a wonderful neighbour and a great friend of mine for years afterwards, took me in his Ford Prefect car. Nowadays a boy of twelve might take no great notice of going to a Munster Hurling Final in Thurles, but for me it was out of this world: it poured rain during the minor match and I got drenched, the place was packed so I saw the ball only now and again, but Tipp won by two points so I went home happy.

Matt was a legend. He went to every match: no matter what the grade, no matter what the destination, Matt Nugent would be there. And he took all of us Lonergans to matches for years. For me, though, nothing will ever compare to going with Matt to Munster senior hurling matches at the Gaelic Grounds in Limerick. Matt would call to our house to collect us at around ten on Sunday morning. Since the match was at 3.30 p.m. and the journey a little over an hour, we were always there well before the time. He would park his car in Mulgrave Street, near the prison – not that I took any interest in the prison back then. Along the Ennis Road, fellows would be playing fiddles and accordions, and the atmosphere approaching the grounds was electric, especially if Tipperary were playing Cork, as we were again in the 1961 Munster Final. In those days there were sideline seats running along both sides of the pitch, and as we were early we got very good seats right in the centre of the field. Matt always brought flasks of tea, home-made sandwiches – or 'sangwidges' – and, my favourite, a big bag of eating apples called 'Beauty Bats'. Nothing ever tasted better than a 'Beauty Bat' in the Gaelic Grounds in Limerick on a sunny Sunday afternoon, an hour or so before the big match.

Cork's Christy Ring was playing in both the 1960 and 1961 Munster Finals, and so – thanks to Matt Nugent – I had the great privilege of actually seeing a legend in action. I have seen a lot of hurling in the fifty years since, and when people talk about who was the greatest hurler of all time – Christy Ring, Mick Mackey or several others – I can honestly say that no hurler ever left the same impression on me as Christy Ring. He was the only hurler I ever saw who could control the crowd by his actions on the field. When Christy Ring got the ball there was a hush and a silence of anticipation; the whole crowd would be waiting for his next act of pure genius.

Matt lived for Gaelic games, and while he was a very busy farmer he never allowed that to interfere with his love of hurling. And into the bargain he was a wonderful neighbour too: you were never short of firewood, a butt of spuds or a lift to a match while Matt Nugent was around.

Emigration was part of life when I was a young lad. As I've already mentioned, my mother's brothers and sisters had emigrated in the 1930s and '40s, and many families in my area in the '60s were also lost to emigration. But emigration had its pluses as well: it gave people extra confidence and opportunities that they would never have got in rural Ireland, and many of them benefited enormously from it.

I recall a fellow who went to primary and secondary school with me and then emigrated to England at sixteen. He was only gone four or five months when he came home on holidays. We were sitting at the crossroads one evening having a chat, when he asked with a bit of an English accent, 'Hey, what do you folks do around here for night life?'

'Night life in Toureen?' we said. 'Never heard of it!'

The start of my 'night life' was going to the pictures in Cahir. In my youth we used to go to the cinema regularly, especially on Saturday nights. Then, in the early 1960s, a new ballroom – the Arcadia – opened in Cahir. All the top showbands came, and the most popular – and my favourite – was Brendan Bowyer, Tom Dunphy and the Royal Showband. When they played, well over 1,000 people, and maybe up to 1,200, filled the Arcadia Ballroom.

I loved secondary school and have nothing but happy memories of it. Though I enjoyed academic subjects like Maths and English and was good at them, there was no question of going on to third-level education. It was just out of our league. I also enjoyed woodwork, and I left the vocational school in 1964 to serve my time as a carpenter. When the apprenticeship I had lined up fell through, I ended up sharpening saws in a sawmill that had just opened close to home. It was skilled work but boring, and after a year or so I went to Dublin to work as a bus conductor.

I enjoyed life in Dublin but I was not happy with the work, so when I saw an ad in the *Irish Press* in the autumn of 1967 looking to recruit prison officers, I decided to apply. I don't know why I was interested because I knew absolutely nothing about the work. I was called for an interview at 45 Upper O'Connell Street in Dublin. The first part of the interview saw me reading a passage in Irish from the school book *Jimím*; in those days candidates for all civil service jobs had to pass an Irish language test. I passed that and was sent to another room and interviewed by three elderly-looking men. I learned later that one of them was the governor of Mountjoy Prison. In early 1968 I had a medical and shortly afterwards I was offered a job in Limerick Prison.

Looking back now on my early years growing up in rural Ireland in the 1950s and '60s, I think it was like every era – a mix of good and bad. Women were often badly treated in those times, and in many ways they were exploited and undervalued. Mothers held families together and worked tirelessly, for little thanks or appreciation. On the positive side, the style of life was often easy-going and relaxed, we cared for and shared with one another, we had great neighbours and enjoyed close friendships with them, visiting their homes and being made welcome. Simple human stuff like that is hugely valuable.

The family has changed pretty dramatically over my lifetime, especially in the diminished importance of the extended family. But the family must be at the very foundation of any caring society. We all need family when we are struggling or when we are broken. And sometimes we need our family just to help us keep our feet on the ground.

A few years ago I was asked to give a talk to parents at the national school in Bansha. It was organized by the Parents' Association and was held in the GAA Community Hall. A few days beforehand I had phoned my sister Cait, and early in the conversation she said, 'I see you're coming to Bansha next week to give a talk.'

'I am – Tuesday night next week.'

'Well, they don't think much of you,' she said.

'Is that so?'

'Yes,' she said.

'Why's that?'

'Because they're only charging €2 to go in to hear you.'

'Ah, they are only covering the cost of the old hall for the night,' I said.

We chatted away for ten or fifteen minutes about all sorts of things and swapped a bit of gossip, and then, when I was about to end the call, I said, 'Well, will I see you next week in Bansha?'

'At what?'

'Are you not coming up to the talk?' I said.

'Do you think I would pay €2 to listen to you?' she said.

And she didn't.

3. Learning the Ropes in Limerick Prison

Limerick Prison was built around 1820 and is Ireland's oldest working prison. In 1968 it was the committal prison for the six counties of Munster and for parts of counties Offaly and Galway. It takes prisoners direct from the courts, both remand (remands are those charged but awaiting trial) and convicted, and it accommodates men and women. In the 1960s it had four wings, or 'classes' as they were called then. A and B wings housed ordinary convicted prisoners, C wing was used to accommodate prisoners committed late at night, and D wing was where the remands were held.

The Sunday after I started working there, I attended my first staff parade. All the officers lined up in a straight line in the hallway just outside the circle gate. I stood at the end. Just after 7 a.m. the chief officer came out the circle gate carrying a huge book. He also had a massive bunch of the biggest keys I'd ever seen on a long leather strap hanging off his arm. He stood in front of us and began reading our names out in order of seniority: Healy, Bourke, Walsh, Ryan. He called my name last, and I remained at the bottom of the list until the next recruit joined us. When our names were called we answered '*Anseo!*' and the chief informed us of our duties for the day.

On that first Sunday morning he told me, 'Assist B class and Mass.' I didn't know where to report to, but someone said, 'Go to your right' as we walked through the circle gate. I went down two steps and I was told by an officer, 'Go up to the second floor, and take off the master locks', pointing as he did so towards the stairs and handing me a huge black key. 'Just turn it once anticlockwise and count the prisoners.'

Off I went, up the steel stairs and onto the landing, not having a clue what I was supposed to do. Some locks turned easily while others were stiff, and the stiff ones would cut the hand off you trying to turn them. I got all ten locks turned, and came back, delighted with myself.

The officer put out his hand for the key and said, 'How many have you?'

'Just one,' I said, handing him the key.

'No, no, not the key,' he said. 'How many prisoners?'

I had been concentrating so much on the locks that I forgot all about counting the prisoners.

'Go back up and count them,' he said, a bit impatiently.

Next thing, a shout came from the circle, 'B class numbers?'

It was the chief.

The other officer shouted, 'Still checking!'

I ran along the landing and counted eight prisoners and two empty cells.

The class officer was looking up from the ground floor. 'How many?' he asked.

'Eight,' I said.

Afterwards I was told that the normal way to report the numbers was to say, 'Eight correct' – 'correct' meaning that not only were all the prisoners in their cells, but also they were alive and well – and when I was giving head-counts to the governor or chief officer, I should say, 'Eight correct, sir.'

I learned early on that it wasn't good to get the numbers wrong. When an officer reported his numbers, the chief checked them against the numbers book in his office. When they tallied he would shout, 'Okay, unlock!' But if they didn't, he would shout, 'Check again!' To be told to check again was not good, as it could mean only one of two things: either you couldn't count or a prisoner had escaped.

The officer shouted out the numbers and the chief said, 'Unlock B class!' The class officer unlocked the ground floor and then gave me the keys to unlock the second landing. It was just as well that the prisoners knew the routine, because I hadn't an idea what was going on. All the prisoners came out of their cells with white aluminium chamber pots, went into the toilet at the end of the landing and threw the contents down it. The smell was brutal. In the years to come, I was to find that the smell was one of the worst parts of prison life for both the prisoners and the staff.

The prisoners then collected water in steel basins and took it back to their cells to wash. Sometimes the water would be hot and other times stone cold: it depended on demand. Prisoners were not allowed to have razors in their cells, and so had to ask the class officer (the prison officer in charge of the landing) for permission to shave. They were issued with a razor, a max smile blade and a mirror. The razor and the blade were shared. One blade could shave ten prisoners.

I just stood there observing what was going on and feeling very awkward. I knew that the prisoners were well aware that I was new and hadn't a clue. I wanted to be 'in charge', but I didn't know how.

Next thing I heard was a shout, 'Fall in for Mass!' With that, six prisoners on my landing stepped out of their cells and went down the stairs to the ground floor. I was told, 'Lock up any prisoners not going to Mass!' I checked that they were locked in and went back downstairs. The class officers told me to go back and check the religion of the prisoners on the cell card on their doors. Both cards read 'nil'. I reported back, 'Two nils.' Refusing to attend the religious service of your registered religion was against the rules (this rule no longer exists), and a prisoner who did so would be placed on report and dealt with by the governor the next day. If the two prisoners were registered as Catholics therefore, I would have had to put them on report, unless they were sick.

Putting a prisoner on report – or, in prison jargon, 'on a P19' – means reporting them for breaching the rules. Prison Form 19 is the official form used when making a disciplinary report. Punishment for breaching the rule about attending religious services would usually be losing evening recreation – being confined to his cell from 5.20 p.m. to 8 p.m. – for a few weeks. Prisoners were never physically forced to attend Mass or religious services. Over the years more and more prisoners registered as 'nils', and they could stay in their cells during Mass. But if a prisoner said that he was sick for Mass, he would have to stay in his cell all day and wouldn't get out until Monday morning.

I was told to sit at the end of a pew in the prison church, alongside the prisoners. A priest from the local parish of St John's came in to say the Mass. A prison officer served the Mass, a job I did on several Sundays during my time in Limerick. One of the main things to look out for when serving Mass was to make sure that the prisoners didn't get their hands on the altar wine.

When Mass was over, the prisoners returned to their cells to wait for breakfast. A prisoner went along each landing with a big wooden tray piled with bread. There were four slices of white bread with a lump of margarine on the top slice for each prisoner. The bread looked fine, but the margarine was horrible. Following the prisoner with the bread was another prisoner carrying a big bucket of tea, and behind him an officer holding a ladle to measure the tea – each prisoner was entitled to one pint of tea. The tea was made in the kitchen, with milk and sugar already added, so if a prisoner didn't take milk or sugar it was too bad. The prisoners had tin mugs in their cells, and these were filled with the tea. But because the tea was always boiling, the mugs got roasting hot and the prisoners couldn't put the mugs near their mouths, otherwise the lips would have been burned off them. It took ages for the tea to cool, and by the time it did it was spoiled. The prison breakfast was dog rough.

As breakfast was being served, the chief came to the circle with two small wooden boxes in his hands. 'Cigarettes!' he shouted. An officer from both A and B classes went to the circle and took the boxes. In each box were cigarette packets with the names of prisoners written on the flaps. In those days, cigarettes were rationed in prison: prisoners were allowed four cigarettes each weekday and six on Sundays. Most prisoners couldn't afford cigarettes, but nearly all of them were smokers. The officer shouted out names and those prisoners who had been sent cigarettes by their families came and collected the packets. They were immediately surrounded by other prisoners begging for a drag. But prisoners would never light up a full cigarette: they would always break them and make up to ten skinny cigarettes out of each one.

Indeed, first thing every morning when the prisoners were unlocked they all scurried around the compounds searching for cigarette butts thrown away by the staff. If they were lucky enough to find one, they would stick it in one of their pockets and break it up afterwards in their cells to make the skinniest cigarettes I ever saw: 90 per cent paper and 10 per cent tobacco. Some were so desperate for a smoke that they would stand close to a prisoner smoking, and as he exhaled the smoke he would blow it straight into the mouth of the other prisoner; he in turn would then try to inhale it.

Writing of cigarettes reminds me of how cruel I was back in those days. The prisoners used to 'fall in' two or three times a day, usually following unlocks, and line up on the compounds to be inspected. Once in line they would be told, 'Put out the cigarettes.' I can remember walking up and down the line looking for any sign that a prisoner was still smoking. You can just imagine how a prisoner would behave if he had just got a lighted butt from another prisoner, the only smoke he was likely to get that day. To try to hold on to it he would stick his hand in his pocket to hide it, and it was when the smoke started coming out of his pocket that I would pounce. 'Take your hand out of your pocket!' I would shout. When the butt appeared, I would order, 'Stamp out that cigarette!' The prisoner would have to throw the butt on the floor and stamp it out with his shoe; I would go off thinking that I was very sharp and feeling like a sergeant major.

The officers went off for an hour for breakfast when the prisoners had been locked up again. All the single officers went to the officers' mess, while the married officers went home for their meal breaks. One of them, Jack Ryan, was always slagging us about the food in the mess. The prison was close to Shaw's meat factory, and as Jack walked towards the main gate on his way home, he would start sniffing the air. 'There's a bad smell today,' he would shout. 'It's either from Shaw's or the mess.'

When I went back on duty on my first Sunday, I was told to 'assist B class and exercise'. The exercise was out in a yard, and my job was to stand at a corner of the yard close to an alarm bell. There was a senior officer in charge and he told me, 'Stand there and don't let any prisoner near the bell, press it if there is any trouble, and keep an eye out for the auld fellow, he'll be around during the morning.' When I looked puzzled he said, 'The governor – you'll know him when you see him. He won't be wearing a uniform.' The governor arrived with the chief shortly after 11 a.m. and stood at the gate, looked around the yard for a minute or so and left. The senior officer walked over towards me and said, 'That's the last you'll see of him today, thank God.'

Dinner was served at 12.30 p.m., and I think that day it was corned beef and spuds. I finished work on my first Sunday at 5 p.m.

Over the next five days I was detailed for a number of duties. On the Monday, I was in the kitchen. The cook officer, John Ryan, handed me a big white coat and said, 'You can pretend that you're a doctor.' I looked on as the breakfast was being prepared, then Jack told me to help cut up the bread for the evening tea. It didn't strike me then that cutting up the bread at 10 a.m. for tea at 4.30 was a terrible idea; I just did what I was told – cutting away, huge loaves, sixteen slices in every one. When all the bread was cut up, we piled it on big wooden trays. The margarine was divided, one ounce per prisoner, and it was put on the top slice.

Then Jack went to a huge fridge, took out a big tray of meat and said, 'Cut that up for the stew and cut off the fat as well.' A few prisoners joined in. One said that he was from Tipperary town. It was the first time I ever thought about meeting fellows in prison that I might know from home. Over the years I met many such people, always a difficult and sad experience.

The dinners served to the prisoners were poor enough. There was Irish stew two days a week, bacon once a week, corned beef, usually, on Sundays and fish on Fridays. For evening tea, along with another four slices of bread and margarine, they might also get a lump of cheddar cheese or a spoonful of red jam.

After just two weeks I was detailed for my first night duty. Night duty was the toughest and worst duty of all. Everyone took it in turns each night. You reported for duty at 7 a.m. on the morning of your night duty and supervised while the rest of the officers went to breakfast. At 9.30 you went to the main gate and relieved the gate officer so that he could go for breakfast. At 10.30 a.m. you were off duty until 7.30 p.m., when you reported back for night duty. You worked through until 7 the following morning. At that time you worked night duty on your own.

At 7.30 p.m. you followed the supervising officer around the prison as he master-locked the cells; you would then check each cell and count the prisoners. At the end of the tour he would ask you, 'How many did you get?' And you would give him your count, praying at the same time that you were right, otherwise you'd have to re-check. There was no way the supervising officer would allow you on night duty until he was satisfied that you had personally checked and accounted for every single prisoner. Before 8 p.m. the four reserve officers would go off duty. The supervising officer stayed on duty until 10 p.m. Sunday was the worst night to be on night duty, as the supervising officer would go off duty before 8 p.m. After that you were on your own.

Just before 8 p.m. you would be given a report book that had to be filled in, a big torch, a wooden baton with a leather strap fixed to it and an electric kettle to make a cup of tea during the night. You brought food with you, otherwise you went hungry. You were also given a pegging clock, which you carried with you in the night to each landing within the prison. A key was fixed to the wall at the end of each landing, and you pegged the clock by inserting the key into it. This marked a piece of paper in the clock, which confirmed that you had been at that point at that time; it was also your safeguard, because if anything happened this was proof that you were awake and were doing your job.

You wore very light shoes or runners so as not to make any noise during the night and to be able to go around the prison without being heard by the prisoners. A prison late at night is a weird and eerie place. First, there is the deadly silence. A prisoner just turning in his bed would be heard all over the prison. A prisoner doing a pee into the aluminium pot would sound like a volcano. Being on your own was just terrible. So that the prisoners couldn't see you going around the prison during the night the lights were turned off, except for one, which was in the circle. You spent the whole night watching out for someone to try to escape – every sound was checked out immediately, and you lived on your nerves. You expected a prisoner to appear any second from anywhere, and you were on your own. I was always so glad to see the staff coming on at 7 a.m. But there was still an anxious wait, as you could not go off duty until the day staff checked the prisoners and informed the chief. The most dreaded thing was to hear the chief say to one of the class officers, 'Check again!' Your mind would race straight away: *Could a prisoner have escaped during the night and I didn't notice?* This was a sacking offence. It was always such a relief to hear the chief shout, 'All correct!' and to go off to bed.

On my second night duty, just after two in the morning I heard a noise coming from somewhere in the B class. It sounded like someone was cutting the cell bars. It seemed to start and stop again, and I couldn't locate the exact spot it was coming from. As soon as I moved it would stop, convincing me that it was definitely a prisoner cutting the bars. I was in bits and didn't know what to do. I was thinking, *Will I call the chief officer on the house phone and risk making a fool of myself if there is nothing wrong? Or will I put off the alarm and hope that someone from the officers' quarters will come over?* I decided to try to find out first which prisoner was cutting the bars, and then I would call the chief. After about an hour, with the sweat dropping off me, I traced the noise to the second landing on B class. I crept along the landing and found that the noise was coming from inside a cupboard at the end of the landing. I pulled the door open, and there in a big galvanized bucket was a little mouse. He had fallen into the bucket and couldn't get out. He was jumping up the side of the bucket but couldn't get a grip. I was never so happy to see a mouse.

I had another bad experience one night in 1969. Just before three in the morning I was on my way to the D class, where the remand prisoners were held, to peg the clock. I had turned all the lights off in the corridor leading to the D class, so that I could see out into the exercise yard. As I was strolling along the corridor, I looked out into the D yard and saw a man climbing up the roof of a lean-to shed in the yard. My first reaction was that someone was breaking into the prison; it never crossed my mind that it might be a prisoner escaping. I ran up to the circle and put off the main alarm. An ordinary alarm clock would have made more noise: I could hardly hear it in the prison, never mind the staff hearing it in the staff quarters. I ran down to D class and started to check the cells. I checked the cell of the highest security prisoner and he was there asleep in his bed. That was a relief. But when I checked the next cell, a bar was cut, the window was half open and the prisoner was gone. It was a horrible feeling. He had put a stool in the bed and covered it up to make it look like a person. After what felt like hours a few officers ran over from the mess, where they were sleeping. I couldn't get out and they couldn't come in because the keys were all locked up, and so I shouted out through a window, 'He's gone over the D yard wall!'

A few minutes later they came back with the prisoner, who they had found hiding at the back of the prison in the coal yard. He had made a rope from torn blankets, which he had tied to a block of wood he found in the D wood yard. He had tried to throw the block over the wall to pull himself over, but it was too heavy and he couldn't get it over. When I saw him on the lean-to shed he was on his way out a second time, having come back for a lighter bit of wood. He had hidden in the coal yard when he heard the alarm.

How innocent I was. I thought I had done marvellous work by being alert and catching him on time, so preventing his escape. However, the talk in the prison was that I must have been asleep since he had managed to cut the bars and I hadn't heard him. The whole thing was turned on its head.

Denis Donoghue was the governor in 1968. The chief brought me over to his office one morning during my first week on the job. It was very formal: he was sitting behind a desk and I stood in front of him, with the chief beside me. In those days when you met the governor you gave him a salute, like in the army. So when I entered the office I raised my right hand to the peak of my uniform cap and then moved it straight down to my right side. He welcomed me and said, 'You'll pick it up as you go along.' The officers were generally terrified of him and everyone jumped when he came into the prison, which was very often, day and night. He lived in a big house in the grounds and had his own keys to come and go as he pleased. He was very energetic and walked at speed around the prison, his arms always swinging.

When he moved to Portlaoise to become governor there in 1969, Mayo man Pat McFadden replaced him. He was a kind and approachable man with no notions about himself. He spoke to everyone when he met them in the prison, officers and prisoners. A lot of the tension disappeared when he took over. Straight away he changed the diet. Out went the horrible margarine, replaced by butter, which was an instant success. He used to say, 'A well-fed prisoner is a happy prisoner.' He was and still is an absolute gentleman.

Chief Officer Patrick Crowley was also a very energetic man and he was always on the move, almost running around the prison. My lasting memory of him is the jangle of keys from the huge bunch he carried with him at all times, about twenty big keys on a long leather strap hanging from his arm. You'd hear the keys long before you'd see him. When he moved on, towards the end of 1968, he was replaced by a Cork man, Flor McCarthy. In contrast, Flor was very easy-going and good-natured, and didn't get excited very often.

At that time officers lived in dread of being half-sheeted. Half sheets were short memos to the governor about a range of matters. In a disciplinary context they were a formal report, usually written by the chief officer or a supervising officer, of some breach of the rules or failure by a subordinate. The governor would write on it, 'For explanation, please', and the chief officer would hand it to the offending officer and ask him to reply to it, usually there and then. Some chiefs and supervising officers were very sneaky and wouldn't tell the officer that they were querying his behaviour, so the first he would hear of it was when the half sheet was handed to him for explanation. Half sheets were issued for the most trivial of things. When an officer got one, word would spread like lightning and it was the talk of the prison. Prison officers had no rights and there were no disciplinary procedures in place, so the governor and the Department of Justice could do as they liked. Officers were sometimes transferred overnight, solely on the basis of a half sheet.

Flor, though, had little time for the tyranny of the half sheet. He dealt with most things directly, which was much tougher than just writing something on a sheet of paper. A dressing-down by Flor was something you never forgot. But that's what he did: every problem or mistake was dealt with at the time and then he forgot it. It was an early lesson in effective management.

Most of the officers were single, and we had a great time considering the wages we were on. I started on thirteen pounds, ten shillings and threepence and I got a big rise in September 1968, when I was twenty-one: my wages went up to thirteen pounds, fifteen shillings and threepence. And we paid income tax as well. As we had to live in the prison, and the gates closed at 12 midnight, we needed a place to stay if we went out for the night. You had to get permission to stay out for a night or go home for a few days, and you would do this by going to the chief officer's office and asking for the signing-out book. When making the application you wrote, 'Sir, I respectfully wish to apply for permission to be away from the prison on the following nights . . . For the granting of same I shall be grateful', and you signed it. The chief officer insisted that three off-duty officers had to stay in every night, and if there weren't three in he would refuse your application. If you ignored him, you were given a half sheet.

In 1969 I attended my first Annual General Meeting of the Limerick branch of the Prison Officers' Association. The Prison Officers' Association in those days had a very low profile and it didn't have trade union status or the power it has today, but it was fully recognized under the civil service conciliation and arbitration scheme. The branch secretary was standing down, and I was elected to the position – why, I don't know. The incoming chairman was another POA newcomer, Morgan Downey. He was very tall, six foot three or four inches and built accordingly. I, on the other hand, was tiny. So the branch was led by 'Little and Large'.

Though working conditions for staff were improving – for instance, since 1967 there had been a proper roster so you knew in good time when you would be on duty or not; before that staff worked day and night, and got time off whenever it was available, or whenever the chief officer decided it was available – they were still poor. There was no such thing as overtime or allowances, and we just got basic pay.

Big Morgan and I had only been elected for a few days when we were called into action. An officer had plugged in the electric kettle one afternoon in the mess and run out for a message. The kettle did not switch off automatically, and it was his bad luck that the governor happened upon the unattended boiling kettle, unplugged it and took it over to the stores. When the officer came back, the kettle was gone. At first he thought that someone was playing a joke on him, but it didn't turn up and nobody knew what had happened. It was the next day before word eventually filtered out that the kettle had been confiscated by the governor. And so our first job as branch officers was to arrange a meeting with the governor to get the kettle back.

He met us the following afternoon, two full days without a kettle and twenty people needing it in the mess. Big Morgan and I were escorted into his office by the chief officer. We stood to attention, explained what had happened and asked for the kettle to be returned. He took two or three different notebooks from a drawer in his desk. They contained details of expenditure on electricity in the mess, along with a whole lot of other facts and figures. He lambasted us about costs and told us that he had received lots of complaints about the behaviour of officers in the mess and went on and on about the outrage of leaving the kettle boiling. Eventually, almost reluctantly, he said, 'Chief, tell the storekeeper to give it back to them.'

We said, 'Thanks very much', but didn't mean a word of it.

Then Morgan said, 'Governor, while we are here, would you consider giving us a fridge for the mess? We badly need a fridge.'

The governor replied, 'You can apply to the stores for it.' We went back to the mess and wrote out an application on a half sheet and gave it to the storekeeper as we collected the kettle. After a long time the storekeeper approved the purchase of a small domestic fridge for the mess.

Our next challenge was getting a public telephone in the mess. We had to make a written application and give the governor all sorts of guarantees before he approved it, including paying all the costs of installing it ourselves and being fully responsible for all the bills. We made a collection and got the telephone.

Looking back now, it's unbelievable to me how much effort we had to put into getting the most trivial of things and how difficult everything was made for us.

Before I joined the prison service, like most people I hadn't the slightest idea what a prison was like, how it worked and what prisoners were like. But I had a belief that they were dangerous and violent. I think this is because I would hear occasionally on the wireless, as a little child, 'A prisoner has escaped from Limerick Prison and he should not be approached as he could be dangerous.' As children in the countryside, we used to be terrified of the escaped prisoner and we were convinced that he would come to Toureen, our little townland. And that perception was still with me when I went into the laundry on my very first day in Limerick Prison. I spent most of the afternoon sizing up the prisoners and trying to figure out what they were really like, how they thought and how they acted.

Almost instantly I realized that they were very ordinary and, in many cases, simple people, a million miles away from the vicious, aggressive and dangerous people I'd imagined. They just looked poor and miserable. Prisoners wore a prison uniform then, unlike nowadays. Sentenced prisoners wore a grey prison suit comprised of old flannel or woollen-type trousers and jacket and a yellow-brown shirt. Remands wore blue, and contempt-of-court prisoners brown. A prisoner was issued with a uniform when he was committed, and he wore it every day until his release or until it was worn out and replaced. It was not laundered. They were not given underpants. They were also issued with heavy shoes with steel studs on the soles. In those days the shoes were made in the prison service, mainly in Mountjoy. They were a half ton weight and were rough and very uncomfortable.

As I got to know and understand the whole system better, I felt that Limerick Prison was similar in many ways to the old county homes or poorhouses that all counties used to have and where many misfortunate elderly and poor people ended up. In many ways, prisons took over from the poorhouses when the latter were closed down. In 1968 Limerick Prison contained a large number of people who were simply poor, odd, mentally ill or physically disabled. They were the homeless, the unemployed, the alcoholics and the travellers. Most of them came from the poorest areas of the cities of Limerick, Cork and Waterford.

My time in Limerick Prison came to an end in 1971. While I was there I experienced all the rewards and frustrations that were to become typical of my time in the prison service. Over the years I have found that one of the great rewards of my job has been meeting the people I've worked with – both the staff and the prisoners – and hearing how their lives are progressing. Even now I run into fellows I knew back in Limerick when I was young and green.

A few years ago, I travelled to a town in County Cork to give a talk to local parents. It was held in the GAA clubhouse at the top of the town. I was due to speak at 8 p.m. and I got there just on time. After pulling into the car park on a wet, dark and miserable night, as I was getting out of the car I saw a man walking towards me. When he got closer he said, 'Hello, do you know me?'

I looked at him and said 'No.'

He went on, 'Well, I met you in Limerick Prison in 1968.'

I said, 'No, I still don't know you.'

'If I told you that I was from Tipperary, would you know me?' he asked.

'No, I'm sorry, I don't know you,' I replied.

And then he said, 'Well, what if I told you that I was the youngest in Limerick Prison at that time? I was only sixteen. I was on remand on a murder charge.'

And then it came to me. 'I know you now,' I said. 'I don't believe it.'

'You were very good to me in Limerick Prison,' he said, 'and I've never forgotten it. This is the first time I've had the chance to meet you again and say thanks. I saw your talk on a poster in the school, but I can't go to it because I'm on a night shift.'

A little girl got out of his car and started to walk towards us. He shouted at her to go back to the car. 'That's my daughter and I don't want her to know what we're talking about. I served over twenty years of a life sentence, but I'm living here now and I have a lovely family. I am working and things are not too bad.'

We shook hands and he drove off to work.

4. A New Challenge in Dublin

In February 1971, I was at home in Tipperary for a few days when I got a message to phone Pat Carroll at work. When I got through to Pat in the mess, he told me that word had come through that I was to be transferred to Shanganagh Castle in Shankill, Dublin, on St Patrick's Day. I was very surprised and shocked at this news. When I went back a few days later the governor, Pat McFadden, confirmed the move.

A week or so after I was notified about going to Dublin I was back home again in Bansha, helping out John Moloney with the underage players in the GAA club. I had taken up refereeing at his suggestion, and was doing so regularly at hurling and football matches in Tipperary. John was telling me about some plans he had for the parish leagues for all the juveniles in the club.

'God, I won't be around,' I said. 'I'm going to Dublin, to Shanganagh Castle.'

'No way – no way will you be going to Dublin. We need you here,' he said.

'I'm being transferred on 17 March.'

'I'll stop it. It'll be no problem to stop that,' he said. 'My best friend, Dan Murphy, works with Paddy Lalor in Abbeyleix.' Paddy Lalor was a parliamentary secretary (a junior minister). 'I'll get Dan Murphy to arrange with Paddy Lalor that you won't be leaving Limerick at all. We need you here in Bansha.'

'Fine,' I said, 'but make sure it works, because there is nothing worse than trying and failing.'

Early in March I heard that my transfer had been delayed until 17 April because my replacement in Limerick had asked for a month's postponement. A few days later I was called to the general office, where the clerk, P. M. Kelly, handed me a circular headed 'Use of Political Influence', and asked me to sign it. I knew then that John Moloney had failed.

I met John in Bansha the following week. 'I got a letter from Paddy Lalor saying that your transfer is to go ahead,' he said, and pulled the letter out of a trouser pocket.

'Shit,' I said, 'that spells trouble.'

Paddy Lalor had written to Des O'Malley, Minister for Justice, requesting that my transfer would not take place. Des O'Malley's office passed it to the Prisons Division, where it had landed on the desk of Dick Crowe, an assistant principal officer and the man who had transferred me in the first place.

And so, on 17 April, I woke at the crack of dawn, caught the first train from Limerick to Dublin and then got the 45 bus from Fleet Street. I knew where it was because I had been there before. After an All Ireland final a few years earlier, a couple of us had called out to have a look at this radical new thing – an open prison for young boys between sixteen and twenty-one.

I got off the bus just after Shankill village and walked the 200 yards to the main entrance off the Shankill–Bray road. The walk up to Shanganagh Castle was impressive, a beautiful avenue lined with trees and shrubs. On the right-hand side of the avenue was a full-sized soccer pitch, and the remainder of the grounds, while still rough, had great potential for development. Close to the house was a tennis court with lovely mown lawns, and at the back of it was an old-fashioned kitchen garden, which was a feature of all big houses and castles in those days. The dormitories, which housed fifty-five people in separate cubicles, were located on the first and second floors of an extension to the main house. On each of these floors there was a big room used to accommodate single officers. I was allocated a place in the big room on the first floor, and I shared this room with two other officers.

I had been in Shanganagh for a couple of days when Dick Crowe turned up. I had this gut feeling that he would be looking for me. Sure enough, an hour or so later the call came: 'Mr Crowe wants to see you.' Up I went to this big hallway, and there he was walking around with his head down in deep thought. He welcomed me and said how wonderful it was that I was in Shanganagh and that he should have told me to bring working clothes as well, as I could be doing anything in Shanganagh: cutting grass with the boys, cutting a ditch or playing football with them. It was all part of the therapy, he said. He told me why Shanganagh was important and what it was going to do in the future, and how I was going to be a significant part of it. And then he came to my transfer. In a very low voice, he asked, 'Why didn't you want to come to Shanganagh?'

'I didn't want to come to Shanganagh because socially it suited me more to be in Limerick,' I said. 'I was only twenty-five miles from home, I was involved in the GAA and a lot of activities and I was quite enjoying it.'

He told me that I would have to decide between my career and sport. 'Why do you think you were selected to come to Shanganagh?' he asked.

'I have no idea.'

'Because Shanganagh needs you,' he said.

And do you know something, I actually believed him: I was so innocent at the time, and I was sort of thrilled with myself to have been 'selected' to go to Shanganagh.

I was just getting a bit relaxed and thinking, *This is it, he is about to let me go*, when he continued in a very low voice, 'You did one thing that disappointed me. What was that?' I pretended I had no idea what he was talking about, but he just kept saying, 'What did you do that I'm disappointed about?' and looking me straight in the eyes. In no time he broke me down, and I said, 'You must be talking about Paddy Lalor. I didn't do that – it was a friend of mine, John Moloney, who did it.'

And he said, 'Don't mind the old fellows in the prison service. Political influence doesn't work.'

Dick Crowe took a personal interest in the development of Shanganagh, and he spent many hours, day and night, there. He was a visionary and knew exactly the type of regime he wanted. He believed that the boys were not bad but simply needed an opportunity to grow and develop, and he was determined that Shanganagh Castle would provide the same type of support and services for them as would any boarding school. There would be no walls, no barbed wire, no caging in of people; they were there on the basis of trust, and they had the choice of either running away or staying.

Open centres are the complete opposite to conventional closed prisons. Prisoners are free to leave at any stage if they wish to do so, and while if they did they would be classified as going unlawfully at large and could be re-arrested at any time, the significant point is that there are no physical restrictions placed on them. There were rules and instructions at Shanganagh Castle and certain areas were out of bounds, but it all worked on the basis of consent.

Most of the boys in Shanganagh had been transferred from St Patrick's Institution, part of the Mountjoy complex. During 1968 a total of 633 boys were committed to St Patrick's but only 19 were serving sentences of more than twelve months, so it was obvious that the vast majority of them didn't require the level of security St Patrick's provided. (Incidentally, St Patrick's had opened in 1956, when the borstal in Clonmel, in County Tipperary, was closed. The Department of Justice decided that the women's prison, which had only a dozen or so prisoners, would be converted for use as a detention centre. With the exception of a section of the ground floor, the remainder of what had been the women's prison was designated as St Patrick's Institution. It was nothing less than a prison for children.)

In Shanganagh the staff wore no uniforms. We all worked in civilian clothes and the boys also dressed casually, wearing jeans, jumpers and runners. This created a very relaxed and normal atmosphere, and was a very important step in deinstitutionalization. The daily regime was structured but very relaxed. The boys were called at eight in the morning or shortly afterwards. They were all expected to get up, wash, make their beds and come down to the communal dining hall for breakfast at nine. After breakfast it was off to school or work, or whatever other activities they were allocated. Most boys went to school and a few worked in the grounds, the kitchen, the dining room or as general cleaners. They were back again in the dining room around 12.30 p.m. for dinner, and then they were free to walk the grounds, play snooker or just sit around until two, when they went back to education and work. At five they had evening tea and then they were free until ten, when they went to bed.

The one big weakness in having dormitories was that we often found it hard to get the boys to settle down for the night. They were like little children, running around and hiding under beds, and all too often they had pillow fights. We were lucky to get out of the place by eleven. Staff duties followed the boys' roster. The duties were pretty straightforward and the staffing levels were low, with only three staff members and one supervisor on duty after five in the evening for up to fifty-five boys.

Dick Crowe spent a lot of time encouraging the staff to have a positive approach and to help the boys in their development. He introduced a mentoring system called 'House Mastering'. All prison officers were assigned two or three boys and were asked to take a special interest in them, to talk to them regularly, encourage them to participate in activities, be a friendly face and the person the boy could go to if he had any personal problems. This concept was very positive, and very helpful for the boys. The main problem Crowe had was getting some of the officers to take it seriously.

One of the objectives that Crowe had for Shanganagh was to try to instil in the boys the discipline of self-control. He believed that the more a young boy is in control of his emotions, his feelings, his actions, the more likely he will be able to control his life in a positive and purposeful way. That is the experience I have had too.

Most of the boys came from urban areas, mainly from Cork, Dublin, Limerick, Galway and Waterford. They were all very poorly educated, had experienced very little positivity in their lives, and had very low self-esteem and self-confidence, but it was obvious that most of them also had huge potential.

The local Vocational Education Committee supplied teachers on secondment to teach in Shanganagh Castle. Before 1968 there were no teachers coming into the prisons, and the only education was provided by a prison officer who was appointed as a schoolmaster, and he would only help prisoners who were illiterate. Bringing the VECs into prison education was a masterstroke, and to this day they make a huge contribution to education in prisons. Two nuns – Sister Veronica and Sister Bridget – also worked as teachers, and the boys got on very well with them. Another nun, Sister James, who was a nurse, looked after all

the boys' medical needs. There were also two full-time gardeners cum
caretakers, Jack O'Neill and Sean Clancy, mature and wise middle-
aged men whom the boys looked up to and took advice from. On the
other hand, the governor, Jack O'Donovan, was old school and author-
itarian, and both boys and staff were on their guard when he was
around.

Only a few weeks after my transfer, I was walking down O'Connell
Street in Dublin one evening and walked straight into Dick Crowe.
He stopped me and asked, 'How are you getting on?'

'Great,' I said.

'If you want to go back to Limerick, you can. There will be a
vacancy there soon.'

'Ah no,' I said. 'I like Shanganagh, I'll stay there.'

Almost every time I met him over the years, he always said to me,
'Only for I dragged you out of Limerick all those years ago, you'd be
still there.' And perhaps I would.

I got to love Shanganagh. I found everything about it exciting,
challenging and rewarding. I loved the open spaces, I loved the fact
that we were encouraged to work closely with the boys, to talk to
them, and above all, I loved the opportunity to play sport with
them, particularly football. We played a lot of football. In those
days most of the showbands took Mondays off, so every Monday,
almost without fail, a team made up of showband members came
to Shanganagh to play soccer and we had some great matches with
them. Staff from the local banks also visited regularly to play the
boys.

The Catholic chaplain Father Ben Mulligan and I used to play with
the boys against the visiting teams and we had a few great battles. In
addition to the more normal work of a chaplain, Ben widened the
role to provide much personal and family support, and he organized
quite a lot of work and social and sporting activities for the boys. He
developed great relationships with the construction industry in the
Bray, Shankill and Cabinteely areas. Once Ben got onto a building
site, he never left without getting a job for one of the boys. He just
had the gift of being able to convince people that they had a social

responsibility. There were times when up to fifteen boys were going out every morning to work in the local area.

The Annual Sports Day was a big occasion and much planning went into it. The morning was given over to athletics and novelty events. The boys competed against each other and against the staff. One year, we decided to play the boys in a soccer match in the afternoon, and Eamonn Darcy, the former Republic of Ireland and Drumcondra goal-keeper, came out to referee it. We lost the match 1–0. We were humiliated because the match was a do-or-die affair and the boys didn't let us forget who won: we were jeered and slagged for months.

Sport made a great contribution to the development of many boys in Shanganagh. Sport is all about giving and taking, and there was an unwritten rule that whatever happened on the football field stayed there. The boys respected all the staff who played football with or against them. It helped to build relationships and to break down barriers, and that was one of the great strengths of open centres. It allowed the staff and the boys to live a far more normal and constructive life than in the more rigid and dividing regime and philosophy of closed prisons.

I decided that the big kitchen garden had great potential and could be developed into a vegetable garden for the castle. At the start of the project, one of the supervising officers, Matt Mannix, used to threaten some of the boys with 'working with Lonergan' in the garden when they were in trouble, and at that stage they hated the garden work. They were inner-city lads who had never been on a farm or in a vege-table garden in their lives. But after a while they got to like it and indeed often asked Matt to work in the garden. And so we dug it up and sowed a load of vegetables, and the boys really got to love it. They actually looked forward to it every morning, working hard, digging, sowing potatoes and cabbage, and doing all the things that I, coming from the country, thought were just normal.

One day I was in the garden with five or six of the boys admiring our work. There were rows of beautiful potatoes with their stalks just breaking the ground and rows of lovely cabbage plants just beginning to sprout up, and the whole place looked immaculate. Behind my back, two or three of them started messing around and then two of them took off chasing some of the others over the garden, trampling on the plants and not realizing the damage they were doing. I just couldn't believe that anybody who had worked so hard and so caringly to nurture the plants to that stage could ruin it. In the space of a few minutes they had wrecked it all through a lack of appreciation or understanding of the value of their own work and the value of the plants in the garden. This also chimed with how they lived their own lives. In a moment of madness, in a matter of minutes, they could wreck all the good they had done and all the hard work they had put in.

In time the garden recovered and the plants grew again, and by midsummer the cabbage plants were just about to develop big heads of cabbage. Then one morning around ten, we went down to the garden and there was nothing left: pigeons had visited during the early morning and had eaten every leaf of cabbage, leaving nothing but bare stalks. It was devastating to see weeks and weeks of work disappear overnight. But I was able to use the destruction carried out by the pigeons as an example of how our lives are often shaken by unforeseen events and how we have to take these ups and downs on the chin because there is absolutely nothing we can do about them. Seeing the bare stalks sticking up out of the ground, headless and leafless, told the story in the most powerful way possible.

Shanganagh Castle had huge potential. My experience was that it changed the course of many young people's lives for the better. But that potential never came anywhere close to being realized, and the responsibility for this rests with the Department of Justice. When Dick Crowe was moved to a different role in the Prisons Division in 1977, nobody took up the cudgels on behalf of open centres or ever again had the same interest in Shanganagh. Sadly few of them could understand its philosophy.

For a number of years the signs were there that Shanganagh Castle was on the way out, as the number of boys being transferred there was reducing all the time. It wasn't that there weren't boys suitable for Shanganagh in St Patrick's, it was that they weren't being sent there. They were often kept in St Patrick's just to keep the numbers of detainees – and therefore staffing levels – at a constant there. I became aware of this through the prison grapevine.

Another problem was that for years officers were not selected to work in Shanganagh; they ended up there by default. Some were transferred there because they had difficulties in other prisons, others for personal and geographical reasons, others still because of seniority. This was a disaster because many of these people had no interest in Shanganagh's philosophy and had neither the interpersonal skills nor the aptitude for it. As a result it was left to a small number of dedicated staff to keep the place going.

In time, the strategy of keeping numbers down in Shanganagh paid off. Because it was catering for fewer prisoners, the cost of staffing and running it was relatively high and the optics were bad. The writing was on the wall for a long time, and the eventual decision to close Shanganagh came about in reaction to an industrial relations dispute between the Prison Officers' Association and the Minister for Justice, Michael McDowell, over his decision to eliminate overtime in the prison service. Shanganagh Castle became a pawn in the dispute, and it was closed in December 2002.

That's what I will remember Michael McDowell for: turning the clock back fifty years or more in our approach to juvenile crime. Not long after closing down Shanganagh Castle, he closed the detention centre on Spike Island in Cobh, County Cork. While I was never a fan of Spike Island – I don't believe that an island is the right place for a detention centre – it had excellent facilities, in particular a wonderful and well-resourced education centre.

Having children locked up for seventeen hours every day in St Patrick's Institution is scandalous, and simply proves that as a society we don't really care about our most troubled children. In 1997 psychologist Dr Paul O'Mahony published research he had conducted the previous year in which he found that 72 per cent of Mountjoy prisoners had served time in St Patrick's Institution prior to their committal to Mountjoy. In 2010 the figure would be comparable. As a society, this is the price – human and financial – we are paying for the folly of these closures and our failure to do something to help these troubled boys to get back on track with their lives while they're still young.

In the early 2000s a suggestion of using Shanganagh as an open centre for women was mooted by the Irish Prison Service (IPS), and I was asked to visit Shanganagh to look at its potential for this purpose. I told the officials it was ideal. I still hold this view. At the time of my retirement there were at least fifty women in the Dóchas Centre – the women's prison at Mountjoy – who were ideal for an open centre setting. At a time of massive overcrowding in the Dóchas Centre, this was and still is a no-brainer. Accommodating fifty women in an open centre would be much cheaper than keeping them in a closed prison.

However, the proposal to use Shanganagh as an open prison for women never really got off the ground and it was quickly shelved. The governor of Shanganagh at that time was totally opposed to the suggestion. And so a great opportunity was missed.

After Shanganagh closed, Dun Laoghaire-Rathdown County Council took the buildings and some of the land to develop for social housing, and about nine acres of the surrounding land were sold to a building developer. Buildings and land remain idle in 2010.

5. An Inspirational Governor

In October 1972, I was asked by Dick Crowe to go to Loughan House in Blacklion, County Cavan, to assist with its launch as an open centre for 16- to 23-year-old men. He felt that it needed a few people who had practical experience of open centres to help to get it off the ground. A number of staff in Shanganagh were asked, but I was the only one who ended up going there, a sort of a guinea pig.

Loughan House had been a seminary. It was situated about two miles from Blacklion, overlooking the Cavan, Fermanagh and Leitrim borders. It was a huge three-storey building. The ground floor was used for classrooms, administration and recreation; the first floor was used to accommodate staff; and the top floor was used to accommodate the prisoners.

I set off for Loughan House on 1 December 1972, along with about fifteen other officers and twenty-six young prisoners who were being transferred from Dublin, mainly from Mountjoy. We got on a bus at Mountjoy shortly after 2 p.m. The journey lasted an eternity. Every light in the distance I hoped was Loughan House, but time after time I was disappointed; we just kept driving along. I kept thinking, *I'll never find my way back from here*. It was 8 p.m., and a dark, wet and miserable night, by the time we arrived. Just imagine the scene – a group of prisoners, a crowd of new staff and nobody really knowing what to do. Madness.

My first morning on duty in Loughan House was a real shock and an eye-opener. Before I arrived, eight prisoners were already there, along with a small number of mostly inexperienced staff. They were very definitely inexperienced in relation to open prisons. Because the prisoners had been there for a while with very little supervision and no structure, they had become unruly and a bit untouchable. They were doing their own thing in their own time in their own way. And so on my first morning, when I went into the first room and tried to wake a young man who was asleep, saying, 'Good morning, right, it's time to get up', he didn't move, open his eyes or take a bit of notice of me. Five minutes later when I returned to the room he was still fast asleep. I shook him and said, 'Time to get up.' With that, he jumped out of the bed, grabbed the safety rail off the side of the bunk and swung it at me. It was some introduction to Loughan House.

Things improved when a bit of structure and organization was put into the place. A regime developed, and the prisoners generally responded positively. There were two guys who were kind of top dogs. They were both well over six feet tall, physically very strong and with personalities to match. In many ways they ran the show before the new staff arrived. These two were very good footballers and were quick to tell us how good they were. My colleague Pat Lindsay was a fullback in the Roscommon Senior Football team. He was also a strong, powerful man with the determination to go with his physique. When the two boys heard about Lindsay's football talents, they challenged him to a game of soccer, staff versus the prisoners. And so Lindsay got a team together and organized a game. Some of the staff were very good Gaelic footballers, but only a few of them played soccer. In addition, none of us really knew each other and so we didn't know who could or couldn't play. The boys were sure that they would beat us.

The prisoners' team was good – particularly the two boys – and it was a tough, dour battle in which we struggled to hold our own. We did our best, but the prisoners won 3–1 and they walked back up to the house that evening feeling six feet six inches tall, while we had to eat humble pie. We felt humiliated but, as in Shanganagh, that one game of football changed the atmosphere in Loughan House immediately. We never again had an ounce of difficulty with the two boys. Indeed, they were a pleasure to work with from that day on. And it was all down to equality on the football pitch. I'm sure, as well, that they admired the fact that we took what they gave us and did so with a smile, never whinging, and equally they took what we gave them and never whinged either.

★

I learned a lot from working for Loughan House's governor, P. M. Kelly. I knew P.M. very well from my time in Limerick and liked him greatly. The more I got to know him, the more I admired him. He was a very sophisticated and well-educated man, but still approachable to both staff and prisoners, good humoured and in tune with ordinary people. Years later, when my first daughter Sinéad was born, we were chatting about the new baby and out of the blue he said to me, 'Now start reading to her straight away.'

'I will when she gets bigger,' I said.

'Not when she gets bigger – right away,' he insisted.

'But she won't understand,' I said.

'That's where you're wrong. Of course she will understand, and if you read to her you will pass on a most wonderful gift, one that will stay with her until the end of her life.'

I took his advice and read to her for years, until one day when she was about four she told me that she could read for herself.

There weren't many that had P.M.'s principles. And he was the only person I ever met who actually worried about the power he had as a prison governor and the dangers of abusing it or misusing it and destroying a prisoner's life prospects. In simple terms, he felt it a great burden to have to, for instance, send a young man back to a closed prison for some misbehaviour. He worried that if by any chance at all he was wronging a prisoner, that wrong would be multiplied several times over because it would be the prison system that had wronged him.

P.M. also took huge personal responsibility for everything that happened, and he taught me some great lessons in this regard. Even if he wasn't involved in the slightest way in a decision or a wrongdoing in his prison, he took full responsibility for it and always took it on the chin.

When Loughan House opened in 1972 it had no clerical staff, and since a young prison officer, Andrew Lang, had a background in office administration, he agreed to work in the general office. One night a prisoner broke into the general office and took all the money in the safe. In those days we were paid in cash and so there was always money in the safe. The next day it was discovered that the money was missing, but we couldn't figure out how the safe had been opened. Andrew lived in Sligo and he used to hide the safe keys under a pile of files and papers in the general office before going home every evening. Then he would lock the door and take the keys home with him. Obviously a prisoner had observed his routine, broken into the office, found the keys, taken the money, locked the safe again and put the keys back where he found them. Naturally, once it was discovered that the money was stolen there was a major enquiry and the gardaí were called in. A few days later the money was found in a bottle hidden in a cistern in one of the toilets, up on the third floor, where the prisoners lived.

P.M. discovered what had happened, the mistakes that were made and the breach of security, and he wrote a report to Dick Crowe in the Department of Justice, then superintending officer of prisons. In his report P.M. outlined the sequence of events leading up to the break-in and how the prisoner got his hands on the safe keys. In the final paragraph of his report he wrote something along the lines of, 'I'm the governor of Loughan House, all breaches of security are my ultimate responsibility and in this case I take full responsibility for the breach of security. Andrew Lang is a young officer with very little experience, there is no fault in the wide world attached to him, he did what he thought was best, and as governor I should have known better and should have instructed him on what was required. And so I take full personal responsibility for this incident.' Never before or since have I witnessed such an example of a person taking overall responsibility for the genuine mistakes or failures of subordinate staff. He was the person I most admired in all my years in the prison service: I will never forget his example and his decency and deep integrity.

In January 1973, I got my first promotion. I was appointed an assistant chief officer, a supervising officer. (The ranks in the prison service are as follows: basic grade prison officer; assistant chief officer; chief officer – class one and class two, with one being the more senior; assistant governor; deputy governor; and governor – classes one, two and three, again with one being the most senior. A chief officer in the prison service is the highest ranking uniform grade. All governor grades wear civilian clothes.) I transferred to the Training Unit at Glengarriff

Parade, Dublin, in September 1975. The Training Unit was a new concept, and again it was down to the thinking and vision of Dick Crowe. He believed that a modern prison service should have a facility where the emphasis would be on preparing prisoners, particularly long-term prisoners, for their release back into society.

The Training Unit was constructed in the grounds of Mountjoy and was a modern and well-built facility that accommodated ninety-six prisoners. There were no bars on the windows and the doors were wooden rather than steel. There was a large communal dining hall where all the prisoners ate together – unlike Mountjoy, where all prisoners ate in their cells. Again, like open centres, the regime was very relaxed. Unlock was at eight in the morning and all the prisoners were out of their rooms until ten in the evening.

The emphasis in the Training Unit was to encourage prisoners to participate in work training, which provided great opportunities to develop skills in welding, steel-turning, electronics and steel fabrication. The workshops were similar to those run by AnCO, the predecessor to FÁS as the state training agency. The instructors were recruited by open competition from the outside, and the training was backed up by a modern education unit, staffed by teachers seconded from Dublin City VEC. The idea was that the prisoners would avail themselves of education and work training and be better prepared to leave prison and reintegrate into the community. Reduced security was also an important part of the regime, as long-term prisoners often suffer from institutionalization, so the scaled-down security would help them adjust to the life that was awaiting them.

In the Training Unit, I teamed up again with P. M. Kelly, whose career had brought him back to Dublin. He was an ideal choice for such a new initiative as he was prepared to take risks with prisoners who had a difficult history and he gave them a second and often a third chance to get their lives back on track.

Both prisoners and staff wore civilian clothes in the Training Unit, and the regime was relaxed. If they put their minds to it prisoners could escape, but few ever did. When prisoners are treated with dignity and respect they usually appreciate it, and over the years thousands have reciprocated the trust placed in them by being transferred to the

Training Unit. It was a great place to work and I certainly benefited from being there.

In the late summer of 1976 the Department of Justice decided to introduce a new grade – assistant governor – and the competition was open to those at the rank of assistant chief officer and upwards. I applied, not with any great expectation of getting it, but I was one of five people selected and I was promoted to the rank of assistant governor in November 1976. At twenty-five, I had been the youngest ever to be promoted to the grade of assistant chief officer. Now, at twenty-nine, I was the youngest ever to be promoted to the grade of assistant governor. I went on to serve for over thirty-three years in the governor grades.

During our training I was sent to Mountjoy for a period. I worked mostly in the general office, where the workload was huge and the clerks were flat to the boards at all times. It must be remembered that in 1976 everything was recorded manually in ledgers. Despite this, we had a bit of craic. One of my colleagues, Eamon O'Reilly, was an awful trick actor. One day he rang in from another office pretending to be an official from the Department of Social Welfare. He asked the young clerk who answered the phone about a prisoner called So-and-so McDonagh. Now, this was a common name in the Mountjoy population, and that day there were ten So-and-so McDonaghs in the prison. The clerk asked 'What's his address?' 'No fixed address,' replied O'Reilly. Then he said, 'He has a scar over his right eye', and the clerk, getting frustrated, shouted back, 'Ah Jaysus, sure all the McDonaghs have scars over their right eyes!' 'What sort of people are ye working in there,' O'Reilly replied, 'that ye can't find a prisoner in the prison? How come the guards can find them on the outside?' By this point the young clerk had about twenty files piled up on his desk and the sweat was running down his face. In the end he just hung up.

I spent a few months working once more in Shanganagh in 1977 before being told in October that I was being transferred back to Loughan House as assistant director (the same thing as assistant governor – because it was a special school, the job titles were director and assistant director). I didn't want to return to Loughan House, mainly because I had recently married, we had just bought a house and my wife, Breda, was working as an official in Dun Laoghaire Corporation. When we got married, we assumed that we would be living in Dublin and the thought of moving never crossed our minds. We certainly didn't want to move up to County Cavan, but I was given no choice really. We rented a house in the village of Glenfarne in County Leitrim, and Sinéad was born there. Despite my initial unwillingness to take the job, I ended up staying almost two years and it turned out to be one of the most positive experiences of my time in the prison service.

For many years up to the early 1970s the secure centre for children under sixteen had been Marlborough House in Glasnevin, Dublin. It became a shambles and had to be closed down in 1972. So in 1977 the government decided to designate Loughan House as a Special School for twelve- to sixteen-year-old boys, until the Department of Education built new secure accommodation at Lusk, County Dublin. At this time a small number of children, mainly from inner-city Dublin, had gone a bit wild and were, to some degree, out of control. District Justice Kennedy was frustrated trying to deal with them in her court, because she had no place to put the most difficult and troubled boys. Newspapers ran stories about the 'Bugsy Malones', and the general public was led to believe that there were hundreds of children running amok in Dublin.

The opening of Loughan House in 1977 attracted huge negative publicity and public criticism, and rightly so. Many of the child-care agencies were totally opposed to a prison taking responsibility for children, and I had no difficulty with that and still don't. But as usual, the focus was wrongly placed and the prison service and prison staff became the target of the criticism, rather than the establishment. To learn the ropes and to get an insight into what was required, all the staff got some child-care training and worked in special schools and children's homes for a number of months. Some of the staff selected were ideally suited for the work; others struggled to cope.

The house had to be totally refurbished, with facilities for education, workshops, medical care and recreation all upgraded. A high wire fence was erected around the perimeter, making Loughan House a secure unit for the first time. All the windows were replaced with Lexan, which was unbreakable, instead of glass, but the window frames were made from wood and were easily broken.

The first boy was committed in October 1978, and he spent almost two weeks on his own in the centre. Over the next few months the numbers increased, and by spring 1979 there were over twenty boys in the house. The agencies of the state had failed these boys prior to their committal to Loughan House – the health boards, schools, local authorities, various professions like psychiatry and psychology, the law and order system. Then, as a last resort, they were given over to us to perform miracles. We took in some of the most disturbed and difficult young boys in the country, in an environment that was totally alien to them. Some of them became reasonably easy to manage – there is a huge difference between being a devious criminal and being a bit wild, and many were just out of control in an innocent sort of way: up to every devilment and fit for anything. These only needed a bit of structure and some discipline in their lives. Other boys were very difficult: they had serious psychiatric difficulties or conduct and personality disorders. Still others were quiet, timid and withdrawn.

From 1978 to the mid 1980s there were never more than thirty boys in Loughan House at any one time, proving that the media had seriously hyped up the situation. The juvenile justice system was not on its knees, and the Bugsy Malones were just a small number of children who had been neglected by the state in the 1960s and '70s.

About three or four weeks after I had arrived I was in my office one night when an officer came in and said that one of the boys was refusing to leave the recreation room to go to bed. I went to the room and there he was standing in the corner, about six staff pleading with him to go to bed. I knew that this was a crunch time: staff would be watching closely how I managed the first serious challenge to our authority. I spoke to him for about five minutes trying to reason with him, but he just refused to move. In the end I frogmarched him to his room. He was every bit as big and strong as I was, and he resisted all the way. When I eventually got him to his room, I had another battle to get him in through the door. It was only at that stage that I realized I was on my own. The staff just stood by and never came to assist me. And that was down to fear – fear that they would be guilty of some wrong-doing if they played any part in his removal. It highlighted the need for leadership, to demonstrate what you could do, what you had to do and how to do it right.

I soon discovered that the boys greatly resented any physical force being used against them. As assistant director I was responsible for the day-to-day care of the boys, and one day they asked if I would see them on their own, without the staff, because they wanted to talk about things that they didn't want to talk about in the presence of the staff. I agreed, and indeed during my whole time in Loughan House I met with all the boys once a week on my own, listening to their complaints and grievances.

At our first meeting their main complaint was the staff 'dragging us to our rooms'. That was the thing that most annoyed them: to be manhandled in front of their peers and to be taken out by force was a humiliation. My response was, 'Well, you have to do what you're told and when you're told to go somewhere, like going to bed at night, you have to go and if you don't, force will be used.' By chance I added, 'But if you give me a guarantee that you will go to your rooms when you are told, I will order the staff not to manhandle you again.' And they said, 'Right, we will give you our word. If you tell the staff not to grab us, we will walk to our rooms when we are told.' They fully honoured their word and this had an extremely positive effect in the house and made a big difference to the staff's relationships with the boys.

To encourage good behaviour, an incentive and reward scheme, based on a complicated points system, had been put in place before the centre opened. It was unworkable and had no credibility with the boys. I came up with a simple system of awarding stars for good behaviour. The maximum number of stars available in a week was five. The star system gave instant rewards: three stars in a week guaranteed a boy one late night, which meant he could stay up until 11.30 on the night of his choosing – to see a film, for instance; four and five stars meant additional late nights; and when a boy accumulated sixteen stars over a three-month period, he qualified for an evening out at the pictures in Sligo or an outing to a local town.

The reward system was flexible in order to meet the needs of each child. The reality was that some boys had no problem maintaining good behaviour, while for others to go half an hour without getting into trouble was a major achievement. I held a multi-disciplinary meeting every Friday to award the stars, and the staff took it very seriously. Some would argue that a boy was making a huge effort, while others would be equally adamant that he was making no effort and was very cheeky. I had to use my casting vote many times. After the meeting I would see each boy on his own to tell him the result, and when a boy who usually struggled got even one star I could see the delight in his eyes. It was a major achievement. The stars were an instant success and helped hugely in bringing about major changes in the behaviour of the boys.

All the boys, without exception, clearly had great potential. However, one of the saddest things for me was that some of them had been neglected from birth, while others needed a lot of help during the early stages of their lives and hadn't received it. They had serious learning difficulties that were never diagnosed or major behavioural difficulties, many had psychiatric problems and some came from chaotic families. Many had multiple difficulties and needed ongoing therapy which simply was not available.

Because of its location in North Cavan, and because most of the boys came from much further south – mainly from Dublin, Cork, Waterford and Limerick – their families had to travel hundreds of miles to visit. Most of them had to rely on public transport, so they got the train to Sligo town, where a van picked them up and brought them to Loughan House. The visit lasted an hour or so and then they were dropped back to the station in Sligo. The whole journey took anything up to twelve or fourteen hours. I could just imagine how difficult it was for the families, who nearly always had to bring with them little children who were tired, often hungry and crying, and sometimes elderly grandparents too.

The choice of location highlighted the lack of concern for the families. Politically it was all about image – *We are going to do something about the Bugsy Malones* – and to hell with everyone else. Little has changed since.

At times the boys were very demanding, and were often cheeky, abusive, unruly and on occasions violent. Some of the rules did nothing to help this, like the lunacy of imposing a smoking ban because, according to the law, children under eighteen could not buy cigarettes. Just imagine what it was like trying to implement a smoking ban in a place that didn't have top security, where staff smoked and often had cigarettes on their person, where the boys' visitors smoked and often smuggled in cigarettes, and when many of the boys had smoked since they were five or six. It was a crazy rule that caused a massive amount of tension, conflict, bad feelings and fights with the staff. After a few months of absolute bedlam and a couple of major disturbances, a decision was made to allow them to smoke but not to buy cigarettes: an Irish solution to an Irish problem.

The boys could be very destructive. On at least two occasions they climbed up on the roof. Loughan House was built on the side of a hill, so it was very high at the back. Despite that, many of them got onto that roof, showing no fear of heights or difficulty with balance. At times like that they caused great difficulties for us, with the whole country watching. Many of them also got over the wire fence, and this caused us a lot of bother as well. There was one little boy in particular from County Galway who, every second night it seemed, got over the wire. He would stay in the woods adjoining the property for a few hours until he was ready to come out to where officers were waiting for him. Irrespective of how he was punished, or what the consequences were, he just continued to do it. There was always a glint in his eye when he was 'recaptured', and he always promised on his return 'I'll escape again', which he did.

Other boys responded to even the simplest of encouragements. Brian was a tiny, pale-faced twelve-year-old when he was committed to Loughan House in the winter of 1978 for stealing from shops and houses. He was the youngest and the smallest boy in the house, and the older boys treated him as a baby, which he absolutely hated. He had little interest in school and it was a battle even to get him into a classroom. He had a very short concentration span and was always looking for attention. He came from a large family with complex issues, and as he was over 200 miles from home this meant that he seldom got family visits. He was a bit wild, but otherwise a normal and likeable young boy. While I was chatting with him one day about his interests, he said, 'I'd love to have little chickens to rear.' The next day I ordered two dozen day-old chicks from a hatchery in Cappoquin, County Waterford. They arrived a few days later, packed in two card-board boxes. Brian was dumbfounded and could not believe his luck. He located a cupboard at the bottom of a stairs as a home for the chicks. He got a tradesman to connect an electric light-bulb and fix it from the ceiling to give light and heat. He got some sawdust from the wood-work classroom for bedding. He placed the chicks one by one under the light, and they all snuggled up underneath it. He talked to them all the time.

Every visitor to the house was invited to visit the chickens. He would open the cupboard door to where they were always sleeping, cuddled up under the light. Then he would say, 'Now I will get them to talk.' He would lift the light away and the chicks would immediately react to the loss of the heat and begin to chirp. 'Now, I told you they would talk to you,' he would say, as proud as punch.

After about ten weeks the chicks grew too big for the cupboard and they were causing a horrible smell. We rehoused them in an outside shed and they were free to walk around the grounds. At first the other boys were fascinated with them. However, once the novelty wore off some of the older boys began to kick out and throw stones and sticks at them. Brian could not understand such cruelty. He did his best to protect them, but it was impossible. The chickens had to be discharged to a new home with a local farmer.

The postscript to Brian's story is that nearly thirty years later he was in the Training Unit in Mountjoy. One morning, Sister Mairéad, a chaplain at the Training Unit, came to my office and handed me a big roll of paper. 'Brian sent this up to you,' she said. 'He has taken up art in prison. He said to tell you that he still remembers the chick-ens.' When I unrolled it, it was a beautiful painting of a landscape very similar to the terrain surrounding Loughan House.

*

I transferred out of Loughan House in late 1979 and returned to Dublin to take charge of staff training in the prison service, a position I was to remain in for two years. When I look back now, I consider that second term in Loughan House to have been the most challenging but rewarding period of my career. The secret of working well in Loughan House was connecting with each boy – just chatting to the boys, trying to understand them, encouraging them, treating them with kindness, explaining to them the benefits of education and how to deal with their own personal difficulties. That, and showing them social skills like how to behave in the communal dining room, how to keep a bedroom tidy and reasonably clean, how to talk to people, how to request things: all the things we take for granted.

And then there was the issue of their futures: what real prospects would they have, especially as most would be returning to the most socially disadvantaged areas in the country, often going back to families that were struggling at best and chaotic and violent at worst, and to parents who had serious difficulties of their own? Brian certainly wasn't the only one who ended up back in the prison system as an adult. I learned in Loughan House that fundamentally life is not fair and that there's no such thing as equality. Some children are born into circumstances where the odds are so stacked against them it is almost impossible for them to overcome the obstacles in their path.

6. Arriving in a Chaotic Mountjoy

In April 1983, I got a phone call one day from an official in the Department of Justice.

'We want you to go to Mountjoy.'

'I haven't any interest in going to Mountjoy. I am very happy here.'

By then I was deputy governor of the Training Unit, where I was working with a colleague, Martin Hickey, on drawing up a two-year strategic plan, and I didn't want to leave it in midstream. We had already had discussions with the Department of Justice about it, though without any great encouragement from it. At our first meeting a senior official said, 'What do you expect us to do about it?' We replied, 'The least we expect is that you are interested and supportive of the idea, and that you will come on board with us.' Despite the lack of encouragement from the civil servants, we were determined to bring out a plan of targets and strategies, and were hugely enthusiastic about the project.

I had been with the Training Unit for two years, having returned to it from the Staff Training Section because I enjoyed my previous experience there so much in 1975. By 1981 the Training Unit was almost fully operational, the workshops were fully staffed, the Educational Unit was in full swing and it had over eighty-five prisoners, many of them on pre-release programmes. The governor was Eddie Doogue. When he was a prison officer in Mountjoy he had worked as a teacher for many years, teaching prisoners who had literacy and numeracy problems. Eddie had almost forty years' service and he was an easy man to work with.

It was in the Training Unit at this time that I first realized the fantastic potential of music and drama in the education and development of prisoners. Claire Wilson, a drama teacher, was invited in by Dublin City VEC to do drama workshops with the prisoners. At the end of her stint as drama teacher in residence she decided to stage a show to celebrate the talents of the prisoners who attended her workshop. She brought in the showband Joanna and Tequila Sunrise to play music, and the prisoners performed various roles. We invited a number of people associated with prisons and a few officials from the Department of Justice to join with the staff and the prisoners for the public performance.

I was totally gobsmacked at the extraordinary talent of many of the prisoners, but I shouldn't have been: music, drama, visual arts and all the creative aspects of life are neglected in disadvantaged areas, and families cannot afford to pay for their children to attend private classes. This means that poor people's talents are untapped, not that they don't have any. Still, it was a revelation that men who had so little going for them could have such skills. At one stage the band was playing a piece of music and a young prisoner jumped up and asked to play the drums. He gave an absolute fantastic performance, eventually doing a solo, hopping the drumsticks on the floor and off the drums but holding the timing. Needless to say he got a standing ovation. As it turned out he was in care as a young boy in Artane Industrial School in Dublin and played in the Artane Boys' Band.

I said to myself, 'There is great potential in all of this. The creative arts must be tapped into for prisoners.' That was true in 1981 and it is still true in 2010. I will come back to the great value of drama in prison, because in Mountjoy Prison in the mid 1980s, at a time of great crisis, it was drama that came to the rescue.

When the official from the department rang to ask me to move to Mountjoy, I explained all that was going on in the Training Unit and why I wanted to remain there.

'We will think about what you have said, but we really feel that you are needed in Mountjoy,' he said. 'There is a lot of change needed up there and things are getting very difficult. And the governor, Pat McFadden, would be delighted to have you.'

The following week he phoned again: 'We want you to go to Mountjoy.'

'Fine,' I said, 'I'll be there next week.'

So on Wednesday, 4 May 1983, I was off to Mountjoy to team up again with Pat McFadden, my boss in Limerick in the late 1960s. The senior deputy governor was another old friend of mine, Laois man Vincent McPherson.

Mountjoy was a pretty chaotic place at that time. First of all, we all shared the one office, all three of us, which made it almost impossible to work. We had no place to have a private discussion with anyone, no place to have a meeting, and no boardroom. There was no clerical backup in the governor's office except for the support of the clerks in the personnel office, so I had to type all my own reports, submissions and letters on an old manual typewriter. There was an ancient telephone system which involved turning a handle to ring and then plugging in cables to connect the call.

One of the reasons for the timing of my transfer to Mountjoy was the imminent opening of the Separation Unit. In the late 1960s and early '70s a group called the Prisoners' Rights Organization was very active both outside and inside the prisons. A small group of prisoners in Mountjoy and Portlaoise became disruptive and set about bringing down the prison system by refusing to cooperate with staff, refusing to work, refusing to go back to their cells at lock-up times, challenging every rule and procedure, bullying other prisoners into joining them, and generally causing as much resistance as possible. A number were identified as the ringleaders, and in 1971 they were transferred out of the prison system and put into military custody in the Curragh, where many remained until 1983. In 1982 the government decided to end military custody and to return the prisoners to ordinary prisons. The old internal officers' quarters at Mountjoy – a dark, depressing three-storey building overlooking the Royal Canal – were refurbished as a high security unit, and this was due to open, taking in sixteen prisoners, a couple of weeks after I arrived.

This was all happening at a time when staff–management relations were very fragile. In 1979, in response to a Dáil question, David Andrews, a junior minister in the Department of Justice, said that overtime in the prison service was not compulsory and that prison officers had the choice between working overtime or declining. That statement caused havoc throughout the service, and prison officers began to refuse to work overtime unless it suited them. Trying to manage a prison in those turbulent days was hell on earth, and prison governors and senior prison officers had a daily struggle to keep the prisons working. Most days prisons operated with a skeleton staff, and it was impossible to provide the normal prison regime. It placed the security of the prison and the safety of the prisoners and staff at high risk.

In Mountjoy it was obvious we were in for serious conflict. The difficulties started over who was responsible for deciding staffing levels. Heretofore this had been decided by the chief officer and staff in the detail office in Mountjoy. In an effort to control expenditure, Vincent McPherson and I decided to examine staffing levels on court escorts and also the number of staff detailed to attend the Dublin courts. We reduced the number of officers on those escorts we felt were over-staffed. The local branch of the Prison Officers' Association was totally opposed to our intervention and decided that officers weren't going to cooperate and would boycott all prisoners who were committed from any courts where we reduced the staffing levels. They called these prisoners 'ghosts', and all staff, up to and including the most senior chief officer, refused to have anything to do with them. They wouldn't lock them up at lock-up times, they wouldn't unlock them, they wouldn't give them their food and they wouldn't check them in the cells. It started after dinnertime on a Friday afternoon in November and it went on until the Saturday morning. By Saturday lunchtime there were forty-one 'ghosts' and only three of us to look after them: Vincent McPherson, who was acting governor of Mountjoy Prison that day; Matt Mannix, a deputy governor in the Separation Unit; and me.

It quickly became unworkable. The 'ghosts' were scattered all over the prison and on all twelve landings. After lock-up at lunchtime on Saturday we said, 'That's it, we're finished. We will not be unlocking any of the "ghosts" in the afternoon – it's getting too big to handle and the security of the prison is now being put at risk.' Vincent McPherson phoned officials in the Department of Justice and informed them of our decision.

After discussing it with the officials, we all agreed that the staff would be asked at the 2 p.m. parade if they were prepared to carry out all their duties, and, if not, told to leave the prison. Vincent McPherson addressed the staff parade and told them what he intended to do. Then he asked the officer at the top of the parade, 'Are you prepared to carry out all your duties as instructed?' The officer said, 'No, I'm staying with the POA', and Vincent said, 'Please leave the prison.' Then he asked the next officer the same question, and when he said, 'No, I'm with the POA', Vincent said once more, 'Please leave the prison', and with that all the staff walked off the parade to the staff quarters outside the prison. Vincent notified the Department of Justice, and they in turn asked the gardaí to go into the prison. After 3 p.m. over 100 gardaí came to the prison and took over from the prison officers.

The prisoners reacted very negatively to the gardaí, and you could feel the tension rising. The gardaí had no knowledge of the running of the prison, and the prisoners exploited this. During recreation on that Saturday evening from 5.30 until 7.30 the prisoners began to break up the recreation hall, and soon a full-scale riot erupted. They broke into the metal workshop, got hold of steel grinders and began cutting through the bars on the windows. This was very dangerous, and for a short time I thought we would lose the whole prison or, worse still, someone would get killed. The gardaí called in their riot squad, and after an hour or so they regained control.

An agreement was reached after two weeks, and the prison officers returned to work. A small number of prison officers worked during the strike and they had a terrible time after it was over. The agreement was that the officers returning from the strike would work as normal, but they refused to cooperate with any of the staff that had worked during the dispute and they would not answer 'Sir' on the staff parade when their names were called like they did before the strike. Officials in the Department of Justice didn't want to know. The one lesson I learned was that strikes are a total disaster, and those who work during them are very poorly thanked.

*

On Friday, 1 June 1984, Pat McFadden retired as governor of Mount-joy Prison, exactly five years to the day after he took up the position. He had served in the prison service for over forty-one years. On his last day on duty he walked around the prison to say goodbye to both prisoners and staff. The previous Sunday he had gone to Mass in the prison and told the prisoners of his planned retirement and wished them all the best for the future. That Friday afternoon, I walked with him up to the old general stores, a rundown building at the front of the prison where Pat had worked for many years. We had to go up an old, dark, twisty staircase to the offices in the stores, and when we got there a few of the staff organized a cup of tea. We stood around having a chat about old times when someone put his head in the door and said, 'You have a visitor.' In came Chris Morris, assistant princi-pal probation and welfare officer, who had responsibility for the probation and welfare service in prisons. He said, 'Governor, I just called up to say goodbye to you on behalf of the probation and welfare service, and to thank you for all your help and support over the years.'

On our way back down the stairs, Pat and I met a member of the clerical staff in the stores, a curmudgeonly character who had worked with Pat for many years. Pat stuck out his hand and said, 'Goodbye and the best of luck.' He walked past us and never even looked at Pat. I just couldn't believe that anybody would do such a thing to a man retiring after forty-one years' service. Pat was embarrassed and hurt, but smiled and passed it off with the comment, 'Ah he never lost it. Bitter to the end.'

We went back down to the governor's office. Pat signed off his governor's journal for the last time, stood up and put on his over-coat. We shook hands inside the main gate, and that was it. There was nobody from the Department of Justice to say goodbye or thank him for his long years of service, and nobody from the establish-ment telephoned to say goodbye or even wrote a few lines of appreciation to him. A prisoner on discharge would have got more thanks.

As I sat in the office I felt angry and thought what a brutal system it was to treat a man of his service, decency and integrity with such coldness. Some weeks later I told a senior official in the Department of Justice how I felt about it. He said, 'Ah you're right, that shouldn't have happened. It was terrible, but I'll make sure that it will never happen again.' All through my career, governor after governor retired – many, like Pat McFadden, with many years of service – and they too walked out the gate without even a goodbye from anybody in authority.

Around 5 p.m. that Friday, Deputy Governor Con Hayes and I received a telephone call to go to the Department of Justice. We drove over to St Stephen's Green, where we were joined by Jim Woods, an assistant governor at Arbour Hill Prison. On the third floor we met the assistant secretary in charge of the Prisons Division, who said, 'The minister has approved your appointment as governor of Mountjoy Prison, if you'll accept it.' I said, 'I'll give it a go.' He handed me a white acceptance form, to sign. I did so, but didn't feel a bit excited. Knowing all the challenges that lay ahead, I knew it was a tough call to be governor of Mountjoy.

Con Hayes accepted appointment as senior deputy governor, as it was called then, and Jim Woods was promoted to deputy governor. They both signed on the dotted line and then we had a short stilted chat during which the assistant secretary asked us what plans we had for Mountjoy. We hadn't had time to think, not to mention plan anything, as two minutes earlier we didn't even know that we would be working together. I said, 'Well, there's a lot of work to be done with the place, and we will sit down next week and draw up a plan of action.' He said, 'Well, good luck with it', and we got up, shook hands with him and took the lift down to the street.

The whole thing was unreal. Here I was on my way back to Mountjoy to take over as governor, with no instructions, no briefing, no outline of what the Department's policy was in relation to Mountjoy, nothing except to go and do whatever I thought was necessary.

I drove home around 7 p.m. I was neither nervous nor excited about my appointment; I just felt that it was a great chance to get the place reorganized. I had ideas about how I was going to do it, but I had already decided that I would not be a dictator and that my style from day one would be to consult, discuss and delegate. When I look back now, it was obvious that I had no idea of the enormity of the job I was taking on, and while I knew that Mountjoy needed to be changed, I certainly didn't realize how difficult it would be and how many huge challenges I would face along the way.

I got home almost an hour later. I had always made a point of keeping work and home life separate, and never discussed work at home. Even that evening it was all very low-key. I told Breda about my appointment, but we had no big discussion about it. Sinéad was then five and Marie was just four, and all they were interested in was going to the park to feed the ducks. That suited me. But before I had a chance to do anything there was a call from an official in the Department of Justice.

'We have just been told that the DPP [Director of Public Prosecution] has decided to charge two prison officers in Mountjoy with the assault of a prisoner during the disturbance last November, and the minister has decided to suspend them from duty tomorrow morning,' he said. 'Will you look after that?'

'Okay, I'll drop in tomorrow morning,' I said.

So my first job on my first day as governor of Mountjoy was to suspend two prison officers. I knew a number of people over the years, including prison governors, who were delighted to suspend officers and got great personal satisfaction out of it. I always found that aspect of the job uncomfortable, because irrespective of the circumstances, or the justification for the action, I knew that officers had families depending on them. Incidentally, the following month the charges against the officers were dismissed in the District Court and they were reinstated.

On Sunday morning, 3 June, I awoke to the news headlines that sacks of letters, written by Mountjoy prisoners but never posted, had been found in a dump in West Dublin. That afternoon the prisoners in the A exercise yard sat down and refused to go to their cells until I spoke with them. I went into the prison to meet them and they demanded that action be taken against the officers who were responsible. I assured them that the gardaí and I would investigate the whole thing, and that nothing would be covered up. They agreed to leave the yard peacefully and went back to their cells. Despite my commitment to the prisoners, neither the gardaí nor I ever got to the bottom of who was responsible for dumping the letters. I had my suspicions, but could never prove anything.

That was how I started running Mountjoy – in at the deep end.

7. Shaking up the Management of Mountjoy

Over the years I was often asked what the title 'governor' means and what, exactly, a governor does. In so far as the courts commit prisoners to the care and custody of the governor of a particular prison, the role has a legal dimension. The governor's responsibility is to ensure that the court order is carried out, so, for example, if a prisoner is sentenced to six months' imprisonment the governor must ensure that he serves that period of time, less statutory remission, or unless he is granted temporary release by the Minister for Justice.

The governor is answerable to the High Court should the prisoner or anyone acting on his behalf decide to challenge his detention under Article 40 of the constitution via an application of habeas corpus. On receipt of such an application the High Court will direct the governor to produce the prisoner in the court to show why he is holding the prisoner in custody – in other words, to produce a committal warrant. The governor must have a legal warrant to hold a prisoner in custody. If the court is satisfied that it is a lawful warrant, the case will be dismissed. If on the other hand the court finds any flaws in the warrant, the prisoner will be released.

Other than this legal obligation, the governor's job is the same as the manager in any large organization. His job is to manage the resources given to him by the state through the Irish Prison Service (the Irish Prison Service, or IPS, took over prison management from the Department of Justice in 1999; before that the service was managed by the Prisons Division of the Department). The governor is expected to manage those resources efficiently and effectively, to get value for taxpayers' money and to ensure that the prison is run in a safe and secure manner. He is also responsible for coordinating the various services in the prison to ensure that all the prisoners have access to them.

The one major difference between managing a prison and managing any other organization is security. Prisons operate on the basis that the prisoners are being held against their will, and they must not be allowed to escape. Keeping prisoners in custody is the responsibility of the governor, because if a prisoner escapes then the fundamental purpose of the prison is not being met. The skill is being able to balance security needs against the need to provide a humane working and living environment for staff and prisoners. I always found great difficulty in getting this right – security versus humanity. When a conflict arose I always came down on the side of humanity, whereas the prison service at management level always came down on the side of security.

A month after I started the job in Mountjoy I had my first challenge to prison security when fourteen prisoners made their way onto the roof of the main prison. In those days there were slates on the roof, so once they got up there they had instant access to very dangerous missiles – big heavy slates that had the potential to cut the head off somebody underneath. The men stayed there through the Friday night and were still there by Saturday afternoon when they called a meeting close to a big chimney on the roof of A wing. Prison officers who had been trying to coax them down were able to hear what was going on. One prisoner took control of the meeting and said, 'Right, the first thing we have to do is to decide why we are up here in the first place.' After a full day on the roof protesting, they still didn't know what they were protesting about. It just highlighted the impulsive nature of many in the prisoner population. They came down late that Saturday evening.

When I took over at Mountjoy the complex comprised five parts: the main prison for adult male offenders, the women's prison, the Separation Unit, St Patrick's Institution and the Training Unit. I became governor of Mountjoy Prison, the Separation Unit and the women's prison. The Training Unit and St Patrick's Institution had – and still have – their own governors. A deputy governor had day-to-day responsibility for the Separation Unit. A female chief officer was responsible for the day-to-day management of the women's prison. Shortly after I arrived, I appointed a deputy governor to have overall responsibility for it.

I don't think it's an exaggeration to say that when I took charge in 1984 the approach to running Mountjoy had hardly changed since it opened in 1850. Everything started and ended with the governor, and all decisions were made by him. There was no management structure and no delegation. All four of the governor grades – the governor, his senior deputy and two deputy governors – worked out of one small office. There was no privacy, no space to concentrate, no place to have private meetings with staff or with anybody else. All telephone conversations were overheard by everyone in the office.

The telephone system was antiquated. There was a switchboard in a small room off the general office, with cables and plugs all over the place. All calls had to be transferred manually, and the operator could listen in to conversations. And, of course, there was no modern technology such as computers, photocopiers or even electric typewriters; everything had to be done by hand. Copying one document could take an hour: you had to mix chemicals, put the document through a sort of roller and then wait ages for it to dry out.

Though there was no secretarial support, everything went through the governor's office. First thing every morning a lorry load of books – all the ledgers and report journals – were brought to the office. The governor checked and initialled them one by one while everybody else looked on.

His next job was to sign a tray full of half sheets, written on foolscap paper. There could be up to fifty of them every morning, reporting bulbs blown in cells or hallways, taps leaking, toilets blocked and so on. Each report was addressed to the governor and signed by the officer, and it would go something like, 'Sir, I respectfully wish to report that the bulb needs to be replaced in cell number 15 on B2 landing.' The governor went through each report, wrote on the bottom of each, 'To the chief trades officer, for your attention, please', then signed and dated it. The chief trades officer would come to the office every morning, collect a bundle of them and detail the prison tradesmen to carry out the repairs or replace whatever was broken.

All the post for the prison, the general office, the personnel office and the general stores was also brought to the governor's office every day to be signed by him and him alone. Operating this way, the governor ploughed a lonely furrow. The question of delegation never arose. The thinking was: *I've got to keep my hands on everything because if I don't something might go wrong, and if a mistake is made my neck will be on the block, so I will not take any risks, and I won't trust anyone. I'll do everything myself.*

Practically from the moment of my appointment I knew that my first step had to be the creation of a modern management structure in Mountjoy. The day-to-day running of the prison had so many different components and was so involved that there was no way I could have my finger on every pulse: I had to let go and use the talent of the staff to achieve my objective of providing a safe and secure environment for staff and prisoners. I had studied management styles and approaches during my time as a trainee assistant governor, and I also got a lot of valuable insights into what worked well during my time developing the new regime in Loughan House. I had come to believe that efficient management was mostly about developing your staff to a level of competence so that they were able and willing to take on responsibility. While my thinking on management would have been fairly unusual in the prison service, it was very much the norm in the private sector. During my early days in Mountjoy I read a number of books on management, the best of which was *In Search of Excellence*. I was also hugely influenced by the example P. M. Kelly had shown me in Loughan House and the Training Unit. He gave me a lot of opportunity when I was a supervisor, and the trust that he placed in me was hugely motivating. I decided that if it worked in my own case it would work equally well with others, and it did. I also brought a good measure of old-fashioned common sense to the role, something I'd had since growing up in Bansha.

Bringing people on board was not easy, as many people had worked in the old system for years – indeed, it was the only system they knew – and they were suspicious and nervous of change. I had one advantage over all the governors who had served during the previous twenty years, however: I had youth on my side. I was only thirty-six at the time of my appointment, and that meant I could take risks and wasn't worrying about my pension or how the bureaucrats would react. My years in staff training also helped, and I knew the value of including people as much as possible, rather than excluding them – which was the norm at that time.

An early success demonstrated the benefit of this approach. Someone suggested starting a small gym for the prisoners, and we identified an area where one could be installed. For the first time ever in Mountjoy the new post – gym officer – was openly advertised so that all staff could apply; the old custom was that a favourite son would be given such a post. When I looked at the applications, I noticed that one was from a man whom some considered a bit militant. The reaction of the senior staff was, 'Oh my God, not him.' But his application was by far the most impressive, and I decided to give him the job.

A day after his appointment he came to me with a list of equipment that he needed.

'No problem,' I said, 'I'll get the stores to order it, but it will have to go out to tender.'

'While we are waiting for it to come in, would you mind if I brought in some of my own equipment to get started up?' he asked.

'Belt away,' I said.

He turned out to be an outstanding gym officer and did wonderful work for years. The best thing about it was that all the senior staff had to admit it was a good appointment and bringing people like him on board was the answer.

The same approach worked for me during all my service: giving people their heads, giving them responsibility and trusting them usually got the best out of them – both staff and prisoners. The amazing thing was that huge changes took place without any significant extra expenditure. Over time we all grew and developed, and the senior staff in the prison during my first two or three years were great people who were completely loyal to me and worked their butts off to make the new approach work.

One evening in late 1984 a group of department officials arrived in the prison to select a site for a number of pre-fab buildings which they wanted to use for workshops in the prison. The buildings had originally been used in the power station at Aughinish, County Clare, and the officials had got them very cheaply; it was clear they were going to impose them on Mountjoy as an excuse for modern workshops.

This was the first I knew of the plan, and I wasn't happy about it. 'Look, Mountjoy needs a far bigger response than putting in old Portakabins as workshops,' I said, 'and we really need to get our act together to respond in a meaningful way to the needs of Mountjoy.' That was the last I ever heard of the pre-fab buildings.

At the end of 1984 I wrote a very forthright annual report outlining the reality of the prison and stating that huge resources and finance were urgently needed to tackle its many, many problems. I referred to the incident with the Portakabins and said that I wouldn't 'tolerate this type of approach again' and that if we were to make the necessary mark in Mountjoy there needed to be full and open consultation on every issue. I highlighted the lack of facilities and the condition of the toilets and wash areas of the prison, saying, 'They are a national scandal and a public disgrace.'

I sent the report to the Department of Justice and I didn't hear a single word from them about it for about four months. Then one day at lunchtime the telephone rang and there was a senior official on the line. After some small talk he said, 'I've got your annual report here.'

'Great,' I said.

'But you'll have to make a few changes in it,' he said.

'Why?'

'You have used some phrases and words that are unacceptable in an annual report. You can't say that you won't tolerate something. And you can't say that something is a national scandal and a public disgrace.'

'But they are a disgrace and that's what I wrote,' I said.

'I know, but you will have to change it,' he replied.

'I have no intention of changing it,' I said. 'You can change it if you like, but it's my annual report, I have sent it to you, it's in your office, you do whatever you like with it.'

That was the end of the call.

The next day Jim Woods, one of my deputy governors, came into my office and said, 'What did you say to that man yesterday? He was just on the phone to me asking if you're all right and wanting to know if you're under pressure.'

'And what did you say?' I said.

'I told him that you were acting normal enough at the moment but you were in a fighting mood, and I asked him why he was asking.'

'And what did he say?'

'He said, "I was just wondering. We're a bit worried. I asked him to make a few small changes to his annual report, and he seems like a man under pressure." And I said, "God, no, he's not under any pressure at all, he's fine, that's his nature. He's going to fight and he won't take things lying down."'

The fact that a senior official had spoken to Jim Woods, my deputy governor, about it was a real eye-opener. This was not about this particular official getting a bee in his bonnet, but was clearly the departmental view of anyone who did not speak in carefully couched, anodyne terms that actually said nothing at all. It just wasn't the civil service way to call a spade a spade. It was clear that crossing swords with officialdom could be dangerous. I could just see how my reputation could be destroyed. *'Well, Minister, Lonergan's finding it hard to deal with the pressure; he's not able for it . . .'*

As I had spent two years in staff training I knew a lot of the younger prison officers and I realized it was vital to get them on board from day one. I had this long-term vision of completely restructuring the operational side of Mountjoy. This would mean getting the staff – and the local branch of the Prison Officers' Association – on board and agreeing to the changes that were needed.

I had to find a way of consulting the staff and of tapping into their knowledge and expertise. I decided to call a staff meeting. Staff meetings for most organizations are fairly routine, but in Mountjoy in 1984 the idea of having such an event was totally alien to the culture. It had never happened. All communication was one way, from the top down, and it was done by written circulars or on staff parades, when staff lined up in the main hallway and were addressed by either the governor or the chief officer. It was autocratic. Staff never had an opportunity to have their say and were not consulted about any issue.

I arranged a staff meeting for 9.15 one morning and notified the prisoners that unlock would be an hour late. The only place big enough to accommodate the meeting was the Catholic church in the prison. It was packed. Well over 250 staff attended, and I addressed them at the start and outlined what I believed needed to be done at Mountjoy and how we would go about it. I gave a commitment that I would consult widely with them and the local branch of the Prison Officers' Association. I assured them that I wouldn't be a dictator and that it was my hope that we would grow and develop together. And then I opened it to the floor and said that if anyone wanted to say anything they should feel free and that I was there to listen.

Standing at the very back of the church was an officer I knew from my days in training in 1980. He put up his hand and said, 'You know, governor, you don't have the confidence of the staff here.' He was referring to the prison officers' strike in Mountjoy in November 1983. As a deputy governor I had worked during the strike, even though I was a member of the Prison Officers' Association. Naturally, a lot of staff felt very bitter towards those who had worked.

I said, 'You don't have a mandate from anybody to speak here except for yourself, so what I am hearing you say is that I don't have your confidence.'

And he said, 'No, no, it's not me, the staff has no confidence in you.'

I repeated again that he had no mandate to say such a thing, that he was here as an individual and only as an individual. Then I went and really put the boot in, 'Now, as far as I'm concerned you have two choices,' I said. 'You can stay in Mountjoy and have confidence in me or you can leave Mountjoy and have no confidence in me. And if you want to leave Mountjoy I will facilitate you in whatever way I can.' Then I said 'Any other questions?'

No one else spoke, so I thanked everyone for coming and went back to my office. Shortly afterwards, Fran Dowling, the training officer in Mountjoy, wandered in with a smirk on his face. 'That went well,' he said, meaning of course that it was an absolute disaster. He was right: I knew I had made a complete bags of it.

While it was a very negative experience and a very bad beginning for staff meetings, I learned a lot from it. I realized that if I was to create an environment of dialogue, I needed to bite my tongue, shut up and take things on the chin. And so my strategy for all future meetings – and I held several – was to allow staff to say what they felt, even if it was critical. My mishandling of the situation highlighted for me that if you are in a position of authority there is a real danger that you will use that authority in a defensive way and destroy your whole strategy. My strategy genuinely was to open dialogue, but there could be no dialogue if I was going to act like a dictator or respond to people's contributions – however hostile – in a dismissive or arrogant way.

Another big lesson I learned that morning was never to humiliate a person in front of his peers. I put the boot in and I damaged the officer's status with his colleagues, thereby doing serious damage to my goal for the meeting. Two days later he put in a transfer request and within a week he was gone from Mountjoy.

From the very start my priority was to develop a management team, and for the first time ever in the prison service I held weekly management coordination meetings, multi-disciplinary meetings where the heads of all the services came together on Monday mornings at eleven to plan. Planning was another new concept. There was no planning – good, bad or indifferent – in any prison at that time, nor in the Prisons Division of the Department of Justice for that matter.

Having all the services working together and discussing a range of issues was new. In the old approach, the teacher looked after education, the chaplain looked after the spiritual needs of the staff and prisoners, and so on, with no input into other services and programmes in the prison. My approach was that while people's first job was to look after their own specialized area, they could also contribute to other parts of the prison. Many people had worked for years in Mountjoy but had only ever been involved in the area in which they worked. The new system broke down these barriers, so that the supervising teacher could join a working group looking at the development of the workshops, while the psychologist could join a working group looking at medical services, and so on.

They all took to the new approach like ducks to water, and I'm certain that everyone benefited. Senior staff got to know the prison much better, and more importantly they got to know each other.

There was much better coordination between the services, greater cooperation and best of all it helped to improve communication throughout the prison. In 1985 we produced the first ever management plan and set of objectives and targets for Mountjoy. We all worked together to try to achieve them, and in the process a great team spirit developed.

At a later date, to reinforce the message that everyone around the table was equal and had an important contribution to make, I introduced rotation of the chairing of the Monday morning meetings: everyone chaired in their turn, and this proved to be very successful.

A practical challenge I faced was to find suitable accommodation to facilitate the new approach. This proved to be very difficult because the accommodation I needed was simply not available. At that time, all the office and administration facilities were located in the main hall on the way into the prison. That was fine in 1850, but as the prison got bigger and bigger and day-to-day administration increased, it was totally inadequate.

After almost two years of lobbying I succeeded in getting the former governor's residence converted into offices. (Right up to Pat McFadden's time, the governor lived in official accommodation in the prison. I never lived in the prison and I always felt that this was a major plus as it allowed me to get out every evening and go home and leave it all behind me.) It took until the end of 1985 to get the house refurbished, but it was a big breakthrough and the first clear sign of major change.

Another breakthrough in the basic practicalities of running the place was the installation of a modern telephone system. In the mid 1980s this was a big deal. After years of frustration, having a telephone on each desk and in all the offices was brilliant. Of course, not everyone was delighted with this innovation. One day Eithne Mulhern, my secretary, put through a call to Assistant Governor Bill Thorpe's desk. It rang and rang and there was no answer, so she ran downstairs to check what was happening, only to discover that Bill had the telephone locked in the drawer in his desk so nobody could answer it. Bill was an absolute gentleman but he was old school and tied in to the culture of protecting yourself from trouble at all costs. When he was away from his desk he locked the telephone away to make sure that nobody used it without his permission. Calls were logged against each extension number, and Bill didn't want to be held responsible for any calls he didn't make.

In 1986 the computer company Wang was brought in to computerize prisoner records in Mountjoy. It wasn't a success. For the best part of the next twenty years, attempts to computerize Mountjoy records were a disaster: time after time, what was installed was incapable of coping with the volume of demand placed on it, or the computers were too slow or completely unreliable. A massive amount of public funds was wasted on this over the years – nobody really knows how much because system after system was commissioned, installed and later abandoned. This phenomenon was not confined to the prison service alone: many other organizations and sections within public services had similar costly experiences. In the five years or so before I retired there were significant improvements in the system, though it is still not perfect and needs to be expanded to cover all prison activities.

8. The Prison Routine

Prisoners are unlocked around 8.15 a.m. in all prisons. In Mountjoy they have to slop out – empty their chamber pots or buckets into toilet bowls. They collect water and wash themselves in their cells. Meals are served on the ground floor in all the wings in Mountjoy, and at around 8.30 prisoners line up to collect their breakfast, take it back to their cells and are locked up again. During this lock-up period the staff goes on a breakfast break. Prisoners are unlocked again around 9.20 a.m., and those wanting to raise some issue or get assistance in some matter attend at governor's parade, welfare parade, chaplain's parade, doctor's parade or dentist's parade. This means they queue up for whoever they want to see. Some go to education, others to workshops, some to the gym and some to work as cleaners on the landings. Family visits start at 10 a.m. each day. A huge number of prisoners in Mountjoy have nothing constructive to do and go to the exercise yards, where they walk around for hours. This is their only outdoor exercise. Or they go to the recreation halls, where they sit around and play cards or watch television or a DVD or just talk to one another. The reason prisoners have nothing to do is that there are not enough workshop or educational spaces for them. Every weekday in Mountjoy, all the prisoners in one wing have to shower, and the showers are in an old building at the back of the prison separate from the main prison. Every prisoner has just one shower a week.

At 12.10 the prisoners line up to collect their dinners – in Mountjoy, prisoners have their main meal in the middle of the day – and take it back to their cells. They are locked in their cells until 2.15 p.m. Again, the staff takes a meal break at this time. At 2.15 the cells are unlocked and the prisoners resume their activities. At 4.15 all prisoners collect their evening tea and return to their cells. They are locked up until 5.20, when they have evening recreation. Again, recreation is normally watching television or a DVD. There is one snooker table for every 150 prisoners, so it is hard to get a game. At 7.15 they collect a pot of tea and a currant bun and return to their cells to be locked up for the night. All cells have either a single or a bunk bed, a small locker or table, a chair, a small television, a cup, plate and a knife and fork – usually plastic. Prisoners who have their own radio can get the governor's permission to have it in their cells. They are allowed to have books from the prison library and some prisoners purchase PlayStations from the prison shop; those interested in art are allowed to have selected art materials in their cells. In Mountjoy the cell lights are controlled from the landings, so the prison officers switch off the lights, usually before midnight. In modern prisons the light switches are inside the cells, so the prisoners can control the light themselves.

This routine changes only on Saturdays and Sundays, as there are no workshops or classes; on these days most of the prisoners go to the exercise yards or recreation halls during periods of unlock.

All sentenced prisoners are entitled to one family visit of thirty minutes once a week. Some prisoners request and are granted a special additional family visit some weeks, and nowadays this also lasts for thirty minutes. Prisoners are allowed one six-minute phone call a day to contact their families or close friends. The calls are recorded and monitored. Calls are only allowed to people who have been checked out and have agreed to take calls from the prison. Telephone calls have proved to be very beneficial to prisoners and their families, and are much appreciated by most prisoners. They allow prisoners to keep in contact with their families and especially with their children or elderly parents, who may not be able travel to the prison to visit. Prisoners can write almost as many letters as they like and they can receive an unlimited number. All letters coming into and going out of the prison are opened, mainly to stop drugs being smuggled in. It was discovered many years ago that drugs were being concealed in the flaps of the envelopes.

All sentenced prisoners, except those serving life imprisonment, can receive a one-quarter remission of their sentence, so if a prisoner is sentenced to four years he can serve three years and get one year off for good behaviour. I'm a total supporter of statutory remission because it encourages prisoners to behave; if there was no such thing as remission, there would be no incentive for prisoners to behave. The governor of a prison can take back remission if a prisoner misbehaves and is placed on discipline report by a prison officer.

This is the basic regime for the prisoner. I know that there is little public sympathy for prisoners or interest in their living conditions, but I have to say – yet again – what a disgrace it is that we still have the inhumane and humiliating practice of slopping out for over 1,000 prisoners in Irish prisons. It is shocking to think that as far back as forty-two years ago it was the stated ambition of the prison service to eliminate slopping out, and forty-two years on it is still there. Being banged up for years in a tiny cell for seventeen hours every day with the smell of piss and shit all around you, and very often, because of overcrowding, having to watch as your cellmate relieves himself in a bucket right in front of your nose, is one of the most undignified experiences a human being can be subjected to. It doesn't make for a very nice working environment for staff either; the smell of human excreta permeates the prison for hours every day. I believe that in all new buildings and in all new refurbishments, in addition to a toilet, a shower should be put in each cell. For prisoners, having a shower is not just an issue of personal hygiene, it's also therapeutic and relaxes them. Anywhere they have been installed they have made a big difference to the lives of the prisoners and the mood of the prison. They should be seen as a fundamental human right and not as a perk or privilege. Human beings either grow or regress through their lives, and in prison it is a massive battle and a great challenge to stop people regressing. If we confine people to prison, we should certainly provide them with the basics to support and sustain them as human beings.

Early in my time as governor of Mountjoy I went down to visit the main kitchen one morning, about 9.30, to discover that the cabbage was already boiling away on the cooker, even though the dinner wouldn't be served until 12.30. Then I found a prisoner stirring the rice in a big boiler; he was plunging his bare arm, which was full of tattoos, right into the rice. After seeing that, the kitchen came in for some changes.

The overall quality of prison food served nowadays has improved dramatically over the years. For quite some time now there has been a self-service system in place in Mountjoy, and this has proved to be both hygienic and cost-effective. In the old days, prisoners were given their rations and they had to take the full amount whether they wanted it or not. Now they take what they want and there is far less waste. The diet has also improved, and the food is cooked and served to a very high standard. Fruit is freely available, whereas years ago prisoners never even saw an apple or an orange. The credit for transforming prison catering must go to one man, Martin Hickey, who introduced training for both staff and prisoners working in prison kitchens, which raised standards and morale. Martin was coordinator of work and training in the IPS.

Another thing worth noting about the Mountjoy routine is that all dining is done in the cells, and that too leaves a mark and is a major contributory factor to prisoners becoming institutionalized.

People often ask me what contact I had with prisoners. How often did I meet prisoners? Did I talk to them? I think some people believe the governor has an elevated position, working well away from the prisoners. In fact I saw and talked to prisoners on a daily basis.

After breakfast every morning, around 9.30, I and my deputies and assistants, whoever was available, went into the prison and met with any prisoners wishing to see us. I moved from wing to wing, filling in for whatever deputy or assistant governor was off duty. On average about forty to fifty prisoners would be seen on governor's parade on each wing every day, but on a very busy day up to seventy prisoners would be seen on a wing. The parades would normally last about an hour and a half. Prisoners were seen one at a time. They came into the little room on their wing that was set aside for this purpose, sat down and made their request or raised whatever issues they had. They might be asking to appeal their sentence, to get the forms to apply to the courts for bail, to get permission to wear their own clothes, to add a new name to their visitors' list, to ask for a special family visit, to request temporary release, to ask for a transfer to another prison, or to complain about something or other. By and large, their issue was dealt with on the spot. It was a great way of keeping in contact with the prisoners, getting to know them as individuals and hearing their issues or problems first-hand.

I also met the prisoners in classrooms, workshops and yards when walking around the prison, and I always chatted to them as I went along. In the old days there was no way a prisoner would approach the governor while he was going on what were called 'governor's rounds'. Back then, when the governor walked around, prison officers stood to attention when he arrived, saluted and told him the number of prisoners in their charge at that particular time. For example, in the workshop the officers would shout, 'Twenty correct, sir!' Nowadays that doesn't happen and governors are not saluted, and rightly so.

From the first day that I was appointed governor of Mountjoy, any prisoner, no matter where I was in the prison, could come and talk to me. At the beginning some staff frowned on this and said that it was undermining their authority. But for me, free and open access to the governor was absolutely crucial, and I know that the prisoners appreciated it. It was also a great safety valve, because it clearly showed me that prisoners were not abused or their problems suppressed. Over the years many prisoners came to see me to discuss personal or family problems.

The secret of managing the prisoners was to treat them with respect, to listen to their story and to be kind to them. Every human being understands the language of kindness, and I actually believe that if kindness doesn't work, nothing will.

Fairness was also crucial. Prisoners who broke the rules had to be dealt with on a daily basis in disciplinary hearings. When a prisoner misbehaved, a prison officer wrote out the complaint on a P19 form and handed it into the chief's office. The prisoner was then given a copy of the complaint so that he could prepare his defence. The following day the governor would read out the report to the prisoner and listen to his side of the story. Sometimes the prisoner would admit the offence and take his punishment; on other occasions he would question the report and challenge the prison officer who made the complaint. The prevailing culture in the prison was, and still is, that the prison officer is always right and the governor should not question the content of his report or his judgement. But I never accepted that culture and always gave the prisoner the benefit of the doubt. I believed that this was one of the most important functions of the governor, and I always impressed on the governor grades in Mountjoy how vital it was to conduct every hearing in a fair and just manner.

On occasions a prisoner would appeal against the outcome of a disciplinary hearing to me, and I would review the case. On one such occasion a prisoner came to see me and said, 'I was set up the other day on report. I was deprived evening recreation for six weeks for taking drugs on a visit, but I took nothing, and I'm going to the High Court.'

I said, 'I will review it and come back to you tomorrow.'

I looked at the CCTV of the visit, and it was very clear that the prisoner had received an item during the visit and put it down his trousers. I printed out six stills of the incident and went back to see him the next day. I sat on the stills, and when he came in I didn't mention them at all.

'You asked me yesterday to check out an incident during your last visit,' I said.

'Yeah, I did. I was stitched up on that visit and I'm going to the High Court.'

'Well', I said, 'I looked at the CCTV and you're guilty.'

'No way. There is no justice in this kip of a jail; I'm taking no more of it,' he said.

I kept talking to him about honesty, his word of honour, how if you don't have this word you have nothing. After ages I looked at my watch and I realized that I had been talking with him for fifty-seven minutes. I said to myself, *This is it. I'm not going on any longer than an hour*.

But with that he looked up at me and, with a grin on his face, said, 'Mr Lonergan, it was worth a try.'

I said, 'Away with you and serve your punishment.'

I never told him that I was sitting on the evidence, because I felt that by getting him to admit his wrongdoing he had learned an important lesson and, above all, I had not humiliated him. That would have been the easy thing to do, to push the prints in front of him and tell him he was a big liar. But I believe that it is never right to humiliate a person, irrespective of the circumstances.

In 1985 I was participating in a management development course with all the other prison governors, and as part of it we were asked to come up with a small project that would make an operational difference in our own prison. Overcrowding was becoming an issue in Mountjoy and, despite strenuous efforts to reduce numbers, many prisoners were sleeping on mattresses on the floor. For my project I decided to address this issue, and after discussing it with senior staff we agreed that we should try using bunk beds to take the overflow. There were eight to ten prisoners on the floor, so I decided to install ten bunk beds, thinking this would resolve the problem of mattresses on the floor for good. We designed a steel bunk bed, had ten made up, and put them in cells spread around all the landings.

It was the worst mistake I ever made, and Mountjoy is suffering the consequences to this day. Within weeks of the ten bunks being put in and working satisfactorily, the powers that be in the Department of Justice found out about it and thought it a fantastic solution for the problem of overcrowding. Very soon, ten more bunks were installed. And then another ten. By the time I was retiring there were over 150 bunk beds in daily use in Mountjoy.

In Mountjoy, the first the governor knows about a prisoner being committed is when the gardaí arrive with him at the gate. A governor has no idea who is coming or how many will turn up on any day. The only information that accompanies the prisoner is the legal warrant, which shows the prisoner's name, address if he has one, the offence he is convicted of and the sentence, and is signed and dated by a judge or court registrar. There is no medical information, no personal or family information, no assessments good, bad or indifferent. The governor has to depend entirely on the prisoner giving him accurate information about himself, his medical and psychiatric history, his addiction problems, if any, and so on. The prisoner goes to reception, is searched and has his personal property recorded, has a shower and is seen by a nurse. He is then assigned to a cell, and that's it.

To try to manage overcrowding, every morning from the mid 1980s onwards – seven days a week – a list of names of prisoners requesting transfers to other prisons or applying for temporary release, along with those we considered suitable for transfer or temporary release, was sent to the Prisons Division of the Department of Justice or, after 1999, to the headquarters of the IPS. All the governor grades in Mountjoy were involved in the soul-destroying work of trying to manage numbers, day in, day out. People might think that it would be a straightforward job to transfer prisoners from prison to prison, but nothing could be further from the truth. Lists of as many as 180 prisoners in Mountjoy were often sent to other prisons for the governors there to select prisoners for transfer, but as few as six or seven were usually the most that we could get transferred. Some of the most modern and secure prisons operated a selection process that was more appropriate for a crèche than a prison. This carry-on was a source of the odd wry laugh in Mountjoy. I remember one morning having a chat about why the rugby player Trevor Brennan hadn't got more international caps. One of my colleagues, Jim Petherbridge, said, 'Yeah, yeah, he is a great player, very aggressive, very strong – and he takes no prisoners, just like the Midlands Prison.' The Midlands Prison had been open for about two years at the time, and we were finding it almost impossible to get prisoners transferred there.

I always operated on the basis that Mountjoy was a prison and its main function was to accommodate prisoners irrespective of who they were. With the benefit of hindsight I was foolish, as Mountjoy was exploited and used by the rest of the prison service. And it was as bad as ever the day I left Mountjoy in 2010.

9. Getting to Grips with Officialdom

Early on in my management of Mountjoy I realized that I would not make much of an impression on my own and that as well as getting the staff on my side I would also need the help and support of the Department of Justice. So, in October 1984, I invited all the senior staff in the Prisons Division of the Department to a meeting in Mountjoy to discuss the future development of the prison. At our management meeting we decided that the agenda for this meeting should consist of four short presentations: I would outline the needs of the management of the prison; Deputy Governor Jim Woods would outline the needs of the staff; the chaplain, Father Harry Gaynor, would talk about the prisoners' needs; and the fourth presentation would be on behalf of the Department of Justice. The three of us presented our thoughts, and then it was the turn of the officials from the Department.

The response by a senior official was, 'Well, the Department has nothing prepared for you. We are not into planning in the Department of Justice. We react if something happens; we respond to it and resolve it. We don't believe in planning ahead.'

We were all shocked by this, but I felt that challenging him would not be a good start to opening dialogue and getting the Department's support. Afterwards, when we were on our own, we all agreed that whatever was going to be done in Mountjoy over the next few years it would have to be driven by ourselves and delivered by the staff in Mountjoy, because if we were going to depend on the Department of Justice, Mountjoy would remain static.

One thing that did emerge during that futile meeting was that most people not on the regular staff of Mountjoy had no idea what the prison was like. I remember a psychiatrist saying, 'I have never seen the toilet areas. I go to my surgery and that's it.' So I decided to draw up a full profile of Mountjoy. I felt that to improve things in the prison, I needed hard data. During early 1985 I interviewed over 400 prisoners using a questionnaire covering areas like levels of education, work record, drug addiction history and mental health history.

All the management team was involved in researching various areas of the prison like facilities, work for prisoners, level of services available to prisoners and the physical conditions within the prison. That, plus the analysis of my questionnaires, would give us a clear picture of the challenges we were facing. In addition to the management team, a few others provided great support, in particular Dr Paul O'Mahony, a psychologist in the Department of Justice, along with his colleague Paul Murphy and the coordinator of education, Kevin Warner. I asked a professional statistician to analyse the figures for me, and when it was all pulled together we produced a very impressive document called 'A Profile of Mountjoy Prison 1985'.

Two of our findings hit the headlines. First, the graphic description of the appalling physical conditions in the prison: urine running down from one landing to the landing underneath, the small number of toilets and the lack of washing facilities. The profile described a feature of daily life in the prison whereby, when prisoners went to the toilet during the night, instead of leaving the contents in their chamber pots they put the excrement into a newspaper, rolled it up and threw it out the window of their cells into the grounds. These were known in the jail as dirt parcels or parcel bombs. The next day the dirt parcels were shovelled into a big wheelbarrow called 'Wanderly Wagon'. The profile noted that this work was always done by members of the travelling community – a form of discrimination that ended immediately. The practice of getting rid of excrement in this way was stopped in the late 1980s when wire mesh was fixed on the outside of the cell windows.

The second thing that emerged and created a big headline was the rapid escalation of drug addiction in the prison. In 1981–2 Dr O'Mahony, along with Tom Gilmore, senior probation and welfare officer in Mountjoy, had carried out a survey and discovered that between 7 and 8 per cent of the prison population had a heroin addiction problem. By 1985 my research revealed that the figure had gone up to 29 per cent.

As usual, officials in the Department of Justice dismissed the report, saying that the statistical research wasn't carried out by a professional researcher and wouldn't stand up. On the contrary, the report was far more accurate than any professional research, because no professional researcher would have interviewed 400 prisoners; they would have based their findings on a representative sample. Regardless of the slight on my efforts, what was really galling was that the Department was – as it had been for years and would continue to be – in total denial about drug addiction. They just tried to pretend that it didn't exist, and they hated people making claims that heroin was a big problem in prisons.

I decided the only way to beat the Department was to play by its rules. I said, 'Right, if my research doesn't stand up because I am not a researcher, I'll get a researcher to do it.' I invited the Department's own man – Paul O'Mahony – to survey the Mountjoy Prison population and identify the levels of heroin addiction. When his findings were published in 1987, he said that 31 per cent of prisoners in Mountjoy had a heroin addiction history, a figure that totally supported my original research. The figure highlighted the fact that heroin addiction was now a major issue in the prison. In those days there were no drug-treatment or methadone programmes in Mountjoy, and prisoners were detoxed over a three-day period. Later on that was increased to seven days. Whether it was three days or seven days, it was absolute hell for the prisoners going through withdrawal symptoms.

Owing to the strike in 1983, the government had set up a Commission of Enquiry into the penal system, chaired by Dr Ken Whitaker. The result of the Commission's enquiries – what became known as the Whitaker Report – was published in August 1985. In 1984 I had led a small delegation of prison governors to make a submission to the Commission.

Dr Whitaker asked me, 'But how could we lever the power away from the Department of Justice? Won't they oppose it tooth and nail?'

'Of course they will,' I said, 'that is an absolute certainty. The only way that any real change will take place is if there is a political will for it.'

The following story illustrates the kind of thing we were up against with the Department. After carrying out a number of reviews of various aspects of how the prison worked, Deputy Governor Con Hayes came up with the suggestion that we should get one-gallon plastic buckets for each of the prisoners to bring water from the toilet area to their cells to wash themselves every morning. The prisoners were currently carrying the water in basins. With men carrying full basins bumping into each other on the narrow landings, they spilt more than they got to the cells. The wet landings were lethal, and prisoners were always slipping and falling. Con felt that small buckets would eliminate the spillages and be much easier to carry. We all thought it was a great idea, and the stores put the supply of 600 plastic buckets out to tender and selected the cheapest quote. We went through the usual form-filling procedure and sent off a requisition form to the Department of Justice for approval.

A couple of days later it came back stamped 'refused'. It stated that after due consideration in the Department it was decided that plastic buckets would present a security risk as the prisoners could flood the prison with water or the handles could be used as weapons.

I wrote back a fairly stiff letter stating that if Mountjoy was to progress, and if I was to be the governor there, then surely a decision to purchase plastic buckets was a matter 'exclusively and entirely for me and the prison management', and if it wasn't, what the hell was I doing as governor of the prison? I was either the governor or I wasn't – and I was happy with either position – but if I was the governor I was going to act as the governor and if they wouldn't let me do that then they could replace me.

I received a letter – or 'minute' as it was called – from a department official a couple of weeks later. 'I acknowledge receipt of your some-what incoherent letter in relation to plastic buckets . . .' it started. But at the end of the minute was written 'approved'.

Dr Whitaker was very approachable and supportive of the prison perspective on things, and he was all for trying to do something that would enable the prison service to come out of the shadows of the Department of Justice. His report stated, 'The Committee is satisfied that the degree to which the detailed administration of prisons has moved into the Department of Justice, to the detriment of discretion and responsibility, and therefore of good management, is excessive.'

His report recommended that policy should stay within the Department of Justice and under the direct control of the minister, but that day-to-day operations should be taken out of the Department and given to a board, which would appoint a chief executive who would be answerable to the board. I and many other serving governors supported this recommendation. As did the Prison Officers' Association.

The recommendation was never fully implemented. In 1999 the Prison Authority Interim Board was appointed, and eleven years on it still has no statutory basis and remains as an interim board. So while the management of prisons seemed to move out from under the control of the Department of Justice, it is currently in no man's land and in many ways the situation is worse than it was in 1985. I will write about this in greater detail later.

On 4 October 1985 we had our first ever death from a drug overdose in Mountjoy. A man called Christy Gamble was found unconscious in his cell with a syringe in his hand. He was removed to the Mater Hospital, but died the next day. It was a tragic death and very tough on his poor mother, who was a lovely woman. A month or so later, on 10 November, a young man was found hanging in his cell and he died later in the Mater Hospital. On 23 December a prisoner on remand cut one of the main arteries in his arm with a sharpened piece of stone and bled to death in a cell in B wing. And then on 17 January 1986 another young man was found hanging in his cell, and was pronounced dead.

Four deaths in the prison in such a short period caused uproar in the media, and rightly so. Suicides in prisons became a highly political issue. There were demands for the appointment of a medical director. I knew that a medical director would have had no bearing one way or the other on suicides in prisons – and this was proved correct when one was put in place years later – but that didn't stop people using it for all sorts of propaganda purposes.

In February I met the Minister for Justice, Michael Noonan, at a social function. 'I can understand one death in Mountjoy,' he said. 'I could even cope with two deaths. But four in such a short time – how come we've had four deaths?' As I understood it, he was saying, 'You are the cause of it. What are you doing to stop people dying?' I considered that he had marked my card.

Around that time we also had some very near escapes with suicides. In one case a man was cut down when he was fully unconscious. The medical staff couldn't find a pulse and thought that he was dead, but they revived him. And then one night a prisoner in C wing drank a cup of the disinfectant Jeyes Fluid. He almost died several times on his way to hospital, but the ambulance people kept him alive and he survived. If these two had also died, I'm sure my job would have been on the line.

Following the deaths, I received a letter from the assistant secretary of the Department of Justice. 'I am directing you to call a meeting of all the medical personnel attached to the prison, to be chaired by you, to examine all the recent deaths in prison and to draw up an appropriate response.' The last sentence read, 'An official from this department will attend in an observation capacity.'

I showed the letter to Father Harry Gaynor, whose reaction was, 'Unbelievable! They're trying to distance themselves from the problem.' That was just what I suspected. I had no role in the recruitment of medical staff, and I had no role in the delivery of medical service; that was the responsibility of the prison doctors. Psychiatric services were supplied on a consultancy basis by the Central Mental Hospital and were controlled and negotiated with the Department of Justice. Overall health policy in prisons was a matter exclusively for the Department of Justice.

But you learn quickly on your feet because if you don't you fall by the wayside, so I said, 'No problem, I'll hold the meeting.' I worked out a strategy with Father Harry and the rest of the management team. At the meeting we highlighted the lack of proper medical services and facilities, the lack of pharmacy services, the inadequate psychiatric service, the lack of facilities in the Central Mental Hospital, the brutal conditions that prisoners were living under in Mountjoy, the lack of occupation and activities, the lack of sanitation and, above all, the total absence of information on new committals: issues that had already surfaced in the profile of Mountjoy, many of which the Department had rubbished.

The meeting lasted for three and a half hours, and we produced five pages of minutes detailing all the issues that were relevant and asking for them to be addressed. And all of them without exception could only be addressed through the direct involvement and commitment of the Department of Justice. The minutes were submitted and I never heard another word about them.

One morning in October 1985 I was called out of one of our weekly management meetings. A medical orderly told me that the result of a HIV blood test had arrived back at the prison and it was positive. We had our first ever HIV-positive prisoner.

Out of the blue, Benny Hogg, a short-term prisoner who was a chronic heroin addict, had requested an Aids test. In those days nobody knew the difference between HIV and Aids, and there was an assumption that if you had HIV, you had Aids. Nowadays many people with HIV live normal lives, but in those days there was a lack of treatment, a lack of understanding and a total ignorance of HIV. Benny received the results of the test without any preparation or counselling. The doctor brought Benny in and said something along the lines of, 'You have HIV. I'm afraid you will get Aids over the next year or so and you have about five years to live.'

I went to see him. Naturally he was in bits, his family was in bits, the prison was in bits and the rest of the prisoners were terrified that they would get the virus; the whole place was chaotic. The Staff Association met immediately and demanded the release of the prisoner because the staff were afraid of contracting the disease, again a fear born of ignorance. That evening Benny Hogg was let out on temporary release. Poor Benny died a few years later.

Within a couple of days, twenty more results had arrived, and fourteen or fifteen of them were positive. The amazing thing was that a few prisoners who received negative results had been using heroin for twenty years, so it wasn't inevitable that if you were a user you had the virus. The Department of Justice decided that we should segregate all prisoners with the virus. Initially, they were put down in the B basement (a floor directly underneath the B wing of the main prison) and then they were moved over to the Separation Unit and eventually, as the numbers grew, accommodated in both the Separation Unit and the B basement.

Not long afterwards, the same thing happened in the women's prison. Some of the women had gone for the test and some had received positive results. The other prisoners and the staff demanded to have them segregated too, and they were allocated a floor in the Separation Unit.

The segregation policy was disastrous. It gave staff and prisoners a false sense of security because they thought, *If the prisoners with HIV are segregated then we are not in any danger*. What people didn't realize was that hundreds of prisoners, drug users in particular, weren't tested at all. Prisoners were terrified to use the same cups or plates or have anything to do with the prisoners with the virus. Staff members were the same. The dentist who had been coming to Mountjoy for many years withdrew his services because he felt that his association with a virus-ridden Mountjoy was going to affect his private practice. (It took two years to sort out an alternative. In 1987 the Dental Hospital came on board, and it still manages the dental service to the prison.) Even prisoners' families operated a form of segregation policy, and when prisoners went home they were given their own cups, plates and cutlery.

In January 1986 the Department of Justice decided to transfer all the HIV-positive male prisoners to Arbour Hill Prison. But the prison couldn't manage them because it was too confined, so eventually they had to be brought back to Mountjoy and put in the Separation Unit and the B basement again. That was where they remained until the Department decided that segregation should end and what we should do was to treat all blood spillage as high risk, irrespective of whose it was. It was a simple solution and it worked. It became international practice soon afterwards.

All through 1985, on top of the coverage of the deaths in the prison, Mountjoy was getting more and more negative publicity. Day after day, editorial after editorial, the press just lashed out at the prison and its failures. If you were working in Mountjoy at the time it was very difficult to keep your spirits and morale up, because all you were hearing was negativity: another suicide, another death, another riot, another disturbance.

I made a number of statements that got publicity: 'They are not my prisons, they are not my prisoners. I am here to manage the prison on behalf of the public, but they are your prisons and they are your prisoners. And if you want things to change then you must support and provide the resources to do it . . . I'm not going to be the scapegoat for the shortcomings of the prison service or the shortcomings of society in general. This is way bigger than me, it's way bigger than any individual, and it requires a national response and not a parochial response or indeed an individual response.'

In desperation – really, to try to change Mountjoy's image, to obtain public support and to help the public get a better insight into prison, how it works and what prisoners are really like – I decided that something had to be done to link the public with the prison. Recalling the great buzz in the Training Unit when Claire Wilson produced a drama project there in 1981, I called Claire and asked her if she would come into Mountjoy to stage a drama to which we could invite the general public.

The play, Tom Murphy's *On the Outside*, was scheduled for 8 April 1986. Male prisoners were cast in the male roles, and actresses from the outside took the female roles. Over 400 people accepted invitations to it. We had no theatre and no facilities whatever for staging a play, so we closed down the main recreation area in the A division and made it, on a temporary basis, into a theatre.

I was down in the hall just after 6.30 p.m., with half an hour to go before the play began, when I got a call to say that a few women prisoners in the Separation Unit were demanding to see me immediately or they would cut themselves up. These women had the HIV virus and had been segregated a few weeks previously in line with the new policy of the Department of Justice. They knew that the play was about to start, and they were determined to exploit it as much as possible. Father Harry Gaynor and I headed over to the Separation Unit. When we got to the landing there was absolute chaos. Six women had cut their arms with blades, and there was blood everywhere. They were roaring and crying and demanding to go back to the women's prison again. Eventually we got five of them calmed down and back in their cells. One young woman was very difficult. She had a tiny blade in her mouth and kept threatening to cut her throat. She showed me the blade on the tip of her tongue and between her teeth, but she wouldn't give it to me. We kept talking to her and asking her to hand the blade over. All of a sudden she took the blade out of her mouth and began ripping her left arm with it. The blood sprayed over us. One of the staff grabbed her and she gave me the blade.

Once the whole thing had calmed down, we walked over to the hall where the play had already started. I recall looking down at Father Harry's shoes and seeing the blood spattered all over them. It's impossible to convey in words the trauma of the incident – the terrible atmosphere in the unit and the awful pain in that young prisoner. And then the irony of heading off to a play that was being staged to change the image of Mountjoy.

The play itself was a tremendous success. The whole exercise – people coming in and seeing Mountjoy, the little reception we held for them afterwards and the quality of the food – helped to change the general perception of the prison. Many dignitaries and media personalities attended, as did the Minister for Justice, Alan Dukes, a welcome surprise to me. He had to go back to the Dáil for a debate, but, even more surprisingly, he returned later to join the celebrations. The media were allowed to talk to the prisoners, to photograph them and to publish comments they made about the play. Coverage the next day was very positive – both supportive of the whole project and very complimentary about the quality of the production and the acting – and there was a buzz around the prison for days afterwards.

We had invited the families of all the prisoners in the play to attend, and that meant an awful lot to them. One of the prisoners working backstage had been in and out of the prison for over twenty years. After the performance, an old man leaning on a stick shuffled over to me and shook my hand. He told me he was in his nineties and he was this man's father. He spoke about how proud he was to see him involved in the play. 'I spent a good bit of my youth in Mountjoy,' he said.

'Tonight is the best night of my whole life – just to be invited by the governor of Mountjoy to be his guest at a play me son is in.'

One other positive story from 1986 – although somewhat bitter-sweet for the team in Mountjoy – was the production of the first ever information booklet for prisoners. It was one of many targets included in our 1986 Management Plan. Not only was it the first ever information booklet in Mountjoy; it was also the first ever information booklet in any prison. A lot of people put a huge amount of effort and work into its production, and prisoners came up with some beautiful artwork to brighten it up. When it was ready I sent a copy over to the Department of Justice with a cover note simply saying that this information booklet was produced in Mountjoy and that it would be distributed to staff and to the prisoners over the next few days.

The next day there was a front page article in the *Evening Press*: 'The Minister for Justice today published the first ever information booklet for prisoners in Mountjoy. The Minister has given directions that the information booklet will be distributed to all prisons.' There was not one word of how it came about or who produced it, and no credit whatsoever to the team in Mountjoy. There and then I said, 'You bastards, you will never do that again.' And they didn't, because I never gave them the chance.

10. Strike

I wasn't long running Mountjoy before I realized that the way the staff was organized was unworkable. The scale of the operation meant that it was impossible to keep track of who was where or doing what. With almost 200 officers lined up for the morning parade, communication was impossible and discipline was breaking down; the parades were becoming a bit of a joke.

After much debate and consultation, I came up with a plan to divide the prison into four units, each with a management team and its own staff. To keep it dynamic, officers would rotate between the units over a three-year period. The other proposed innovation was that all posts – existing and future – would be advertised in the prison and open to everyone to apply for. Prior to this, some staff held down posts for years and once in a position practically considered it theirs for life. Now all staff would get a fair crack of the whip.

I felt – and still do – that I made every reasonable effort to consult with staff. I wrote to all of them asking for their views and suggestions but I got no response, even from the local branch of the Prison Officers' Association. It was a feature of my relationship with the local branch that it showed no urgency about any proposal until implementation was imminent, and then it made every effort to block it. This is exactly what happened. I heard nothing from the POA until the new structures were about to be introduced in February 1986, and then all hell broke loose.

The POA branch officers requested a postponement of a month, so that their national officers could hold discussions with the Department of Justice. This was another peculiar and frustrating aspect of running a prison: in disputes, local branch officers would deal with local management, unless they couldn't agree on something; then the national officers of the POA stepped in. However, instead of talking to management, the national officers would go to the Department of

Justice and talk to officials there who might not even grasp the nub of the matter. Decisions would be made behind the governor's back and without his input. He was told what had been agreed and he could like it or lump it. On this occasion, however, I felt so strongly that I picked up the phone to the assistant secretary in the Department and told him that not proceeding with the restructuring plan was not an option.

Right up to the evening of 4 March 1986, there was still no agreement. I decided to go ahead and introduce the changes the following day. I was at home when I got a call to say that three prisoners had made their way onto the roof of the Separation Unit. I returned to the prison. Just as I was walking towards the Separation Unit, I was told that the headline story on the *Nine O'Clock News* was: 'Three prisoners have climbed onto the roof of the Separation Unit in Mountjoy, and at a meeting tonight in the prison the staff has voted no confidence in the governor.' The no-confidence vote was over the restructuring plan and had nothing to do with prisoners on the roof, but the impression was being created that they were linked. The whole thing was a clever bit of media manipulation.

After all that, the outcome of the discussions in the Department of Justice was that the restructuring was a local matter and that it should go ahead. And it did, as planned, on 5 March.

The management structure I introduced in 1986 remains in place to this day. I am convinced it was the most significant and meaningful change I made in Mountjoy. It put a bit of shape into the place, it facilitated delegation and it gave all staff a sense of identity within the prison. At the end of the year, staff in each unit organized a Christmas night out for themselves, which demonstrated that they had developed that sense of affiliation to their unit that I had hoped for.

Until 1986, men's prisons were staffed solely by male prison officers and women's prisons by female officers. That year the rule changed, and officers could work in either men's or women's prisons regardless of their gender. Before the new ruling was introduced, some governors opposed the change. They said they were concerned about the safety of female officers working with male prisoners. They need not have worried: the transition went very smoothly and both men's and women's prisons benefited greatly.

Somehow, female officers helped to normalize things within Mountjoy and the other men's prisons. The women who came into the prison did – and continue to do – magnificent work. While it wasn't easy for them going into a male-dominated culture, they seldom had problems with the prisoners. They were able to relate to male prisoners in a way men could never do, and through their presence alone the men behaved differently. The prisoners often confided in them about personal and family issues, something they seldom did with male staff. They would ask their advice if they had relationship problems with their wives or girlfriends or worries about their children. Generally the language and the banter in the prison improved, and all the men – officers and prisoners – tended to behave in a less crude and aggressive way. On occasions prisoners would come to the support of a female officer when she was having difficulties with other prisoners. Something similar happened in the women's prison: many women there responded very positively to male officers. Either sex could work as chaplains, teachers, probation officers, doctors, nurses, psychologists and librarians too, in either men's or women's prisons, with a similar positive effect. Balancing the gender mix in prison communities works well and has a lot of potential.

Occasionally I saw female officers imitate their male colleagues rather than having their own independent approach. It is vitally important that when women work in male prisons they are confident in their own unique qualities and principles, and that they retain their femininity. They must not get swallowed up in the male culture, because if they do the value of their presence in the prison system is wasted. Equality is not the same as behaving or reacting like men. They are there in their own right and have as much, if not more, to contribute to the culture of prisons by being themselves.

Finally, it is worth noting that governors' worries about women's safety turned out to be groundless: female prison officers have never been seriously physically abused or injured by prisoners targeting them simply for being women.

*

For three years through the mid 1980s, the Prison Officers' Association and the Department of Justice attempted to come up with a comprehensive new roster system for all grades in the prison service. I took part in the working group examining this roster system as a member of the management (Department) side of the discussions. As with all such matters, the issues were complex, and I won't go into them here. By 1987, however, we were still stuck on one key issue: changing the shift arrangements. While we were still teasing this out – and without saying anything to the working group or to prison governors – department officials made a submission to the government that the prison service's £16 million annual overtime bill could be halved if 300 extra prison officers were recruited.

Though there was an embargo on recruitment in the public service, the government approved the proposal. But the Department had not done its homework. Now it had to have a new roster, one that took account of 300 extra bodies, in order to meet its commitment to government. When the Department tried to impose a new roster, the POA, inevitably, resisted being pushed into a corner, and in mid April 1988 declared that its members would go out on strike.

I was totally opposed to strikes on the basis that whatever the problem, a solution can always be found, and it is far better to find that solution than strike. Strikes cause lasting bitterness and damage to morale, and staff often return to work united against the management. And then there is the massive headache of people who decide to work while the strike is going on. A number of people, especially staff at senior grades, felt a loyalty to the state, to the prison service and to me as prison governor, and they worked during the strike. Before the strike I let it be known to senior staff in the prison that I didn't expect any of them to work out of loyalty to me and that it was a decision that they should make for themselves. I pointed out that there would be a price to pay later if they did decide to work.

I was very mindful of what had happened to people who had worked during previous strikes, particularly in 1983: they got no thanks or appreciation from the establishment and were labelled 'scabs', ostracized by their colleagues and suffered greatly in the job and indeed outside of it. As late as 2010 in Mountjoy, when a man was having a retirement do, I heard the comment, 'No, I'm not going – he worked in '83.'

A few days before the strike in 1988, two officers from the women's prison – both conscientious and excellent officers – came to me and said they were thinking of continuing to work. My strong advice was that they go out with their colleagues. I explained that should they work during the strike they would be isolated when it was over and would have a dog's life. I told them that their peace of mind, their general well-being and the whole atmosphere they would be working in on their return would be a million times better if they took part in the strike. They took my advice and didn't come to work.

Those who did work in 1988 had the same experience as those who worked in 1983. They were expelled from the POA and from prison-related sporting organizations and social clubs. This had serious financial consequences for some, as they were also expelled from insurance schemes the POA had negotiated. There was one scheme whereby, if the spouse of an officer died while the officer was in service, they received a lump sum payment. A few years after the 1988 strike, a senior officer who had worked during it – indeed, he was invaluable to the gardaí and the army who came in to run the prison, and only for him I doubt we could have survived at all – lost his wife. Because he had been expelled from the POA and was not eligible for the lump sum payment, he applied to the Department of Justice for the equivalent amount. The Department turned him down, saying there was no question of making such a payment. It is not an exaggeration to say that he had served his country at a time of crisis and he received no thanks for it.

The outcome of the 1988 strike was that Professor Basil Chubb of Trinity College was invited in to draw up a roster that would be acceptable to all parties. He came in, listened to both sides and came up with a roster that everyone agreed to. This roster had been on the table before the strike, but the Department of Justice wouldn't accept it. The month-long strike, which had been hugely costly and caused irreparable bad feeling, had been a waste of time and effort.

11. Taking on Portlaoise Prison

My transfer to Portlaoise Prison was a bolt out of the blue. In the autumn of 1988, word was out that Ned Harkins was about to retire as governor there. 'You might have to go there yourself,' said a Department of Justice official jokingly as I was leaving a meeting in the Department one evening in October.

I laughed and said, 'No way, I'm struggling where I am.'

I never gave it another moment's thought until I was back in the Department for a meeting about a week later. There was some discussion about Portlaoise, and an official said, 'We might have a problem with Portlaoise this time. It needs an experienced governor.' Later he turned to me and said, 'Is there any chance that you might go there? There's a big job to be done and I know you're the man to do it.' After discussing it for a bit I said, 'If none of the other governors will go there then I will consider doing a stint, but all the governors must be asked first.'

A couple of days later he called me and said, 'There's no serving governor interested or willing to go to Portlaoise. It looks like you'll have to go.'

In a strange way I embraced the idea of going there. It was the state's top security prison where members of the Provisional IRA and other subversive organizations were held. I had never worked with political prisoners, and there were so many stories about them, I felt I should do so if I was to complete my experience of being a prison governor. There was also a credibility aspect to my decision: in 1968 I had signed on to serve in the Irish prison service and I felt it was my duty to answer the call now that the service was in difficulty. Finally, I wanted to prove that I had the balls to run Portlaoise, because I knew I had a lot of critics in the prison service who felt that I was 'too soft to run a tough jail'. I firmly believed that softness or hardness were not essential personal qualities needed to manage a prison.

As Portlaoise was a top security prison, one of the very first decisions I had to make was about the level of personal security I needed and what was I prepared to go along with. I didn't want to have our lives disrupted by increased security around the house, and I certainly didn't want to raise any fear or anxiety in our daughters Sinéad and Marie, who were now in primary school. So we decided immediately not to move to Portlaoise, and the only extra security measure that I took was to have a house alarm installed. I would commute every day from Dublin to Portlaoise, and otherwise life would go on as normal.

The agreement was that I would go to Portlaoise for two years and return to Mountjoy at the end of my secondment. My brief was to evaluate the prison, look at the staff situation there, identify somebody who could take over as governor – regardless of rank – and groom them to take over at the end of my time there.

On my way out of the Department that evening, I met an official I had known for years.

'I hear you're going to Portlaoise,' he said.

'It looks like it,' I said.

'Well, I hope you go. It would be a charity to go down there. It needs an outsider to go in. It's crying out for change – the place is in bits.'

I drove down to Portlaoise in early November to have a look around. Deputy Governor Mick Horan met me on the road outside. Getting into the place was a nearly a day's work in itself. First there was a steel gate right out on the Dublin Road. Once you got through it, you then entered the search area. The search was a bit like going through airport security nowadays: I removed my jacket and shoes, was scanned with a metal detector and got a rub-down search. After the search area it was gates, gates and more gates before you got into the prison grounds; as far as I can remember I went through five of them. I had expected Portlaoise to be a big place with plenty of open space, but unlike Mountjoy the grounds were very small and tight and it felt a bit claustrophobic. The place was dominated by drab old buildings, rusty razor security wire and wire-mesh fencing.

I glanced back towards the main gate, and it was only then that I registered the soldiers in a watchtower close to it – armed soldiers on sentry duty. When I mentioned this to Mick he said, 'Oh, I forgot to tell you, if they ever tell you to halt going in or out, make sure you stop and tell them who you are.'

I said, 'Why, what will happen if I don't?'

'They could shoot you,' he said, with a big grin on his face.

I thought to myself, *This is no Mountjoy*. Indeed, it was anything but: it was dark and depressing and I was already feeling down.

The governor's office was a Portakabin. The ceiling was low and the windows were covered with some sort of brown sticking paper. Mick said it was to stop the prisoners seeing in. The lighting in the office was brutal, and to make matters worse the walls were painted in a dull yellow. When I walked towards the chair behind the desk, the whole place shook.

I said to Mick, 'This is the pits. If this is the governor's office, what's the rest of the place like?'

'It gets much worse,' he said.

A door at the end of the office led into another Portakabin – the office of the deputy governor and assistant governor. Next to that, a bigger Portakabin housed the general office and the personnel office. Some of the conditions in Mountjoy might have been poor, but the offices there were like palaces compared to these.

'This is far worse than I ever thought. It's the Calcutta of the prison service,' I said.

'You'll get used to it,' Mick said.

The tour continued on to the main security block, E block. Again there were more gates – three, I think – before we actually got to E block itself. Then, to get into the compound, there was another elaborate security procedure with two gates. The prisoners on E1 – the first floor of the block – were known as 'The General's men' because many of them were associates of crime boss Martin Cahill, 'The General'. But there were other prisoners too: some from the general prison population, some who had disassociated from the subversive groups, and a small number of individual paramilitaries. In total there were about twenty-five prisoners on E1. Facilities were sparse. There were no activities, no education, no work and limited access to outdoor recreation.

We went up an old steel staircase to E2, where a number of smaller groups of subversives were located, the biggest being the INLA (Irish National Liberation Army). There were also members of the Official IRA and the IRB (Irish Republican Brotherhood). Up more stairs were E3 and E4, where the Provisional IRA prisoners were held. In those days between eighty and ninety Provisional IRA prisoners were in custody in Portlaoise. Facilities were almost as poor on these landings. The prisoners had a workshop, a school and a laundry, but again the overall standards were much lower than I had expected.

The most striking thing of all on each of the landings was that the prison officers sat in strong steel cages. This was to protect them from being attacked and the keys taken from them forcibly. They monitored the landings and if they were concerned about anything they either used their walkie-talkies to contact the control room or set off an alarm if it was more urgent. They had no direct access to or physical contact with each other or with the prisoners. They were very much on their own, and would spend up to six hours at a stretch on these posts.

Then we visited what was called the South End – the Segregation Unit for prisoners who were abusive, disruptive or violent. Again, there were no facilities whatsoever, just a compound and cells. The main prison kitchen was near the South End. It had been built in 1900, at the same time as E block, and very little refurbishment and few improvements had been carried out in the meantime. It was small, poorly equipped and generally in a state of disrepair. The doctor's surgery was a little building on its own. It was well over 100 years old, and once again the facilities were antiquated and totally inadequate. The tour ended with a visit to the general store. I had never seen a building in such poor condition. It was a two-storey building, and when we got to the second floor we were welcomed by a flock of pigeons flying out through the roof. I could see clear blue sky through it. Yet the store was in use every day and catered for the needs of over 170 prisoners.

I left in the mid afternoon. Driving back to Dublin, I was in shock:

I couldn't believe that the condition of the prison was so bad. I had expected it to be a modern and well-equipped facility, especially as it had such a high profile as the state's top security prison. Over the years I had formed the impression that money was not spared in Portlaoise and that management there got whatever it needed. I thought that the key problem in the prison would be managing relationships – between management and the staff, staff and the prisoners, and management and the prisoners. Clearly I was way off the mark. I recalled the comment of the official from the Department: 'It would be a charity to go down there . . . the place is in bits.' How right he was: it was literally in bits.

By the time I got back to Mountjoy, I was fired up. I felt genuinely sorry for everybody in the prison – both the staff and prisoners – and I thought, *This is a challenge and I can't fail*. The problem was where to start.

12. A Staff in Dire Need of Support

Within a month of taking over as Portlaoise governor in mid November, I held a general meeting for Portlaoise staff in the Killeshin Hotel. They had never met as a group, except perhaps at POA meetings, and because identity is important I thought that it would be a good beginning for everyone to be able to look around a room at their colleagues and say, 'This is us; we are the staff of Portlaoise Prison', and feel a sense of affiliation. Allowing for officers on duty that night the attendance of 330 people represented a turnout close to 100 per cent.

Mindful of the complete mess I had made of my first meeting in Mountjoy, I was determined not to repeat the experience. I told the meeting that I would be in Portlaoise for two years and my objective was to try to help to improve things in whatever way I could. I said that I had no agenda and no fixed perceptions. I would assess the situation over time and respond as objectively as I could, with no vested interest and no favourites. I told them I would be completely honest with them. I distinctly remember saying, 'But really it's about you. It's about your lives, it's about your workplace, it's about your futures, and if I can do anything to help you, I will; but at the end of the day the people who will make the real difference are yourselves, not me.' And then I opened the meeting to the floor.

The room erupted. It was oozing with frustration, anger and feelings of hurt, neglect and abuse, feelings that had obviously been festering and building up for years. The hostility and bitterness of the strike was still raw, and boy did it come out at the meeting. Several speakers said things like, 'I'll never forgive the scabs the longest day I live. I'll never forgive them.' They spoke with a viciousness that was upsetting. The staff who had worked sat there in silence and took it on the chin.

I challenged some of the critics. Several times I said, 'If you feel like that, it's your choice and you are going to have to live with it. If that is your choice so be it, but consider what it's going to do to you as an individual. My advice would be if you feel that bad then get the hell out of the job because feeling like that will eat away at you and destroy you. You have to move on. If you are going to have any future, any enjoyment, any job satisfaction, you cannot continue holding those sorts of grudges. The grudges will eat you up and they'll destroy you and make your life a misery. There is no job worth that.'

After the meeting ended we had tea and sandwiches and a chat. Ending on a social note gave people time to mingle and to discuss what had happened, and it was good to see that there was a buzz in the air. I think it's fair to say that this meeting had huge psychological benefits for all the staff and management in Portlaoise. Though the mood had been very blunt and angry, the meeting had unleashed a huge amount of frustration that had built up for many years. There was something very special about it.

During the meeting one officer had stood up and asked me, 'Have you seen the back gate?' When Portlaoise had become a top security prison in the 1970s, the back gate – the gate between the prison compound proper and what had previously been a prison farm – had become a target for subversives. They had once tried to ram it open. Since then two big steel girders had been fixed directly in front of the gates. Each girder was about two hundredweight and was sunk three feet down into a cement base. Several times a day, when vehicles entered or exited, officers on the back gate had to haul the girders out of their bases to allow access through the gates, and then fix them back into position once the gates were closed. The officer wanted to know if I thought it was fair or right that they should have to go through this every day.

First thing the next day I went to the back gate and saw the whole procedure with my own eyes. I asked the trades to look at the possibility of coming up with some sort of lift or hydraulic system to move the girders, rather than officers having to do it manually. In the interim I told them to take the girders out in the mornings and put them back at night so that at least they would only have to go through this palaver twice a day.

I thought this was quite a routine decision – no big deal at all – but the benefits were enormous and quite amazing. First, it gave the staff a clear indication that I was listening. Second, they accepted that I had a genuine interest in their welfare. It proved to be a tremendous morale booster for all the officers, but in particular for the man who had raised it at the meeting. It became a watershed decision and a signal for change.

Another thing that emerged from the meeting was a need for training and personal development. Many officers had worked in the prison for over fifteen years and had gone through tough times and never had a day's training, even though the training headquarters of the entire Irish prison service was just down the road in Beladd House. For many years there had been outright hostility between the staff and the Provisional IRA and other subversive groups. Prisoners would refuse to be searched, especially to be strip-searched, and officers were under orders to carry out the searches by force. The staff felt isolated, used and unsupported. There was so much feeling about this that it needed to be dealt with as a matter of urgency.

Throughout 1989, with the help of Department of Justice psychologists, Des O'Mahony and Eddie McElduff, we ran five-day training courses at Beladd House. The first two days of the course were given over to grievance and griping sessions. Eddie ran the groups and he let officers vent and get everything off their chests; the feedback from this was very positive. The staff training and development officer Eamon Kavanagh and his assistant Fran Dowling ran the Wednesday and Thursday sessions, which were dedicated to practical issues – for example, identification of illegal drugs and explosives, and dealing with prisoners who had psychiatric disorders – as well as stress management and other personal issues for officers. Friday afternoons were earmarked for a session with me.

I met every group and every single officer in Portlaoise during those thirty-six weeks. My sessions were mainly to allow the officers to tell their stories. Most of the sessions were tough. I found it hard going sometimes to just keep cool and not become defensive, because their frustrations and anger were sometimes misdirected. I kept telling myself, *Just listen. Even when what you are hearing is misinformation, it doesn't matter. The therapy is the listening. The clarifications and the explanations can be done another time. Now it's all about hearing their stories.*

From the feedback I got then, and from talking to officers in the years since, I know that that course was probably the first time in their careers that they had had the opportunity in the prison service to reflect on their jobs, vent their anger and frustration, think a little bit about life and, above all, just be heard. Over twenty years on, it is still remembered warmly. The course proved just how badly members of staff need personal attention and support. I'm fairly certain that they never again got such an opportunity, which is a disgraceful neglect of staff welfare by the IPS.

Throughout these difficult and challenging early days in Portlaoise, I was lucky to have a great team around me. They were outstandingly supportive and also very flexible when it came to implementing new systems and approaches that in many ways were alien to them. It really was remarkable.

Just to give an example. One morning I was called to an urgent security meeting in the Department of Justice. They had information that the prisoners were digging an escape tunnel and that the start of the tunnel was under a toilet in the yard. When I got back to Portlaoise and told the deputy governor, Mick Horan, he said, 'Leave it with me.' Three hours later he walked into my office wearing overalls and covered in muck. 'You have nothing to worry about,' he said, 'there's no digging going on under the prison. I was down in all the shores under the prison and nothing has been disturbed.' And he was right. Mick's support, his courage, his wisdom and his loyalty were second to none. Subsequently, he worked with me in Mountjoy as my senior deputy governor and he retired as governor of the Curragh Prison.

Paddy McPherson was assistant governor. I had known Paddy for some years and I knew that he had an enormous amount of experience in prison administration. There was always great craic when he was around, and he would lighten up the place even when it was full of tension or dark and gloomy. Mick Horan and Paddy McPherson were an outstanding combination and one of the most loyal pairs I ever worked with during my career.

Chief Officer Paddy Powell had been on duty in 1985 when the last major escape attempt took place. He tried to physically stop prisoners forcing their way out of E block, and an armed prisoner had aimed at him and twice pulled the trigger. Thankfully, the gun didn't go off. That was Paddy: he put himself on the line and always did his job without fear or favour. Paddy was assisted by another two outstanding chief officers, Paddy O'Keeffe and James O'Reilly.

So I had a great team, five loyal and capable men, who all had great experience of Portlaoise and understood it inside out. They were a pleasure to work with and the real beauty was that they weren't yes men and always told it as it was.

Over the years, I have heard a lot of negative comments about the 'old staff' in Portlaoise, in other words the staff of the 1970s and '80s. Some of those making them were johnny-come-latelies to the prison service and perhaps knew no better, but what really drove me mad was to hear some of my contemporaries leading the charge. It was nauseating to hear them criticizing the staff for their 'lack of flexibility' and 'lack of interpersonal skills' with prisoners. The bloody cheek of them: they had many opportunities to serve there in the 1970s and '80s, but they ran miles away from it. The staff who worked in Portlaoise Prison during these tough times served this country with courage and distinction. They were used and then neglected by the state over the years, and their treatment was nothing short of a national scandal.

13. The Subversive Prisoners

Until the early 1970s, IRA and subversive prisoners were imprisoned in Mountjoy and presented no real security problem. However, as conflict in Northern Ireland escalated, the threat presented by the presence of IRA prisoners also escalated. Now the prison service – an unarmed civilian system – was coming up against people willing and able to use explosives and firearms to escape. In October 1973, a hijacked helicopter was forced to land in the D yard of Mountjoy and three prisoners escaped in it. The government was under huge pressure internationally to take action against Provisional IRA activists in the republic, and the incident caused a huge political storm both in Ireland and abroad. A decision was made, almost immediately, to remove the subversive prisoners from Mountjoy and transfer them to Portlaoise, which more or less overnight was to change from being a medium to a top security facility, complete with army support. Armed sentries were posted all around the boundary walls to prevent attacks from outside or escapes from inside.

The prison service didn't know what hit it. It was like calling out 'Dad's Army' to deal with the war. Portlaoise was in no way equipped to deal with the challenge of a well-trained prisoner population versed in all types of sophisticated guerrilla warfare tactics. It was not the service's fault; it was just a situation that had never been envisaged. Everything – from staffing levels to the prison buildings to prison officers' training to management resources – was totally inadequate. Overall it was a complete shambles, and everyone involved in the service at that time deserves great credit for managing to hold the fort.

When I got to Portlaoise in 1988 it held two sorts of prisoners: the security prisoners (members of the IRA and other subversives) housed in E block; and prisoners who were transferred to Portlaoise to work in the prison, called the Portlaoise Work Party. They were ordinary prisoners who had no subversive connections, and had been chosen to work in the kitchen and the grounds and so on. For security reasons subversive prisoners were not allowed to do this work, and in any case they were selective about the prison work they would do: they cleaned their own landings and toilets, and washed their own clothes, but they wouldn't do any other type of prison work. Only prisoners convicted in the Special Criminal Court were committed directly to Portlaoise Prison. All others were committed to prisons like Mountjoy and then transferred to Portlaoise to make up the work party. The work party prisoners got extra remission and were kept completely separate from the subversives. They were housed in D block, which was part of the old county jail and was hundreds of years old. It had been closed after E block was built in 1900, but it reopened in the mid 1970s when Portlaoise became a top security prison. It had been closed because it wasn't fit for human habitation; it reopened in the same condition.

In the decades before the outbreak of conflict in the late 1960s, IRA prisoners had automatically been granted political status. They didn't have to do ordinary prison work, they were allowed to wear their own clothes, they were permitted food parcels and they were allowed to organize themselves on a paramilitary-type basis – to march and to give commands and to have a commanding officer who spoke for them. All these traditions were in place on the basis that they were political prisoners – freedom fighters and not criminals. In the 1970s the government refused to give them political status, which resulted in huge conflict and culminated in thirst and hunger strikes.

Eventually the Minister for Justice, Des O'Malley, resolved the clothing issue by allowing all prisoners to wear their own clothes, provided they could have them washed and laundered on the outside. And in most prisons to this day all prisoners who wear their own clothes have to get their families to wash them every week or so. As forbidden items had been smuggled into the prison in food parcels these were not permitted when I got to Portlaoise, but prisoners could purchase food in the prison tuck shop or it would be purchased for them out in the town by prison staff. Other agreements worked out between the subversives and management covered things like strip-searching and being let out on temporary release. For example, the agreement on strip-searching was that in return for being allowed open family visits in an ordinary visiting box, instead of behind wire mesh screens, they would allow themselves to be strip-searched afterwards. While they still refused to remove their underpants, they didn't physically resist the staff doing so.

The change in the clothing policy created a huge security headache. Anything coming in from the outside was a security risk; for example, prisoners were able to smuggle in explosives and other contraband in the soles of their shoes. When wood was delivered to the prison for the craft workshop, explosives and guns were concealed within it. The prison service just didn't have the means of counteracting such a sophisticated operation.

It was only after some spectacular escapes and attempted escapes from Portlaoise that the necessary staffing levels were put in place. The gardaí were called in too, and for years, as well as soldiers, a significant number of gardaí worked in the prison every day.

The higher the level of security, the greater the consequences if an escape took place, and even a breach of security was regarded as catastrophic. The governments of the 1970s and '80s made it very clear what the consequences would be if there was a serious breach of security at Portlaoise: all associated with it would be sacked. The commandment in the prison was 'Thou shalt not escape', and everything else was secondary. It was an approach that nearly caused a tragedy.

Two prisoners had a falling out over a word processor. One decided to take his revenge by setting fire to the computer. As it wasn't burning quickly enough, he threw on a bag of sugar, not realizing that the sugar would melt instantly and cause a minor explosion. When the staff heard the bang and another prisoner shouted, 'Explosion!', everybody dived on the floor thinking it was an attempt to blow open the gates or the wall. Within seconds the fire in the cell got out of control and thick smoke began to billow out, causing havoc for the staff and the prisoners. Black toxic smoke filled the whole of E wing within minutes, and everybody in the area was choking and gasping for air. The officer on the main security gate leading into E wing was locked in the security cage and couldn't get out. Although he had the key, the lock was on the outside of the cage, and with all the smoke he found it impossible to pass the key through the tiny hole in the cage to the officer outside. Finally he got it through, but it fell to the ground and the officer couldn't find it because of the smoke. The upshot of all this was that a number of prison officers and prisoners were taken out of the South End and E block unconscious and close to death. We were very lucky that nobody died.

The incident highlighted the fact that good fire evacuation plans are almost totally incompatible with top security procedures. That was the most frightening and the most dangerous incident that happened in my time in Portlaoise, and the lesson was that good fire evacuation procedures should never be sacrificed, even in the interest of security. Getting the right balance was almost impossible, because politically it was totally unacceptable to have any serious breaches of security in Portlaoise and that was my first and really only priority; however, as the governor of the prison I also had a clear responsibility for the safety and well-being of both the staff and prisoners. Nevertheless, when I was pushed I had no problem coming down on the side of humanity; in other words, I would prefer to see a prisoner escaping from custody rather than getting killed in the process. And I felt the very same with the staff: I never expected a prison officer to sacrifice his or her life in preventing an escape.

I had every opportunity to talk to D block prisoners because the D wing operated as an ordinary prison where the governor's parade was held every day and the prisoners came to make requests and to discuss different issues. It was quite a different story with the subversives. None of them ever came to the governor's parade – indeed, there was no governor's parade. The Provisional IRA prisoners had an OC (oifigeach ceannais) or commanding officer and a deputy OC who acted as spokesmen for their members. These and other 'spokesmen' were the only E block prisoners I communicated with, and I had no opportunity to talk to the other prisoners to find out how they really were.

The spokesmen came to see me on a regular basis, at least once or twice a month. They would send over a written agenda a few days before the meeting, which was held in my office. The first agenda they

sent through had about twenty-two different items on it. The nature
of the items varied – from minor things about equipment for the
school or recreation area, to more substantial matters such as temporary
release requests. That was typical.

From early on it was obvious that in some ways the spokesmen felt
the same as the staff – frustrated and very annoyed about small things.
And they had huge grievances about family visits. As previously noted,
to deal with the possibility of contraband being smuggled in, prisoners were strip-searched before and after visits. They were prepared to
cooperate with the searches, except the removal of their underwear;
however, staff were obliged to complete the search and this always had
the potential to cause trouble. All it took was an awkward prisoner or
an awkward prison officer. During my time there I think we got the
balance pretty right with the visits, however, and I didn't see any major
conflicts.

Though governments in the 1970s and '80s stuck to the line about
refusing to give subversive prisoners political status, they did grant
them many privileges that other prisoners did not, and still don't,
receive. When being granted temporary release, it didn't matter how
long the sentence was or how much of it was served; once it was
covered by the agreement on temporary releases, they got it. They
didn't have to work in the prison except to carry out some small clean-
ing duties in their own quarters. They were allowed to do craftwork
and then give it to their families and friends. They were allowed to
buy extra items of food in the prison tuck shop that other non-subversive
prisoners weren't allowed. The Provisional IRA prisoners had a
central account that they could use to make purchases, and on a regular basis they were allowed to order takeaway food from the town.
The OC would give the order to the prison staff, who would give it
to the fast-food outlet. Then the prison van would collect it, bring
it back to the prison, have it checked out by security and delivered to
the prisoners. The cost of the food would be taken out of the Provisional IRA account. It was known in the prison as the 'Cumann
Cabraigh' account and it was used by the Provisional IRA prisoners
for various purposes, including helping any of their members who
had no money of their own. They were also allowed late lock-up

once a week. I can vouch that every single extra privilege they received was approved from on high, at least at ministerial and sometimes at cabinet level.

The 'guarantee' was also unique to the subversives. All temporary releases of subversive prisoners were granted subject to the guarantee. Indeed, this was always written on the applications. What it meant was that the Provisional IRA or the INLA gave their word that the prisoner would comply fully with the conditions of his release. And he always did. On many occasions, even though they were usually serving shorter sentences, ordinary prisoners were refused temporary release for family occasions similar to those being attended by subversive prisoners. There was no question that it was a two-tier system.

The guarantee applied within the prison too. If the prisoners required material or equipment for educational or recreational use, they would give the guarantee, it would be granted and they always honoured it. When they were staging their annual commemorative Easter drama, for example, they would look for electric cable for the lighting. I would say, 'I take it the guarantee applies', and they would say yes: the cable could be there for days and they would never abuse it or attempt to use it in an escape attempt. They would still try to escape; they just wouldn't use the cable.

The spokesmen often asked me to reduce the heavy escorts used when one of their men needed treatment in the local hospital.

'There is no need for the army to be all around the hospital,' they'd say.

I always said, 'No problem, will you give the guarantee?'

'Ah now,' they would reply, 'you know we can't do that.'

'Well, in that case I won't be taking the army off the escorts.'

At the end of my very first meeting with the Provisional IRA spokesmen, one of them asked, 'When are you going to take those criminals off of E1?' He was referring to the prisoners associated with Martin Cahill. It highlighted their mindset: they saw themselves as freedom fighters and definitely not as criminals. That psychology played a huge role in keeping the Provisionals, and indeed other subversive groups, motivated for many years. As well as that, and in contrast to ordinary prisoners, they were actively supportive of one another within the prison. They had a sense of camaraderie and discipline, and nobody outside of themselves knew how this was imposed and controlled.

When I look back, it is obvious that after the big escape attempt in 1985 the whole approach and philosophy of the Provisional IRA changed, and while they were never passive, they became more cooperative and less resistant. During my time in Portlaoise a sentence review group was established by the Minister for Justice, and this forum led to the release of many long-term Provisional IRA prisoners. One of the conditions applying to a prisoner's release was that he would disassociate from the movement. A regular feature of life in the prison from 1989 onwards was high-profile Provisional IRA prisoners arriving at the gates of E1 with their kit and stating that they had disassociated from the movement and wanted to be released. In hindsight it was the beginning of the peace process, but we did not know that at that time.

14. Returning to Mountjoy

While buildings and physical conditions are important, they are far from being the be-all and end-all of what makes a prison a safe and humane place. Which was just as well when it came to Portlaoise. We made many submissions to the Department of Justice about improving things. D and E blocks, the store, the kitchen, the surgery and the offices all needed major reconstruction. We didn't get very far. However, during my time in Portlaoise the trades staff carried out a lot of work in refurbishing D block. While it was still a kip when I was leaving, and didn't have anything even closely resembling acceptable standards, it had much improved toilets, showers and food-serving facilities.

However, the relationships between management and the staff, and the staff and the prisoners, had improved immeasurably. One officer was overheard telling a visitor that he used to hate getting up and going to work, and now he looked forward to it. That we had come so far in such a short time was a tribute to the team who had supported me so resolutely.

Obviously all this time I knew that I had to decide who would take my place when my two-year term was up. After a while I decided that the person best equipped to take over – who had the capacity to bridge gaps and to try to bring the place forward, despite all the difficulties and hostilities – was Paddy McPherson. I felt he had the right personality for the job. He was flexible, mature and intelligent, as well as strong and big enough to be able to walk away from things that were ingrained in the system and say, 'That was then, now is now, we need to move on.'

This created a difficulty, because as the deputy governor Mick Horan was the senior man. I told him how I was thinking and he said, 'I totally agree with you. He should never have been passed over in the first place. He was always the man for the job, he is the man for

the job, and I'll be delighted to work with him. I have no problem.'
His was an unbelievable attitude, and it just proved the quality of the
man. The great thing was that he fully supported Pat McPherson when
he took over, and never showed the slightest disappointment or bitterness. And I know that Pat greatly appreciated Mick's attitude. They
continued to be great friends as well as colleagues.

Getting out of Portlaoise proved a far slower process than getting
into it. The department officials I had dealt with when going to Portlaoise were honourable and decent people and they treated me very
well and fully honoured all the commitments they gave me at the time.
But now the timetable had changed. Paddy had to be promoted from
assistant governor to deputy governor and then to governor class 2
before he could take over from me, and this didn't happen until May
1992. During my first two years in Portlaoise my intention was to
return to Mountjoy and take over from the senior deputy governor
at Mountjoy, Jim Woods, who had been acting governor of Mountjoy
while I was away. Just towards the end of those two years, on the
assumption that my departure from Portlaoise was imminent, I was
called to a meeting in the Department of Justice to discuss my next
move. A proposition was put to me that when the time came perhaps
I should consider going to work in the Department of Justice, in
prisons operations, carrying out a role and a function yet to be created.
I said, 'It will depend on the job. If it's a real job and if I am doing
something useful then I would be interested, but if it's not a real job,
I'm not interested.'

Discussions on the nature of this position went on for well over
a year. Eventually, when I was well into my fourth year in Portlaoise, I decided that I had to be more determined in getting this
resolved, so I put on a bit of pressure. Finally, department officials
came up with a job that was unacceptable to me: to go into the
Prisons Division in the Department and assess the training needs of
the service, advising officials on security and other prison issues. It
was very clear that I would have no real responsibility and definitely
no authority to do anything. I declined the job and said I would go
back to Mountjoy.

★

When I returned to Mountjoy, all the governor grades that had served with me before I went to Portlaoise were gone. That was to be an ongoing problem – the regular turnover of management staff due, mainly, to promotional opportunities. It meant starting all over again with a new management team.

During my absence there had been a serious riot in 1991. Over seventy prisoners got onto the roof of the prison and spent many hours wrecking it. They pelted staff below with the lethal slate roof tiles, and when they were done the roof was destroyed. But some good came out of it, as the slating was replaced with a far more secure material that couldn't be broken up and used as missiles. That was the last time prisoners went onto the roof at Mountjoy.

Another improvement that was on the way was a new main kitchen. For reasons that were never clear to me, it was going to be located right inside the main gate of the prison, which not only created a huge security headache – with prisoners working close to the main gate and the staff detail office – but offered no natural light. When I raised these objections I was told that it was a fait accompli and that it was too late to change either its design or location. Since the building was going ahead anyway, I decided then to take a more positive approach and I fought like a tiger to have a second floor built on top of the new kitchen as an auditorium. Having had a number of hugely successful drama productions at the prison, I was convinced that drama had unlimited potential as a therapy and an activity for prisoners.

Eventually department officials agreed and so we went about designing a small auditorium to seat around 250 people. The three key things the experts we consulted stressed were acoustics, lighting and having a good high ceiling. The architects came back with a perfect plan: a beautiful little theatre – a high ceiling, a lovely stage, with lighting and a sound system built in. I was delighted. This would be a facility that would really make a difference.

One day a prison officer who was supervising the building site came up to my office and said, 'Do you know that they have reduced the height of the building?' I was shocked. He said, 'Yeah, it's finished now. They have cut down the height because of costs.'

It turned out that to save a few thousand pounds officials had decided that the height of the building would be reduced by five feet. But while the ceiling was much lower than in the plans, they had still built the stage to the original specifications. It meant that people's heads were touching the lights and you could smell burning hair. It was a total disaster. For safety reasons then, the stage, which had been five foot high, had to be reduced to less than a foot and a half off the floor. Of course it was now so low that people sitting anywhere from four or five rows back couldn't see it clearly. Unbelievable stuff, but not a bit unusual for the prison service.

The kitchen and auditorium opened in December 1994. The auditorium proved to be a great asset, and the educational staff have used it for music classes ever since. And the new kitchen provided modern cooking facilities for the first time. We recruited a qualified chef, which was a first for Mountjoy. The results were immediate, the standard of catering reached very high levels and the prison kitchen was soon competing for national hygiene awards and winning them.

In December 1995 I faced my second serious fire. A seriously mentally ill prisoner in the Medical Unit managed to set fire to his padded cell. Prisoners were very good at concealing contraband – it wasn't a bit unusual for a prisoner to hide drugs or a syringe or a cigarette lighter in his back passage – and this prisoner had smuggled either matches or a cigarette lighter into the cell when he was moved there. When the staff noticed the smoke coming from the padded cell they rushed to the door, unlocked it and tried to get the prisoner out. However, he didn't want to come out, so they had to drag him from the burning cell and place him in another one. By the time they had done this the fire had got out of control and it ripped through the whole building.

It was my second time to come across flash fire – where fire runs along ceilings and floors and spreads with great speed. That was what had happened in Portlaoise too. The Medical Unit was full of prisoners and they were all locked in their cells and the staff couldn't get to them. The cells began to fill up with foul smoke. Firemen arrived on the scene. They tried breaking the glass in the cell windows to let in air but the windows were fitted with Lexan and the firemen were unable to break it. As a result the smoke couldn't get out of the cells.

The firemen did not consider it was their job to unlock prison cells, so prison staff had to do it using prison-issue breathing apparatus that was designed only to enable staff to snatch and grab a prisoner from a cell. They succeeded in pulling nineteen prisoners, some of them unconscious, from their cells and to safety. All the staff on duty that night did heroic work and put themselves at serious risk, particularly Chief Officer Liam Davis and Assistant Chief Officer Seamus Cramer. In the aftermath it was discovered that everything that could go wrong had gone wrong on the night: the air flaps that should have closed off the air supply actually opened up, the material in the padding was highly toxic, and the issue of who would unlock the cell doors proved almost fatal.

All through the 1990s the number of prisoners in Mountjoy continued to increase, as did our constant but usually futile efforts to find them places in other prisons. Towards the end of 1996, however, we had the unusual experience of the Department of Justice instructing us to transfer ten prisoners to the new Curragh Prison that was coming on stream. Officials accepted that it was not yet ready for prisoners, but said that the minister wanted it open before the end of the year. Ten prisoners also transferred from Loughan House to the new Castlerea Prison at the same time and for the same reason.

15. Siege

It was Saturday, 4 January 1997, just after 6.30 p.m. I was sitting at the kitchen table at home having a bite to eat before I was due to head off to a function at my local GAA club, Kilmacud Crokes. The phone rang. It was Killian Flynn, a chief officer in Mountjoy. 'We have a bit of trouble in the Separation Unit. Some of the prisoners on E3 have locked staff in the recreation room and won't let them out.'

Driving the six miles from Stillorgan to the North Circular Road, I was trying to get my head around what I would do when I got there. I had never managed a hostage siege, nor had I any formal training. But we had had a hostage negotiations strategy in place in Mountjoy for a number of years, and I had read some material on hostage-taking and knew the principles of best practice on managing such a situation. Being an optimist I felt that I would solve it straight away. Then I began to have second thoughts. I knew how dangerous a hostage siege could be, especially in the early stages. I thought about the staff and the dangers they were in. What if somebody got killed or badly injured?

Jim Woods, my former colleague in Mountjoy, was now working in the Prisons Division of the Department of Justice, and one of his jobs was to develop a national hostage negotiations strategy. I felt I needed to talk to someone of his experience, and called him from the car. He lived near the prison and volunteered to come in immediately.

I got to Mountjoy shortly after 7.30 p.m. and went straight to the Separation Unit. I ran up the two flights of concrete stairs, jumping over every second step, until I reached the third floor, E3. When I got there it was absolute bedlam. There was shouting and music blaring at top volume coming from the recreation room. The prisoners were roaring that if anyone tried to storm the room, they would stab the hostages with infected blood-filled syringes. Officers outside the room confirmed that they had seen the prisoners with two blood-filled syringes and steel bars, and that a knife was being held to the throat of an officer. I thought to myself, *This is no ordinary prison disturbance; this is serious stuff.*

When I had been told the names of the six prisoners, I realized that I knew five of them well. I had met them several times one-on-one, most recently shortly before Christmas. Some had been looking for financial assistance for themselves or their families for Christmas, and I arranged something for them. One had asked for a transfer to Portlaoise Prison. Though I knew that at least two of them were addicted to heroin, highly strung, unpredictable and, in certain situations, likely to be violent and dangerous, I had felt a little relieved. *At least I know them and I get on okay with them*, I thought. *This will be a help.*

Yet as I stood there outside the room, my earlier optimism vanished. Six maverick prisoners were holding four prison officers as hostages, and they were in total control of the room. I had lost control of part of the prison, and I felt uneasy and vulnerable. A prison can only work safely when the governor is in control. It is a psychological thing, that feeling that someone is in charge. Staff and prisoners very much depend on this, as it gives them confidence and assurance. When the governor is not in control, as was the case in the Separation Unit that Saturday night, people feel insecure, unsafe, unsure and frightened.

The prisoners claimed afterwards that what they had intended to do was to break through the ceiling of the recreation room and get onto the roof of the Separation Unit to protest. The focus of their protest was unclear – they seemed to be protesting about everything. They didn't realize that above the false ceiling it was solid concrete, and when they couldn't break through it they panicked. They barricaded themselves inside the room, holding the staff as hostages. They warned that if anyone came near the door they would 'smash up' the hostages.

The recreation room was about nineteen feet long and thirteen feet wide, with only one entrance, a solid steel door. The only other point of contact was a small steel-framed window overlooking the recreation room from a tiny office. This window was about six feet off the ground and had eight small panes of glass. The staff had broken one of the panes to allow them to speak to the prisoners. But the prisoners had stuck a black plastic bag on the inside of the window, preventing anyone from looking into the room.

When I went into the little office, two supervising officers were standing on chairs at the window trying to talk to the prisoners. The prisoners were firing cups, plates, pieces of broken chairs and fireballs made of newspapers at the window and shouting and roaring abuse at them. The loud music was making it very difficult for the staff to talk to them or to hear what was going on inside. Then the prisoners turned off the lights, plunging the room into total darkness. It had all the signs of a full-scale riot except that it was much worse as the lives of four officers were at serious risk.

One prisoner came to the window and shouted, 'Two of them are going to snap if they don't get Physeptone now.' Physeptone, better known as methadone, is a prescription drug given to people addicted to heroin to help to stabilize them.

Another shouted, 'I'm not a hard man, but if you storm the door I'll smash all their fucking legs and arms.'

Jim Woods and I had a conversation to work out a negotiation strategy. My first priority was to save lives; the second was to prevent injury of hostage or prisoner; the third was to get the hostages released as soon as possible; and the fourth was to demonstrate that hostage-taking does not work. These four principles formed the basis of my entire strategy during the crisis.

I went back to my office in the main prison after 8 p.m. and took up the role of siege commander. The commander is in charge of the whole operation, and all decisions are made by him. An important rule in hostage negotiations is that the commander has no direct contact with the hostage takers. This is to prevent them from blackmailing or putting undue personal pressure on the commander. The commander appoints negotiators to deal directly with the hostage takers, and they relay all requests by phone back to the commander, who decides what the responses will be. This worked very well throughout the weekend.

An incident room was set up on the floor beneath the recreation room. Senior Deputy Governor John Brophy took control of the incident room, and over the weekend he was assisted by a number of other governor grades and prison officers. During the siege, six assistant chief officers acted as negotiators. They were Tommy Hughes, Pat McCabe, Sean Dempsey, Seamus Cramer, Greg Fleming and Martin Delaney. They displayed great patience, wisdom, communication skills, sound judgement and many other qualities throughout the siege, way beyond what could have been expected of them. They had no training whatsoever in hostage negotiations, but they did have years of practical experience in dealing with difficult prisoners. They were brilliant during that weekend, and I will always be indebted to them.

Staff service officers – basic grade prison officers who have been trained to provide a welfare support service to their colleagues – got to work immediately and contacted all the families of the hostages to tell them what had happened. The staff service officers did great work not only on Saturday night but all through the siege and afterwards. They provided invaluable support for the families at a very, very stressful and difficult time.

The prison-service control and restraint team reported to the Separation Unit soon after the siege started. This was a group of about twenty prison officers who were trained to physically control and restrain violent or disruptive prisoners. They were supported by members of the Mountjoy trades staff, who had equipment that could force open locked cell doors. The presence of the control and restraint team along with the trades staff made me feel confident that should we need to use force to enter the room, we had the men and the means to do it. The only uncertainty was how long it would take.

For the rest of Saturday night I kept in close contact with the incident room. I knew after a short time that the prisoners were not an organized or unified group. Their demands were all over the place. Because of this it was a very dangerous situation: a group with an agreed set of objectives and demands is more straightforward to deal with than a group of individual mavericks. It was impossible to gauge what they really wanted and why they were holding officers as hostages.

During the siege the prisoners demanded the following: black plastic bags, a roll of Sellotape, Physeptone, Valium tablets, cups of tea, paper and pens, crisps, a bottle 'to piss into', cigarettes, burgers and chips, blankets for themselves and the hostages, sandwiches, nasal spray, flasks and flasks of hot water, coffee, bottles of water, bottles of 7up, tea bags, spoons, bars of chocolate, daily newspapers, cartons of milk, and telephone calls to their families. Over the course of the first evening, most of the items requested were actually given to them and with the exception of the blankets they were all pushed in through the small broken window. The blankets caused a huge hassle for the staff, and after long-drawn-out negotiations the prisoners opened the door to pull them in, all the time holding the officers as the ransom to stop staff bursting into the room. They wanted to send out statements to the media that they were innocent of their crimes and that they were being brutalized in prison, which we agreed to deliver.

At 9.45 p.m. one of the prison doctors prescribed Physeptone for the two heroin-addicted prisoners and this was put through the window too. That had an immediate calming effect.

Around 10 p.m. they agreed on some demands and told the negotiators that they were ready to talk. They were asking for transfers from Mountjoy to other prisons, and they wanted to talk to an official from the Department of Justice; all inter-prison transfers have to be approved by the Department of Justice and they knew this. They also wanted to see Sister Caoimhín, a Dominican nun from Ballyfermot, who was a regular visitor to the prison and a genuine friend to prisoners. They wanted her to be there when they came out so as to ensure that they wouldn't be beaten up. I thought, *This is good news – they are thinking of giving up*. They also asked to see Joe Costello, a local Labour Party TD, and formerly head of the Prisoners' Rights Organization.

I contacted the Department of Justice and asked for an official to come to the prison. After 10.30 p.m. an official spoke to them about transfers. He pointed out that only one of them had previously applied for a transfer. The prisoners responded by ranting on about their conditions, transfers to other prisons, that they were innocent, and then said that they were staying there until Sunday. They said they wanted their solicitors brought in before they came out. The negotiators told them that it would be very difficult to get solicitors at such a late hour on a

Saturday night. When they told one prisoner, 'We are doing our best to contact your solicitor', he said, 'You can contact fucking Houdini if you like.'

Sister Caoimhín was away for the weekend in the Dominican convent in Wicklow Town, and the gardaí got her to the prison shortly after midnight. Sister Caoimhín, the department official, Jim Woods and I went to the Separation Unit. I stood well back so that they couldn't see me. Sister Caoimhín talked to the prisoners through the broken window. They were very respectful to her and asked her to contact their families. Sister Caoimhín went to an office in the main prison to do that, and returned half an hour later to tell them how she had got on with the calls. While they hadn't given up and released the hostages, at least they were now more settled and less dangerous, and they told the sister that she could go home and come back tomorrow.

Around 2 a.m. I returned to my office and Sister Caoimhín went home. I felt confused and a bit frustrated. A few hours earlier I had thought that they were about to give up, but now it seemed they had no intention of coming out. I began to accept that it was going to drag on into Sunday.

An important part of hostage negotiations is for the negotiators to try to get something in return for every request granted; the principle of give and take must be at the very heart of negotiation. So when the prisoners requested water, the negotiators asked to see the hostages. Sometimes the prisoners agreed and allowed them to come to the window one at a time; other times they refused.

At a very early stage I decided that if any of the hostages were attacked, injured or humiliated in any way, then I would order the control and restraint team to enter by force. For instance, at one point the prisoners had threatened to strip the hostages naked and make them stand on a table. If this happened I was going to send the control and restraint team straight in. I gave clear instructions to Willie Connolly, who was in charge of the control and restraint team, that under no circumstances were they to attempt any forced entry until they got direct instructions from me.

The media were being briefed on a continuous basis by officials in the Department of Justice. From how the incident was reported in the newspapers on Sunday and Monday, it was clear that journalists were being told that all decisions about the negotiations were being made by civil servants in the Department of Justice and that I was simply following their directions. A security journalist I ran into towards the end of January told me, unprompted, that this was indeed the impression given by the Department. For the record, nothing could be further from the truth. As the siege commander I was personally and fully responsible for all decisions, and rightly so.

Around four on Sunday morning the prisoners told the negotiators that they were taking a rest and would not be talking again until 8 a.m. In a way this was a relief. While four officers were still held as hostages and at risk, at least things had settled down, and we all needed a rest and time to think. I was expecting a few hours of peace and quiet and I was thinking about how I would approach Sunday morning.

At 6 a.m., however, all hell broke loose. The Sky News headlines had it that one of the prisoners had been involved in the murder of journalist Veronica Guerin. He became highly agitated and felt that we had fed Sky this false information. He demanded that his name was removed from the broadcast or the hostages would 'fucking get it'.

Chief Superintendent Dick Kelly, who was attached to Fitzgibbon Street Garda Station, the headquarters of garda operations for Mountjoy District, spent most of the weekend at the prison and was a great support. Dick got on to Sky News and succeeded in getting them to tone down the broadcast.

Around 8 a.m. things settled down again. There was little progress. The negotiators kept asking the prisoners to release the hostages. The prisoners were less aggressive, but they said that they were there for the long haul. The negotiators had a very tricky job trying to keep dialogue going. Several times the prisoners told them 'no more talk' and roared, 'If you talk to us again we will smash their fuckin' heads in.'

Around 10 a.m. the prisoners made a new demand. They wanted to telephone their families. I allowed each a telephone call to a close family member. I felt that it was worth a try: their families might encourage them to give up and come out. In return the prisoners agreed that the negotiators could see the hostages, and they brought them one by one to the window. This provided a reassurance that, physically at least, they were okay. The calls were monitored in the usual way. The first couple of calls went smoothly. One prisoner told his mother that 'Lonergan is a fair man but he is part of the system.' But another call proved to be a bit of a disaster: a father started to encourage his son to hold out and to continue their protest. That was the end of the experiment with family phone calls.

I was asked to go to the Department of Justice on St Stephen's Green at midday. I met the Minister for Justice, Nora Owen, a number of her senior officials and Deputy Garda Commissioner Noel Conroy. I outlined my key objectives of saving lives, preventing injuries, getting the hostages released as soon as possible and showing the prisoners that hostage-taking doesn't work. I also told the minister that I had decided that if any of the hostages were injured or subjected to humiliating treatment, I would order the control and restraint team to enter the room by force.

'John, before you make that decision, will you contact my office?' she said.

'No, Minister, I can't give you that undertaking. If something erupts and the hostages are in danger I will have to respond instantly and I cannot wait to consult with you or the Department.'

Noel Conroy supported my position, saying, 'No way can the governor be expected to consult anybody in such a situation. He has to use his own judgement.'

The minister agreed.

While I was out of the prison, a man from the Northern Ireland prison service phoned Willie Connolly and offered us the use of equipment that he said could cut through a steel cell door in less than one minute. He said he would be delighted to bring it down and show the trades staff in Mountjoy how to use it. Willie reported to Jim Woods, who had taken over the role of siege commander in my absence. Jim asked the Department of Justice official to clear it with the Department. The official called the Department in front of Jim, and Jim took it that it was cleared. He told Willie Connolly to call his contact in the Northern Ireland prison service to accept the equipment and thank him for their support.

The equipment arrived in the prison on Sunday afternoon around 3 p.m. Our trades staff got to work with it straight away. Within an hour they told me that they were confident they could cut through a steel cell door, similar to the door leading to the recreation room in the Separation Unit, in thirty-five seconds. This was brilliant news and it gave me great confidence that from now on if we had to enter the room by force it could be done in a little over half a minute.

Shortly after 6 p.m. I got a call from a senior Department of Justice official.

'John, what is this about equipment coming from Northern Ireland?'

'Yeah, yeah, it has arrived. It's fantastic. It can cut through a door in thirty-five seconds. It will be brilliant should we need it.'

'That shouldn't have happened. You shouldn't have taken in equipment from Northern Ireland without going through the proper channels. This is serious. The Taoiseach's office, indeed the Taoiseach himself, should have been informed. The Taoiseach should have given permission,' he said.

For a few seconds I was speechless. Then I repeated, 'This equipment is great. If we have to enter the room by force, we will be able to do so in thirty-five seconds. Anyway, it was cleared by someone in your department.'

'Who?' he asked.

'I don't know,' I said. 'Listen, I have a lot of difficulties and problems on my mind at this moment, and one of them is not government diplomacy or how the Taoiseach feels about this equipment. It's invaluable, it's a major help to us and that's it.' And I hung up.

A few minutes later the official rang back. He said, 'John, forget about it.' I took him at his word and put it out of my mind.

Throughout Sunday the prisoners made many demands and issued media statements asserting their innocence and highlighting grievances. One wrote out a statement for the twelve o'clock news stating that he was an innocent man and had killed nobody. There was still no consistency in their demands. They kept changing their minds. They argued among themselves. Sometimes two were in favour of something and four against. It made it impossible to get common ground to negotiate on. It was very frustrating and it was the cause of the siege continuing into Monday.

Sunday night was calm, free of incident, and the prisoners went to sleep early. At 7 a.m. on Monday they demanded copies of all the newspapers. I said, 'No problem giving them the papers, but we will check them first. I want to make sure there is nothing in them that might cause any difficulties for the negotiators or for myself.'

Dick Kelly, Jim Woods and I went through the papers. Everything was going well until we came to the *Irish Independent*. On page six was a story headlined, 'Army Rangers are Steeled for Action'. The sub-head read, 'Crack squad from Curragh consulted on how to end crisis'. The story went on to say that the army rangers from the Curragh had visited the Separation Unit on Sunday, assessed the situation and were convinced that they could blow open the door leading into the recreation room. The story was correct, but its publication was a disaster. With this information the prisoners would be in a position to stop us entering the room forcibly. They could tie the hostages to the back of the door, and then there was no way the door could be blown open or cut through. I decided we had to withhold the *Irish Independent*. Dick Kelly said that he would see if there was a country edition that hadn't run the story.

After 8 a.m. the papers were handed in to the prisoners. There was no response for a long time. But after 10 a.m. came the dreaded demand, 'We want the *Independent*.' I told the negotiators that the *Irish Independent* wasn't available and to do their best to deflect the prisoners' interest in it. They continued to demand a copy of the *Independent*, however, and as time wore on they got more and more abusive, more and more determined to get it, and threatened to smash up the hostages if they didn't get it. They made some of the hostages stand on a table and, using the cable from the television as a rope, formed nooses around their necks. Things were getting very dangerous. The gardaí couldn't find an edition of the *Irish Independent* that didn't have the 'blowing open the door' article.

At 12.50 on Monday afternoon the prisoners gave the negotiators an ultimatum. 'If we don't get the *Irish Independent* by 1 p.m. we will start to cut up the hostages.' They began to fire the broken legs of chairs at the window, knocking things over inside the room, shouting and roaring, smashing up tables and banging the walls with steel bars. They had gone mad. I briefed officials in the Department of Justice, telling them of the ultimatum and the dangerous situation we were now entering.

At 12.55 p.m. the phone rang. It was Nora Owen.

'John, there is a showdown?'

'Yes, Minister, there is. They are demanding a copy of the *Irish Independent* but there is an article on page six that I have decided not to give them because it would undermine our options to enter by force.'

'John, do you think it's a good idea to have a showdown over an article in a newspaper?'

'They are not getting it,' I said.

'Fine,' she said.

Then it hit me: *If this goes belly up, if one of the hostages gets injured, I am on my own and my days as governor of Mountjoy are over.*

One minute to go: the deadline was almost up. The phone rang. It was from John Brophy in the incident room. 'Governor, they have gone mad upstairs. You will have to give them the *Independent*.'

I said, 'John, I'm ordering you not to give them the *Irish Independent*, end of story.'

I hung up.

The deadline came and went. The negotiators couldn't hear a sound. No talk, no noise. They had cut all contact. Two p.m. came and went. Still no talk, no contact, no sign of movement, nothing. The tension was unbearable, and there was absolutely nothing I could do but wait it out. The negotiators felt that if any of the hostages had got beaten or injured they would have heard screams or some sort of noise. They were reasonably satisfied that the hostages were not hurt.

At around 3 p.m. one of the prisoners came to the window to look for food and drinks. The negotiators asked to see the hostages in return. They agreed and brought them to the window one by one. They were all fine. This was a tremendous boost for the negotiators and for me. I felt that now we had the upper hand psychologically: the prisoners had made serious threats but hadn't carried them out. I began to feel that it would end shortly. How wrong I was.

At 5.30 p.m. on Monday, John Brophy called from the incident room to say that the prisoners were looking to speak to me on the phone. At this point the negotiators were finding it impossible to talk to the prisoners, who had become very abusive and aggressive. The situation was becoming more dangerous, and the negotiators were really concerned about the safety of the hostages. I talked it over with Dick Kelly and Jim Woods, and decided that I would talk to the prisoners on the phone from my office.

'Lonergan, get fucking over here immediately,' were the first words I heard when the call came through.

'Hey, I don't speak to anybody like that, and nobody speaks to me like that either,' I said.

'Sorry, Mr Lonergan. Can you come over to the Separation Unit now? We want to talk to you.'

I told him I couldn't go over. We spoke for over half an hour. I asked him time and time again to end the siege and release the officers held as hostages, and said, 'What you are doing is crazy, and the sooner you all come out the better for everyone.'

'If we come out, will we be beaten up?' he asked.

'The one guarantee, and only guarantee, I will give you is that none of you will be beaten or abused when you come out,' I said.

'Will we be charged?' he said.

'Very likely,' I said.

'Will you allow our solicitors to come in to speak to us? We want to let them see us before we come out.'

'I have no difficulty allowing your solicitors in, provided you end this madness immediately,' I said.

'If you let our solicitors in, when we see them on the landing, we will release one of the hostages as a gesture.'

A second prisoner came on the phone and also asked for his solicitor, saying, 'We have not harmed the officers.'

Their solicitors, including well-known Dublin solicitor Michael Hanahoe, were contacted and arrived at the prison shortly after 10 p.m. I went with them to the Separation Unit and up to E3. Michael Hanahoe went into the little office, got up on a chair and spoke through the window to the prisoners; shortly afterwards one prison officer was freed. Then he spoke to the prisoners again, saying, 'You are committing a serious and stupid crime for no reason whatsoever and the only advice I can give you is to give up now and to come out. The longer you are in there, the more serious it is getting.' They started to argue with him. Then he said, 'I want you to meet together now and discuss this question: "Why can't we come out now?" Discuss it and come back to me.'

A couple of minutes later they came back to the window and told him they were coming out. Their final demand was that an independent person would accompany each one of them to the cells downstairs, where they would be searched and locked securely awaiting a decision on their transfer requests. Amazingly one of the prisoners asked that I would accompany him to the cell.

First they released the prison officers, one by one. They were told to throw away their weapons and to come out with their hands up, which they did. They were escorted individually down the two flights of stairs. I walked down with the prisoner who had asked for me. On the ground floor they were searched by prison officers and placed in single cells. The siege was officially over. It was shortly after 11 p.m.

The released officers were examined by a doctor and then seen by a team of psychologists led by Mountjoy's senior psychologist, Colm Regan. Shortly afterwards they were taken to a private room and reunited with their families. They continued to need counselling for many months. They paid a big price for just doing their jobs as prison officers.

Later that night, five of the prisoners were transferred to Portlaoise Prison. One remained in Mountjoy as he had a court appearance at

Kilmainham District Court the following morning. On his way into court his father shouted, 'Did they beat you last night?' The prisoner shouted back, 'They never touched us, Da.' This was captured on television and shown on the RTÉ news that night.

Nora Owen telephoned immediately after the siege ended to say congratulations and that she was on her way to the prison. I asked her to make sure that when she was paying tribute to the staff, she paid special tribute to the negotiators. I said to her, 'After the officers who were taken as hostages, the negotiators were the other heroes of the weekend.'

While the hostages met with their families, the rest of the staff on duty assembled in the prison auditorium. The minister expressed her sympathy to the officers taken as hostages and their families. She also paid a glowing tribute to the negotiators. She was brilliant. I spoke after the minister and thanked the many people involved in so many different aspects of managing the siege and bringing things to a successful conclusion. I ended by saying that while it was a terrible incident, everyone should take pride in how well it worked out at the end.

Walking out the main gate after three on Tuesday morning, I said to Jim Woods, 'Well, that was one rough weekend.' It was only when I was driving home that it struck me that I hadn't slept for three days.

At a press conference on Tuesday morning at eleven, a journalist asked, 'What caused the big showdowns and flashpoints?' I said, 'Believe it or not, the most dangerous time was a dispute on Monday morning over an article in a bloody newspaper', and I went on to explain why. I also said that 'we were all learning and we all made mistakes'.

That evening I went home at five. After a cup of tea I joined the Kilmacud Crokes senior and intermediate hurlers on Sandymount Strand for the first night of our winter stamina training. Ploughing through the wet slushy sand on a cold and bitter winter's night was tough going, but it felt great.

The next morning the *Irish Independent* went for me. My comments at the press conference were quoted fairly by their reporter, Tom Reddy. However, most of its editorial page was given over to an attack on the remarks I had made relating to the *Independent* story. The paper appeared to take great offence, and obviously believed that I was blaming them for prolonging the siege. The editorial said my comments were 'ill-judged and ill-directed'. An article by high-profile columnist Sam Smyth was headed 'Shooting the messenger' and he said I was naive to have remarked that the paper's story was unhelpful. Security correspondent Tom Brady's article was headed 'Governor's "media" criticisms fall down under scrutiny'. The *Irish Independent*'s sister paper, the *Evening Herald*, also had a go at me on its front page that day.

In his article Tom Brady wrote that first thing on Tuesday morning the paper had received a telephone call from 'a senior prison source' in the Department of Justice thanking it for its coverage of the hostage siege. He said that senior colleagues of mine were shocked at my 'outburst' in the press conference.

A few days later a group of prison governors met senior department officials in the Department. The officials refused to confirm or deny that such a phone call was made to the *Independent*. More tellingly, they refused to issue a statement of support of my position.

Jim Woods raised the issue of the fuss they had made over the equipment from Northern Ireland. Jim was adamant that clearance was sought and received from the Department. At first the officials disputed this and then, as usual, they closed ranks. The best the governors could get was that perhaps there was some misunderstanding or that during the phone call between the department officials on Sunday morning, the one in Mountjoy had somehow forgotten to mention the source of the equipment.

A few days after the siege ended, prison officers began looking for a scapegoat. There were strong rumours that they were going to have a vote of 'no confidence' in me. The word was that some officers believed I was personally to blame for the siege because of my approach and philosophy as governor; they felt that I should be much tougher on the prisoners. Others felt that I should have used force on Saturday night and finished it there and then. I suppose this was a natural response, as they wanted to do everything in their power to get their colleagues out as quickly as possible. But equally I had to be responsible and follow a strategy based on saving life and preventing serious injury. After a week or so it fizzled out and we all moved on. I remember thinking, *You can't win in this job.*

16. Taking Women Prisoners out of a Hellhole

I'm the first to admit it, but I have a soft spot for the women in prison. Why? Because most of them are mothers, and I apologize to nobody when I say my ultimate admiration is for mothers. There is something distressing about seeing mothers locked up in prison and their children outside.

The women's prison at Mountjoy was opened in 1858. When the government closed the borstal in Clonmel in 1956 and put the boys into this old building, the female prisoners were put into the basement. The conditions were awful, with no integral sanitation and no washing facilities in the cells. Worse still was the fact that the women were often four or five to a cell; it was so bad that one cell was known as 'the black hole'.

The only outdoor area was overlooked by the boys in St Patrick's, and they continually shouted abuse at the female prisoners and the staff. The Education Unit was a small Portakabin. There was an old laundry with big white enamel sinks and a flagstoned floor where the clothes were washed by hand on wooden washing boards. The women used to wash all the clothes for the men's prison too. And there was an old sewing room off the laundry where the women made towelling for all the prisons. It was boring and very monotonous work. It was brutal, the culture was horrible, and it was a disgrace how the staff and the prisoners were treated.

By the 1980s another major problem was the huge number of female prisoners with serious heroin problems. Many used to shoot up in the cells. If non-drug users were in the same cells they were often forced to join in and take drugs as well, and on a number of occasions prisoners had their arms cut by cellmates. Young women were at high risk of sexual abuse, and many were forced into having sexual relationships with their cellmates. While there was little evidence of sexual coercion being much of an issue in the men's prison, for some reason it was a big problem in the women's prison. Management's concern was not about homosexuality, but about harassment and abuse. Overall the conditions at that time for female prisoners in both Limerick and Mountjoy were appalling.

When I went to Mountjoy as governor in 1984, coming out the gate of the women's prison after my first visit I vowed, 'If I do nothing else as governor of Mountjoy, I'm definitely going to do something to civilize this hellhole.' I appointed my senior deputy governor, Con Hayes, to take special responsibility for the women's prison. Con and Chief Officer Catherine Comerford, who had been in charge of the place since 1979, did a marvellous job. They made a series of minor changes that were of huge significance.

They allowed the women to wear their own clothes instead of the depressing drab prison uniforms. They got a professional hairdresser to come in to do the women's hair. Before this, prisoners used to hack off each other's hair. They decided that they would allow the women to use make-up. Being allowed to dress properly, have a decent haircut and wear make-up helped the women to feel good, to feel like women again. There is no way anybody could ever measure the value of that. They introduced knitting machines and arranged training for the women. And they began to train and develop the staff too. In a short time huge changes took place, and the whole atmosphere had improved. Catherine would not have had the authority to introduce any of these changes on her own initiative in preceding years, but once Con Hayes was on board, and I was actively encouraging change without worrying about having to get department approval for everything, she more than embraced the new possibilities.

The final change that was crucial at this time was the introduction of a female doctor. Prior to this, whichever doctor or doctors were in the male prison also looked after the women's prison, and they were always men. For all sorts of reasons (and no personal reflection on the medical personnel themselves) – having been treated badly or sexually abused by men, embarrassment, just not liking men – many of the female prisoners hated going to see a male doctor. The appointment of a female doctor meant they could see a fellow woman, a person who would understand them, someone they could trust.

Though the conditions and the facilities in the women's prison remained brutal, Catherine Comerford, Con Hayes and their team proved that the conditions are only a small part of the equation; what is crucial is how people are treated.

In the late 1980s, the Department of Justice started a refurbishment of the building that contained St Patrick's Institution and the women's prison. The plan was to extend the women's prison to two floors – the basement and the ground floor – while the top floor would be for the boys. I was away in Portlaoise at the time, but I know there was no dialogue or consultation with the staff or the governor of Mountjoy about the design of the new facilities.

Despite the fact that prison governors from around the country had pressed for a new women's prison during a meeting with Minister Ray Burke, the minister and his department ploughed on with the plans.

When I returned to Mountjoy in May 1992, I went straight up to see the new facilities for women. To say that the refurbishment was a dog's dinner would be a total understatement. Everything that could be wrong with it was wrong. It was wire, wire, wire everywhere; the place was completely dominated by wire and security. Alcatraz had nothing on it. They had got rid of every blade of grass from the grounds and tarmacked the whole place. The little pathway out to the exercise yard was enclosed by a huge twenty-foot-high steel cage. It was more like a set-up for controlling dangerous wild animals in a zoo than a facility for human beings. It was a disgrace, a backward step and totally unsuitable for women prisoners. I decided that I would have to do something about it.

Luck was on our side when Máire Geoghegan-Quinn was appointed Minister for Justice in early 1993. On her second day in office she came to see the refurbished prison. She stood in the yard surrounded – over-whelmed, really – by wire mesh, reaching thirty to forty feet into the air. She looked at it, turned to a senior official from the Department and said, 'Who is responsible for this?'

'I don't know,' he said.

'It's a disgrace,' she said.

Inside the prison she went into a cell. The beds had a concrete base with a three-inch-thick mattress on top. She is a tall woman, but when she stood on the bed to look out the window she couldn't see out.

'This is terrible,' she said. 'The women are better off where they are than coming into this.'

There and then she decided to build a new women's prison. She set up an advisory group to help plan and design the facility. To chair the group she appointed Frank Dunne, an assistant secretary in the Department of Justice. He was a brilliant choice, a man of great intelligence, vision and integrity.

Within the prison I set up our own working group to devise a philosophy for the new prison and to identify the services and facilities it should have. The opening statement of the report we produced said that the new prison should revolve around 'treating all women in prison with respect'. The report went on to say that the women should be allowed to decide their own futures, and that the job of the staff and the services was to support them in their choices. We emphasized the importance of developing an environment of 'normalization' – aiming to create living conditions for the women in the new prison that would mirror as closely as possible living conditions outside. The more normalized conditions are for people in prison, the smoother their transition back to mainstream society.

We also said that the needs of women in prison are fundamentally different from the needs of men. In many ways they are the opposite. Men present a greater security challenge: they are much stronger, they often behave more aggressively and they escape from prison more frequently. Women, on the other hand, seldom escape using force or try to get over the walls. Neither do they damage the place; they usually keep the prison immaculate, treating their cells as their homes. This was a very big factor in the design of the new prison.

Both prisoners and staff were asked what they would like in a prison in terms of work, education, recreation, living accommodation and security. Asking prisoners for their opinion on such matters was a new concept then, and still is, in the prison service. My experience is that when people are asked for their views they feel valued and respected and take far more interest in the outcome.

While all this consultation and thinking was going on inside the prison, the minister's advisory group under Frank Dunne was doing equally valuable work outside it. The group included Catherine Comerford and me from Mountjoy, three senior officials from the Department of Justice, two Office of Public Works architects, and the well-known public affairs activists Ann Taylor and Carmel Foley. Frank was an excellent chair. We were coming up with ideas and suggestions that were totally alien to the old prison mentality, and he was genuinely concerned at times, particularly about protecting the minister and the Department from ridicule if anything went wrong. But the great thing about him was he listened, he heard and on most occasions he went along with the consensus of the group. And once he agreed with something, he was totally committed to it. I have met very few of his kind in all my years dealing with the Department of Justice. He was an exceptionally intelligent, straight and honourable man.

Ciarán McGahon, an architect from the Office of Public Works, sat in on our meetings in Mountjoy to get a gut feeling of what we were saying. This proved to be of immense value, and I believe that it should be an absolute requirement when planning any prison facility in the future. Ciarán was an exceptional visionary and absorbed everything he heard at our meetings and at the minister's advisory group. But he was also able to interpret what was being said in a practical way, given that he had very limited space to play with in the site we had earmarked for the building in the Mountjoy complex.

Confined site or not, he did a marvellous job in creating a building that is secure but does not feel like a prison once you're inside the main gate. There is a sense of light and openness, and relatively speaking a lot of grass and shrubs. In a way the new prison was a revolution: a prison designed specifically for women and the first purpose-built prison for women in Ireland. It had no wire mesh, razor wire, steel doors, gates or barred windows. There were no cell blocks. Instead, it comprised six ordinary houses that could each accommodate anywhere from ten to eighteen women. Each house had a kitchen, dining room and a large sitting room. There was a big communal dining room for the entire jail for main meals – dinner and the evening meal – but the women were to have breakfast and snacks in their houses. The logic was very simple: they would have two choices, stay in bed and have no breakfast or get up and make their own, just like people on the outside. This worked a treat.

The idea of the sitting room was so that the women could sit around and socialize in a group, just like any group of people sharing a house or flat. Each woman also had her own room with a toilet and shower. If you really want to show that you respect every woman in prison, a good starting point is to give her decent living and washing facilities. Many people, including many members of prison staff, felt that a shower was a luxury, but of course it is anything but: a shower is a basic necessity. The best innovation was putting showers in every room. In addition to the practical benefits, it is amazing what a shower can do for a person who is feeling frustrated, depressed, anxious or down in the dumps. It relaxes them, refreshes them and makes them feel human. The showers in each room have paid for themselves over and over again in defusing people's feelings of anger and aggression, and there is also a therapeutic benefit. Every modern prison should have a shower in every cell.

There was a slight security issue – unavoidable, given where the new building was situated, with its boundary wall running along the North Circular Road – with people trying to throw stuff over the buildings into the yards, mainly drugs.

The prison was built for a relatively small sum, around £14 million. As well as the prison, the project included the building of a locker room for staff, office accommodation, a suite of offices for the probation and welfare service, and a visitors' waiting room with a crèche.

The idea of the new prison was to encourage growth and development in all women who were in prison. Rather than calling it a prison, we wanted to give it a name that would convey this new vision. We ran a competition between staff, prisoners and friends of the prison to come up with a name. A teenage prisoner, Tara O'Callaghan, suggested that it should be called the Dóchas Centre, *dóchas* being the Irish word for 'hope'.

Two months before Dóchas opened, a number of women were transferred there from the old prison to clean it up and get it ready for the opening. We decided that the prisoners would have a central role in the opening proceedings and that it would be nice if, just before Minister John O'Donoghue officially opened the centre, one of them read out the vision statement we had agreed. One day, as Deputy Governor Kathleen McMahon was doing her rounds, she asked a 26-year-old prisoner, Clare, if she would take on the job, and gave her a copy of the statement. A few minutes later, when Kathleen was back in her office, there was a little tap on the door. It was Clare. 'Miss McMahon,' she said, 'why did you ask me to read the vision statement on Wednesday?'

Kathleen replied, 'Because you've been down here for eight weeks and you've worked very hard, and we all think that you deserve to represent the women on Wednesday.'

'Thank you very much, Miss McMahon,' Clare said. 'But do you know something? This is the first time ever in my life that I was selected for anything.'

This is what Clare read out on the day of the opening:

We are a community that embraces people's respect and dignity.
We encourage personal growth and development in a caring and safe environment.
We are committed to addressing the needs of each person in a healing and a holistic way.
And we will actively promote close interaction with the wider community.

The Dóchas Centre officially opened in September 1999. In the December the old women's prison closed. A few days before it was due to close, I was walking up the compound when Ruth, a young prisoner I knew well, came up to me and said she wanted to be the one who locked the gate on it for the last time when all the women moved that Friday.

'No way, that's my job,' I said jokingly.

'Well, I am entitled to lock it,' she said.

'And why would you be entitled to lock it?' I said.

'I'll tell you why: my grandmother served time here in this prison, and so did my mother and my sisters. My father is in prison and so are all my brothers. That's why I'm entitled to lock the gate for the last time on Friday.'

On Friday, 24 December 1999, Ruth locked the gate after the last of the prisoners left.

Tara O'Callaghan, who gave the Dóchas Centre its name, was one of those transferred from the old prison. A short time later she was released, having served her sentence. A few months later she died from a drug overdose. But Tara's memory lives on: it was her idea that the new women's prison should be a place of hope. I am certain that the Dóchas Centre has given hope to hundreds and hundreds of women since 1999.

17. The Fragile Miracle of the Dóchas Centre

The Dóchas Centre's first chaplain, Father Eamon Crossan, once described it as a miracle. In many ways he was right. On its opening, one cynic said, 'Give it a week and it will be burned to the ground.' It faced a lot of opposition from the Prison Officers' Association too. They were unsure about how the new regime was going to operate, and there was disagreement over staffing levels. Yet now, well into its eleventh year, it is still standing and it has grown and developed out of all recognition. I doubt if there is a similar type of prison any place in the world.

Shortly after it opened, Marian Finucane's radio show was broadcast live from the centre. The most profound moment during the programme occurred after Marian had described the small fountain inside the main entrance. A listener phoned in to express her annoyance at having such a fancy thing in a prison. Marian asked one of the prisoners to respond. The young woman said, 'Well, that woman doesn't know what she is talking about. The pump for that fountain only cost two or three hundred pounds, but the value of running water to us is huge: when we see the running water we think of freedom.'

To say that our first Christmas dinner in the centre was chaotic would be an understatement. Some of the women had hardly ever sat down with others to have a civilized meal before, and in the old prison they ate in their cells. They just didn't know how to behave in that context and were jumping up and down, running out to smoke and grabbing stuff off the tables. They just had no idea what was expected of them.

In 2005, President Mary McAleese was guest of honour at our Christmas dinner. The women worked really hard in preparation for the meal, dressed immaculately, had their hair and make-up done and behaved impeccably. You could hardly have distinguished between prisoners and other guests, up to and including the President. It was a real sign of how much both staff and prisoners had developed in five years.

Just before my retirement in June 2010, over 90 out of the 125 prisoners in the Dóchas Centre were attending the Education Unit every day, availing themselves of a range of courses provided by the Dublin City Vocational Education Committee.

We said from day one that the dream was to create a community made up of the women, the staff and, we hoped, people from the wider community who would come in and befriend prisoners and get to know them, connecting with them as fellow human beings who as part of their life's journey were in prison. Traditionally religious sisters visited the women's prison, and they still do, but the extension of the pool of befrienders to lay people has really helped the centre achieve its aim of creating a normalized living environment. Befrienders came on board informally from the early days of the centre. Most were known to someone closely associated with the centre, such as staff members or chaplains. If we got a letter from someone we didn't know, either I or the governor of the Dóchas Centre, Kathleen McMahon, would interview them and decide if they were suitable. The befrienders usually visit between 5 p.m. and 8 p.m., or during weekends. Some just come to visit someone who has no family or friends, or perhaps to befriend a foreign national. Others come to help with craftwork or some other activity. All befrienders are subject to the same security procedures as anyone visiting the prison.

So many fantastic staff contributed to making the Dóchas Centre what it is today. The most significant of these was Kathleen McMahon, who retired as governor of the Dóchas Centre shortly before me. Kathleen's career in the prison service started in the mid 1970s, and she transferred to the women's prison in the early 1980s. In the early 2000s, Kathleen was appointed governor of the Dóchas Centre and she was responsible for its day-to-day management, though I was still its overall governor. Kathleen understood the purpose and philosophy of the Dóchas Centre early on; she identified with it and set out to live that dream – and back then that was what it was, a dream. She spoke to the women every day, listened to them, reassured them, made representations for them and, above all, treated them as her equal in human terms. She and her colleagues set an extraordinary example of giving generously without expectation. Another woman who must be mentioned alongside Kathleen is Sister Mary Mullins, full-time Catholic chaplain for the past eight years, who also supported the philosophy of the centre wholeheartedly.

The Dóchas Centre was often a difficult place to work, and could take its toll emotionally and psychologically. Every year since the centre opened as many as fifteen women who have spent time there have died after being released. Most died from drug-related illnesses or overdoses, but others died from pure neglect. I recall running into a young woman called Adrienne when she was on her way out of the prison in April 2005. We walked out the gate together and down the North Circular Road until we came to a public telephone box. She was going to call her boyfriend to come and collect her. She was over the moon, just delighted to be free. 'Goodbye now, Mr Lonergan. I won't be back ever again,' she said as we parted ways. An hour later I was back in my office when Kathleen McMahon rang me to say that Adrienne was dead. Her boyfriend had collected her, they had got home, and she went to her room, where she collapsed and died from a drug overdose. Things like that take a lot out of staff and prisoners.

For the Dóchas Centre's tenth anniversary in autumn 2009, President Mary McAleese was invited to come in and celebrate the occasion. She planted a tree in one of the yards to commemorate the ten years, and she visited a number of the houses and met all the women. As usual she was brilliant with them and her speech was perfectly pitched.

However, there was a shadow over the day. The Dóchas Centre had been developed on the basis of building a community where everybody was equal. Over the years we put that into practice, making sure that everyone participated in whatever activities there were. For the tenth-anniversary event we planned to have two women – one Irish and one foreign national – welcome the President and then say a few words about what the Dóchas Centre meant to them. When we outlined the plan for the day, the director general of the IPS, Brian Purcell, expressed reservations and said he would have to think about it. A few days later we got an email from the IPS office outlining the programme for the day. Brian Purcell would come down to welcome the President, and there was no mention of the women. We sought clarification from the IPS and were told that no prisoner was to speak on the day. In one email, the culture of the Dóchas Centre – the very thing we were celebrating – had been turned on its head.

The Dóchas Centre has received, at best, lukewarm support from the IPS. Many years ago, a senior official from the IPS had stood in the tea room in the general store's building in Mountjoy, looked over at the Dóchas Centre and said, 'It's too good for them' – and sadly he meant it. For some time that has been the attitude of the IPS to women in prison generally. They seem to believe that the women are getting something that the men are not. Instead of using this as a spur to improve conditions for men, a determination to take away some of the advances in the conditions of the women appears to have taken hold.

From late 2009 onwards, the Dóchas Centre struggled to maintain the high standards it had set over the previous decade. Many times officials from the IPS compared the conditions for women in the Dóchas Centre with those in Limerick Prison, saying, 'We can't have women here living in single rooms when the women in Limerick are doubled up.' Eventually this was used as the justification to put two women in each room in the Dóchas Centre. When we were designing the Dóchas Centre, it was agreed to build the rooms so small that they could not house two women, the idea being to prevent this from ever being considered an option. However, the IPS ignored all advice – and the size of the rooms – and brought in ugly black steel jail bunks.

Doubling up in single rooms seriously erodes the values promoted in the centre – women having privacy, their own space and above all personal safety. If you are in prison and you have to share accommodation with another prisoner, you are never on your own, not for a minute. People crack up when they don't have their own space. But it looks now as if doubling up is going to be part and parcel of the regime in the Dóchas Centre for years to come.

Another thing that appears to be changing – and again, not for the better – is the general approach to security. Over a decade ago I made a decision that we would no longer handcuff female prisoners, except in exceptional circumstances – in other words if she was an escape risk or was likely to attack staff in an attempt to escape. The decision came about after I was coming into work one Monday morning in the mid 1990s and saw a female prisoner being escorted out to the Mater Hospital in handcuffs. I knew her background and, more to the point, I knew that on that very weekend she had been out on temporary release with her family. She had returned to the prison under her own steam on Sunday night. Yet here she was on Monday morning, handcuffed, supposedly for fear she would try to escape. I realized that it was a crazy situation and more about asserting power and control and humiliating the prisoner than having any practical purpose. I made a governor's order stating that 'In future all women going on escort to courts, hospitals and on transfer to other prisons shall only be handcuffed if the chief officer directs.'

I am pessimistic about how long this will continue to be the practice, however. There were occasions in the recent past, before I retired, when handcuffs were back on the agenda – some staff members requesting to handcuff certain prisoners going to court, and women in the courts handcuffed on their way to the cells underneath. There are a lot of men in custody who really don't need to be handcuffed either. I have seen horrible examples of abuses of power by members of the Garda Síochana, bringing in prisoners who present no security threat with hands handcuffed behind their backs. Is there any need to handcuff a 75-year-old? Or a man with a broken leg? I have seen both. Those in authority should decide to use handcuffs solely on the basis of the security threat. If a prisoner presents a security or safety risk then handcuff him or her; if a prisoner doesn't, don't.

I was speaking at the UK conference in the mid 1990s where the British prisons minister, Ann Widdecombe, defended the shackling of a young female prisoner during childbirth. I spoke immediately after her. I said, 'To shackle a young mother during childbirth is nothing short of an abuse of power. I've been around a long time and have worked with women prisoners for many years, but so far I've never heard of a woman escaping from custody while giving birth.'

For most of my time as governor of Mountjoy we succeeded time and time again in keeping mothers and babies out of prison. We believed that this was the best solution for both of them. Over the years, numerous officials in the Department of Justice and various Ministers for Justice went along with this approach. Now it seems to be the case that it doesn't matter if you have a baby or not, it doesn't matter if you are pregnant or not, if the sentence is there you serve it in jail. That is sad, and another retrograde step.

In recent years it has also become more and more difficult to obtain temporary releases for women in prison. There is a saying that the difference between men and women in prison is that in most cases men leave all their personal and family problems outside, whereas women bring all their personal and family problems with them. I came across hundreds of examples that supported this theory. Women in prison are nearly always responsible for children, and this is an additional reason for granting them temporary release.

The whole temporary release situation needs to be looked at independently. The present system lacks transparency, and prisoners and their families have no idea what criteria are used in the granting or refusal of temporary releases. Indeed, I didn't know myself what criteria were used. A prison governor cannot release a prisoner for any reason unless they have served every day of their time, even if they have been jailed for the most minor offence. Yet a civil servant with little or no knowledge of the prisoner, or the situation in the prison, has the power, delegated by the minister, to release prisoners. Every day – day in, day out – prisons around the country email hundreds of names of prisoners to the IPS headquarters for temporary release, either for personal reasons or to relieve overcrowding. As prisoners come towards the end of their sentences, their names are submitted repeatedly. They come back time and time again – refused – and then, out of the blue, one day they are released. It is as ad hoc as that. It is never clear how decisions are arrived at, how a prisoner qualifies or why he is refused.

Years ago, in the 1960s and '70s, by and large if a prisoner's father, mother, son or daughter died, the prisoner was given temporary release to attend the funeral. Now it is almost a rarity for a prisoner to be released for the funeral of a close family member. They are usually only allowed to go to the morgue, in handcuffs. Holy Communions and confirmations are the same: requests by the prisoners to attend – fathers and mothers – are often turned down, even when they have less than twelve months to serve. It makes no sense whatsoever and it ignores the child's rights. These are one-off events in a child's life that can't be reproduced later on, so every effort should be made for the child's sake to ensure that the parent is present.

There is talk of the Dóchas Centre being relocated to the proposed new prison complex at Thornton Hall in north Dublin. It is easy to change buildings and resources, but changing people is a slow, painful process. The centre we have took a long time to establish itself and to grow and progress. Those who drove the Dóchas Centre forward from 1999 until today were dedicated and special women and men. If and when the Dóchas Centre is relocated, officials would do well to remember that it takes more than a building to bring out the best in people.

18. Who Are Our Prisoners?

In 2007, a group of mature students from All Hallows College visited Mountjoy as part of a social studies course. They talked to ten prisoners – five men and five women – about their life experiences. The discussions went well, both sides sharing all kinds of personal stories over ninety minutes. As things were coming to a close, a young prisoner who had stayed silent put up his hand to speak.

'Yes, Mike,' I said, 'do you want to say something?'

'Yes, I do want to say something, but what I want to say you won't want me to say,' he replied.

I said, 'Mike, I don't mind what you have to say – say whatever you like.'

'This is my life story,' he said. 'I'm the youngest of a family of eleven. When I was two my ma left one day, and I've never seen her since. My sister reared me because my da is an alcoholic. When I was seven, I was sent to St Joseph's in Clonmel. When I was eleven, I was in St Laurence's in Finglas. When I was sixteen, I was sent to St Patrick's Institution. Now I'm twenty, and I'm doing five years in Mountjoy. I have spent all my life in and out of special schools, institutions and prisons, and nobody ever came to help me or to do anything for me. The only person who ever did anything for me is my sister. That's what I've got from society. Fucking nothing.'

And that, in a nutshell, is the story of so many of the men and women who end up in our prisons – people who never had a hope of developing into responsible members of society, because society put no value on their lives and left them to rot.

I realize that being the victim of a crime is a devastating experience. Despite what people think, I do not underestimate the pain and trauma that has often been caused by the men and women who come into the prison system. Many victims of crime suffer for the rest of their lives, and some never recover from the devastation of injuries inflicted on them, whether physical, emotional, psychological or sometimes all three. While I was never the victim of serious crime, my car was stolen once and it has been damaged and broken into a number of times. One evening I was in our sitting room when I saw a young fellow jump up on the bonnet out on the road, and he continued to jump up and down on it until I burst out the door to chase him away. He ran for his life, and thank God I didn't catch up with him because at that moment I'm sure that I would have been tempted to assault him. Trivial as they were, my experiences gave me an inkling of how I might feel if something more serious occurred. My reaction was always the same: I was full of anger and mad for revenge, but once I cooled down I was able to put it all into perspective and accept that under no circumstances could I take the law into my own hands. But I can empathize with people who are the victims of serious crime, and understand their anger and frustration. I still believe that the answer isn't an eye for an eye.

In 1994, Joe Duffy came into Mountjoy and broadcast live as part of Gay Byrne's radio show. He brought together six victims of crime and six prisoners to discuss and debate crime. The dynamics in the group were amazing: from huge tension at the beginning to a rapid thawing as the programme progressed and both sides listened to each other's stories. One of the most striking things that emerged was that several of the prisoners admitted that the thought of their victims had never even crossed their minds as they committed crimes. This was the first time they had been confronted directly by the people their crimes had hurt, and the first time they had heard about the cruel consequences of their behaviour. Equally, the victims saw the prisoners as individuals, and were able to differentiate between their criminal behaviour and the normal human beings they were at the back of it all. Many of the victims said things like, 'You are so young' or 'You could be my son' or 'Why are you wasting your life in here?' After the first commercial break the tension disappeared and the prisoners sat on the floor in front of the victims chatting away. The whole thing was most revealing and showed the potential benefits of having direct contact and direct communication between groups of people who hold totally different points of view.

There is no conflict between being sympathetic to victims of crime and speaking up for prisoners. The media can spin any concern for the prisoner and his family as a lack of support for the victims of his crime. However, they are separate issues and should be kept separate. It is up to the gardaí to pursue those who commit crimes, and the courts to punish them. Once they are in prison, the pursuit has ended, the day of judgement is over and the punishment is being administered; they have been deprived of their freedom and forced to live a regimented life in a small space with hundreds of others, often for long stretches of time. It is the job of prison staff to keep prisoners secure and look after them in a civilized way, not to take it upon themselves to make the punishment even harsher. Indeed, ideally prison staff shouldn't concern themselves at all with the severity of a prisoner's crime, nor have it in mind when working with him or her. That has already been dealt with in the sentences the prisoners receive.

The more severe crimes attract the most publicity and the longest sentences. The prison service needs to have more strategies in place to help long-term prisoners. There is a perception that people can be locked up and treated as robots, and then after ten years or more they can be released, cured of their criminal ways. But life is not static and we all either grow and develop as human beings or we regress. I am sure that most long-term prisoners actually regress while they are in prison, and that is no surprise. Imagine spending at least seventeen – and as many as twenty-three – hours of every day locked up in a tiny cell, often having to share it with someone who is driving you mad.

One of the greatest scourges for a prisoner serving a life sentence is they have no idea when it is going to end, or if it ever is. The one consolation for other prisoners is that they have a definite release date. Every prisoner should know where he or she stands, even if that means telling them that they will never be released. The English system of setting a tariff – a specified number of years – is a much better approach. I have seen ministers sit on decisions over releasing prisoners on life sentences for years, and then their successors making their minds up instantly on assuming office. The courts should decide the tariff, not the politicians, and the prisoner would then know where he or she stands. I say this mindful of the pain and trauma suffered by the families of victims. The courts should take this pain into account when deciding the sentence; this would help victims too, as they would know exactly what the sentence was.

Imprisonment must never be looked upon as anything other than a severe punishment. After a serious health problem, it is the next most traumatic experience someone could go through, not just for the prisoner but for their family and on occasions for a whole community. Contrary to the idea that crime pays and that prisoners have a lot of wealth stacked away for when they get out of prison, the reality is usually quite different. Most prisoners that I knew over the years had no nest eggs and were nearly always broke. Of course there are exceptions, but the vast number of people in prison are poor and come from the most socially disadvantaged areas of our society. If a child from a middle-class or a respectable area gets into trouble, by and large every effort will be made to try to prevent that young person from getting a conviction – and rightly so; I fully support the view that young people should be protected from criminal convictions if at all possible. On the other hand, if a child from a very socially disadvantaged area gets into trouble, it is often believed that he will benefit from a period in a special school or in St Patrick's Institution – the reasoning being that he will get an education there or that the discipline will be good for him.

I have seldom met a happy prisoner, except when their circumstances were so appalling on the outside that they were actually better off in prison. And if anybody feels better off in prison than outside, it says it all about how awful their lives must be. Most prisoners suffer greatly while they are in prison. It's a real punishment, locking somebody up in a cell for seventeen hours on average every day.

Because Ireland is a very small country, parochial news is also national news, so it's easy to get the impression that prisons are full of violent, vicious and brazen young men, an image very much associated with gangland crime. While, of course, there are a number of this type in prison, this number is very small in comparison with the overall prison population. A young person might give two fingers to the media on his way into the prison van, but once inside, life is tough and few take it in their stride. I am convinced that serving a long stretch in prison, irrespective of who you are, leaves a psychological mark. Though I found some of the gangland criminals tough and highly dangerous, I also found that they had some humanity within them. I believed, too, that irrespective of how they behaved I should always deal with them in a humane and respectful way, and that is what I did.

People often asked me whether the prisoners who committed horrible and violent crimes were downright bad. Of course, I met people in prison who were very dangerous, but when I asked myself whether they were basically bad or had underlying personal, mental or psychological problems, I always came to the same conclusion: 'Ordinary, sane people don't behave in such a manner.' Human beings can be very cruel to their fellow human beings in certain circumstances, and I am certain that the environment and the culture we live in has a huge influence on how we behave. In addition, many people have serious and genuine mental health problems from birth, and often this is at the root of their behaviour. Finally, if a child is brutalized during childhood, as many children are, then it is no surprise that they too act in a violent manner when they grow up.

I met many thousands of people in prison over the years, but I always found a bit of kindness and humanity in all of them: maybe when they talked about their parents or their family or an occasion of tragedy in their local area or whatever. There was a bit of goodness. I never met a wholly good person on the outside either.

My heroes in life are the people who stand by the imprisoned, usually members of their immediate families – their mothers, fathers, children, grandparents – and on many occasions close family friends. To stand by a family member who is in prison is never popular, but it's the one time in life that a person really needs their family. I think of mothers in particular, turning up week after week to visit their children. I can't think of a more humiliating experience. They never give up, and that really is unconditional love.

The families of the imprisoned have committed no crime, but you wouldn't think that when you see how they are treated by society and on occasions when they come to visit the prison. I always said to staff that a welcome, a bit of kindness and a word of encouragement is so much needed by those visiting prison. It is a traumatic experience to visit a close family member in a prison, especially for young children. Nowadays, with the arrival of drug sniffer dogs, it is much worse. The IPS and the dog handlers claim that the dogs don't jump up on people, but time and time again I saw them jump up at visitors, including children. The official line is that everything that can be done to stop drugs getting into prison shall be done, irrespective of the consequences. Though this approach is popular with the public, I certainly don't agree with it and I never will. I have sympathy for those who argue that every human effort must be made to keep drugs out of prisons, but I don't believe it should be done at any cost. Security can be used as a reason for doing almost anything, and unless there are some balances in place, innocent people get hurt and damaged.

It is especially difficult for people visiting someone in prison for the first time. It's a tough call, to arrive at a prison like Mountjoy, to be searched and sniffed over by a dog and then arrive in a crowded visitors' room where maybe fifteen or twenty other people are already chatting away comfortably. Then your son or your daughter arrives. That's the moment when it really hits home. Apart from victims of crime, who could not reasonably be expected to feel compassion for those involved in such a scenario, I cannot understand how the rest of us could get any satisfaction from seeing such pain and suffering or wish that it was any worse.

Hardliners might say that prisoners should have thought of the damage they would do to their families before committing their crimes; my concern is about their children, who didn't commit any crime. They must not be associated with the wrongdoing of their father or mother and they have rights too, one of them being to have a positive relationship with their parents. Prison rules state that no physical contact is allowed between prisoners and their visitors, even infants. I believe that it's a fundamental human right for parents to hold their babies, even in prison, and certainly it's a baby's right to be held and hugged by his or her parents.

Just before Christmas 2007 I was standing outside the main gate of Mountjoy when a young mother and her son of about six came across from the visitors' waiting room on their way in to visit his father. I said hello, and the mother introduced me to her son as 'the boss of the army'. She had obviously told him that his dad was not in prison but in the army. When the little boy heard this he said, 'You can do me a favour. You can let my dad home for Christmas.'

I knew that his father was only two or three years into serving a life sentence. The little boy would be twenty years old or more before he would ever see his dad out for Christmas. The innocence of the little boy, the devastation of crime, the consequences of it and nobody outside the immediate family understanding or caring – it was all there before my eyes. Children are always the innocent victims of crime. Children of victims can be left with lifelong trauma. But the children of prisoners suffer greatly too.

I recall Bishop Brendan Comiskey contacting me when I was governor of Portlaoise, wanting to know if a prisoner there who was serving a long sentence could get out for his son's confirmation. I told him there was no chance of that. Then he asked if we could have the ceremony in the prison. I agreed, so one day the bishop, the boy, his mother and a few close family members came to Portlaoise and we had the confirmation in the prison chapel. After the ceremony they all sat down together for a celebratory meal prepared by the prison's home economics teacher. As they started to eat the little boy turned to his father and said, 'Daddy, do you know something? This is the first time ever, in my whole life, that I had a meal with you.'

Another woman I ran into at Christmas 2007 was a woman I knew well, a grandmother in her seventies. I had known her for over twenty years because all seven of her children – all of them heroin addicts – had been in prison. Over the years she came to see me several times to discuss their situations, especially when they were very sick. Now they were all dead. She was back to visit her eldest grandchild, at the start of another cycle of visiting jails.

The family might have a special place in our constitution, but it has yet to find a significant place in prison. The design of the visiting boxes where the visits occur is totally family unfriendly. Just imagine seven families in one visiting box all trying to have private conversations, all packed into a small room with little children running around. In

Mountjoy we introduced special family visits for long-term prisoners, particularly prisoners serving life sentences. We got a small Portakabin, fitted it out with easy chairs, put in tea and coffee-making facilities and extended the visit to over an hour rather than the normal thirty minutes. Prisoners were searched before and after the visit and they never abused the more relaxed approach. These visits proved to benefit the prisoners and their families greatly.

In the mid 1990s, Helen Haughton from the Quakers and Anthony Lenihan, an activist with the Guild of St Philip Neri, offered to provide tea and biscuits for people who were waiting to go into Mountjoy to visit prisoners. At that time everyone would be packed into a small waiting room waiting for their name to be called out so they could go into the prison proper for their visit. We got a pre-fab, and every day Helen, Anthony and a group of volunteers came to serve tea and biscuits to the visitors. This was the first time that such a civilized service was provided for prison visitors.

As part of the construction programme in the late 1990s, we created a purpose-built visitors' centre, which has developed over the years and today provides great support to the families of prisoners. It is up there with the best anywhere in the world. Visitors are welcomed, given refreshments and provided with a comfortable place to wait and a well-managed crèche if they have young children, and if they want they can have a chat with one of the staff in the waiting room and get some reassurance. Most prisons have visitors' centres nowadays, and this all came out of Helen and Anthony's initiative.

What creature comforts there are in prisons are few and modest, and none compensates for that loss of freedom and control and the separation from loved ones. It is the job of prison staff to make sure that prisoners stay in prison for as long as the court orders, and to look after their basic human needs in the meantime. A progressive prison system also does its utmost to help prisoners to grow as human beings. I have seen men and women grow far beyond my wildest expectation. They have responded to basic human kindness, compassion and positivity. So many have been educated, not necessarily in the classroom but simply as a result of how they were treated. An enlightened system helps prisoners to develop the emotional, social and educational or vocational tools to make a better fist of living decent responsible lives when they get out, whatever the challenges and temptations facing them. And that is not just good for them, but for all of society.

Men and women appreciate it when they are shown respect and when trust is placed in them, and that is what the open centres, the Training Unit and the Dóchas Centre provide – an environment where prisoners can prove themselves, which they do. Getting the message 'I believe in you' – possibly for the first time in their lives – is a powerful thing, and the vast majority of prisoners respond positively to it.

Enormous numbers of people have no idea of what some people have suffered in life, the struggles they have had to endure, and the uphill battle it is for them to cope and survive; their lives are totally miserable and abnormal in every way. Not everybody is born into the right circumstances, with the stability, the intelligence and the talents to live the type of life that the general public expects them to.

A few years ago in the Dóchas Centre we had a middle-aged woman from the west of Ireland. She had committed no crime. She was mentally ill and homeless and had been shouting and roaring on the street and wouldn't move on, so the gardaí arrested her. When she got to court the judge – recognizing her vulnerable state and realizing it was her only hope of getting medical treatment – sentenced her to three months' imprisonment. During her sentence she had her fifty-fifth birthday. The staff and some of the prisoners baked a cake, put some icing and a few candles on it and brought it into the communal dining room at teatime, singing 'Happy Birthday'. The woman became very upset, broke down and cried her eyes out. When she calmed down, one of the staff asked her why she had become so upset. 'Because this is the worst day of my life,' she said. 'I'm in prison, I'm not feeling well, my family have all left me. And today is the first time in my life I've ever got a birthday cake.'

I have met men and women in prison, and after getting to know them and becoming aware of the difficulties they had in life, my conclusion is often, 'It is amazing they are as good as they are, considering what they have been through.' Sometimes there was no love or kindness in their lives. Sometimes they were treated like animals –

abused, beaten up, neglected, ostracized, raped, brutalized. We get high and emotional about the abuse of children in the 1930s to the 1970s in the hellholes we created for them – the orphanages, the convents, the industrial schools, the reformatories, the psychiatric hospitals. Yet when we encounter the troubled people who came out of those places, how quickly we forget about what was inflicted upon them in our name and demand from them standards of behaviour that are totally unrealistic. We must never forget that as a society we created all those institutions and in doing so we all have a responsibility for the savagery that many of them inflicted on our own children, and indeed, the savagery that some of those children subsequently inflicted on others. Our prisoners are us.

19. Opening the Gates of Mountjoy to the Public

When, at the height of our troubles in the mid 1980s, I said Mountjoy was not my prison, nor the prisoners my prisoners, but the public's, I meant it. I believe that prisons belong to society. From that time a series of initiatives – some planned, some spontaneous – opened the gates of Mountjoy to the public and helped to get this message across. To encourage people to know and understand the reality of their prisons and their prisoners, I was glad to do anything I could.

Drama was a wonderful way of bringing the public into the prisons, and after our first success with *On the Outside* in 1986, the Mountjoy play became an annual event. Audiences saw that prisoners were just ordinary people. Yes, they were in prison for committing crimes, but they were also talented men and women capable of cooperating, working hard and putting on a quality play. We always had a little reception afterwards to allow the public to mingle with and chat to the prisoners. One night during the run of a play featuring women from the Dóchas Centre, I overheard a member of the public saying, 'Oh my God, they are all so young, they could be our own daughters.' I heard comments like that regularly and my response was always, 'Yeah, that's true. Of course, they *are* all somebody's daughters.'

Among our memorable productions over the years were *The Risen People* by James Plunkett, *Da* by Hugh Leonard, *Philadelphia, Here I Come!* by Brian Friel, *Juno and the Paycock* by Sean O'Casey, *The Lonesome West* by Martin McDonagh, *The Factory Girls* by Frank McGuinness and a number of John B. Keane plays, including *Many Young Men of Twenty*, *Moll* and *The Field*. John B. attended *Many Young Men of Twenty* and was highly complimentary about the production, becoming a great supporter of the drama project. One year an English touring company worked with the prisoners to put on *West Side Story* in a marquee in a prison yard.

The prisoners benefited enormously from these productions. There is something uplifting and generous about entertaining others, and for prisoners, who are so often ostracized, condemned, abused and vilified, it is fantastic to give pleasure and be the recipients of praise, applause and ovations. For long-term prisoners, especially those serving life sentences, the drama project was a godsend; it broke the boredom of prison life and it was one of the few things that they could look forward to from year to year.

I have so many wonderful memories of prisoners who surpassed all expectations in those productions. Most moving of all was when they surpassed their expectations of themselves. Paul was the understudy for the part of the Bull McCabe in *The Field*. He was from Dublin and I doubt if he had ever stood in a field in his life, let alone had a grasp of the culture of rural Irish life as depicted in the play. He had to step in at the last minute, and on the opening night I sat there thinking, 'If the Bull McCabe goes down, the play is sunk.' A few minutes into the play, the Bull comes on. I needn't have worried, Paul was electrifying: at the interval Tim Dalton, the secretary general of the Department of Justice at the time, and a Kerry man himself, turned to me and said, 'God, I wouldn't like to cross that fellow.'

One night during the run, I met Paul after a performance and he told me the play had changed his life: 'I have been coming in here for years and nobody ever asked me how I was, but yesterday up on my landing the class officer asked me how I was getting on and said, "You are brilliant in that play." Nobody ever told me I was brilliant before. And another officer asked me, "Can I do anything for you?" Jaysus, no one ever asked me before whether they could do something for me.' Later on that year I was asked to present a cheque to representatives of Temple Street Children's Hospital on behalf of the prisoners, and I discovered that Paul was one of the main organizers of a marathon in the grounds of Mountjoy, coinciding with the Dublin City Marathon, to raise money for the hospital.

Paul was in the Training Unit the following year and I asked him to that year's production as a guest. I have never met anybody who was so thrilled with an invitation. He shook my hand repeatedly and kept saying, 'Thanks for having me here as your guest.' As far as I know he has never been back in prison.

Another last-minute substitution who turned out to be a star was the prisoner who ended up playing Bridgie Andover in *Moll*. Jean had to step in when the woman who had been cast in the part absconded while on temporary release. (And no, we were not shocked: prisoners don't turn into model citizens overnight just because they get a small bit of positive attention; change is an even slower and more difficult process for the prisoner than it is for the average person.) The play was due to end on a Saturday night. Jean was due for release on the Friday morning, but she volunteered to stay on until Sunday to finish playing the part. On the Monday morning one of the staff in the Dóchas Centre told me, 'You should have seen little Jean leaving yesterday morning. She didn't walk out the gate, she danced out through it.'

Tommy, who played Rashers Tierney in *The Risen People*, was a very talented actor and another natural on the stage. The morning after the opening night, Gay Byrne said on his radio show that Tommy's performance as Rashers was outstanding, as good as David Kelly's legendary depiction in the TV series *Strumpet City*. A few days after the staging of *The Risen People*, we met with all the cast to reflect on their experience. Tommy said, 'If I was born in Foxrock I would have got drama classes and I could be a professional actor now.' And I said to him, 'But you'd never have played Rashers Tierney as well as you did the other night if you came from Foxrock.'

Over the years the plays were performed for the other prisoners, usually in the afternoons. In the early years they behaved very badly during performances. They kept interrupting and shouting at the cast, getting up and walking out of the hall, throwing orange peel at the stage and generally messing about. They slagged all the male prisoners as they appeared on stage, calling them sissies, and they jeered at the women.

Prisoners from all the wings were rowdy, but those from the A wing, which accommodated most of the hard-core prisoners – hard men and veterans who had seen it all – were notorious for their behaviour, and for the first few years the cast hated playing for them. Then one year a prisoner from A wing got a part and he was brilliant. From then on their whole attitude changed and they began to listen to the lines, and enjoy and understand and respect the acting and the actors. When a prisoner started talking or acting the clown, the other prisoners would shout, 'Will yez shut up and listen to it!'

In 2005 at the performance of *The Lonesome West*, the prisoners from A wing were by far the most attentive and best-behaved audience. At the end they gave the cast a standing ovation. It was unbelievable to see such a reaction, and it was one of the best feelings I ever had. That was real progress: they had learned to understand, appreciate and enjoy drama. I didn't know it then, but it was to be our last play.

A new attendance roster for staff was introduced in 2006, and there was no overtime available to allow us to work the way we needed. For two weeks – during the final preparations for the play and while it was running – at any given time we needed the same four or five officers to be available to monitor everything and to attend performances. The new roster, which worked on the basis of annualized hours, provided no flexibility for any 'extra-curricular' activities like the drama project, and it was not possible to get approval for a special overtime arrangement. I tried to see if three officers could work the extra time, bank the hours and take time off at a later stage, but the Prison Officers' Association would not agree to this. The end of the drama project was simply collateral damage along the way to making the new arrangements, and neither management nor the union cared about it.

It is a bit sad for me, at the end of my time in Mountjoy, to have to accept that it is unlikely the plays will ever be reintroduced. Certainly, at the moment there is no support in the IPS for initiatives like the Mountjoy annual drama project. Indeed, financial considerations aside, I am certain that if I had tried to start the project in 2010 rather than twenty-five years earlier, the answer would have been a blunt 'no'.

Another way we tried to bring prisoners and public together was by having students visit Mountjoy on school tours. This started by accident. I was giving a talk to a group of Leixlip teenagers attending Youthreach, a training programme for early school-leavers. Marian Quinn, the course organizer, asked me to come down and talk to the trainees about the dangers and consequences of crime, about drugs and generally about how to stay clear of the law. It was a group of about twenty-five, and I had an hour to talk to them and for questions and answers. It seldom happens to me, but a few minutes into the talk I knew I had lost them. They were messing about, kicking out, shuffling the chairs, knocking the caps and hats off each other, throwing paper missiles across the room and generally acting the maggots.

Out of pure desperation, I said, 'Would you like to visit Mountjoy?' Instantly they stopped messing and just stared at me in shock. 'You're joking, Mister. Can we? Oh please, can we?'

I had them back in the palm of my hand. They quizzed me up and down about everything to do with Mountjoy, and we had a good discussion about crime, drugs and prison for the rest of the hour.

A week later they came into the prison. They were very different boys and girls from the ones I had met in Leixlip: all the giddiness gone. They walked around the prison during lunchtime, visiting the wings, the yards, the visiting box and going into a vacant cell. I had asked a sensible and mature prisoner to talk with them about his life of crime, what it really feels like to be locked in a small cell for seventeen hours every day, what he missed most of all and his regrets. He told them that prison was a waste of time and to cop on. He said, 'I thought that I was tough, but to be honest with you I have cried many nights in my cell when I'm locked up. I don't let the other fellows see me crying, but I feel very lonely in here. I miss my son, he's only two, and I hate myself for letting me ma down. She hates coming up here and she was never in trouble in her life. I was here for me twenty-first and that is when you miss being out: it's brutal in here for your twenty-first.'

One young girl asked, 'Does your girlfriend come to see you?'

'No, no, she won't come up here. She is from a good family and won't come up. Me ma brings me son up to visit.'

'What are you in for?' a young lad asked.

'For nothin' really – we were smoking hash in the park and we got caught and I got two years,' he said. 'But I was in trouble before. I was in Pat's a few times for cars, joy-riding, that sort of thing.'

'What do you miss most?' a young boy asked.

'Me son and me ma,' he said with a little tear in his eye.

You could hear a pin drop. He was having more influence on them than any teacher, any parent, any youth leader or any prison governor. He said that when he was twelve and thirteen he thought he was smart and that he could do drugs and not get addicted. One lad had a bit of a smirk on his face when he mentioned drugs; it was obvious that he had used. But the prisoner handled it very well, acknowledging that when he was their age he was exactly the same and thought it was all a joke. But he left them in no doubt that drugs were a disaster and to stay clear of them. And he spoke about the hellhole that Mountjoy was and how he hated having his young child coming up to visit him there. He said, 'My son leaving after the visit is the worst thing about prison. That's when it really hurts.'

As they walked out the gate after the visit there wasn't a word out of them. I was surprised how much the visit affected them. Even though the tour was conducted in a quiet and relaxed way, and it was not used to try to frighten them deliberately, they seemed almost traumatized. But it had shown them the stark and brutal reality of prison life.

The following day, Marian got them to write down their thoughts. They wrote about the razor wire on the tops of the walls and their feelings of fear when the big gates banged shut behind them on their way in, and how trapped they felt. They thought that the cells were small, dark and frightening, and that the smell of piss in the jail was rotten. The highlight for them was hearing a prisoner speak about his life in prison. It was clear that they had heard him, believed him, understood him and didn't want to be him. To this day Marian is convinced that that visit to Mountjoy saved at least three of the boys from going to prison as young men.

As a result of that experience, visiting Mountjoy Prison became a regular feature of Youthreach programmes and its successor, Copping On. Then schools became interested, and eventually we were running eight tours a week, visiting both the men's prison and the Dóchas Centre. Students travelled from all over the country, from as far north as Donegal and from the most southern parts of Cork and Kerry. Usually, once bookings opened for a term, we were booked out within two days. It was particularly popular in transition year, and many students and teachers told me the trip to Mountjoy had been the highlight of their year.

I never believed in using the prison tours to put fear into the students. That could backfire, as some young fellows might think that it was a challenge to prove how tough they were. The prison tours were intended to be both educational and experiential – to give students a real sense of the atmosphere of a prison. It didn't matter from which side of the social divide the students came; seeing and smelling a prison was quite a shock to most students and teachers. When they came from poor or disadvantaged areas, where they were more used to people going to prison, the visit left its mark in a different way: any glamour surrounding it disappeared. A prisoner telling them about prison life, drugs, violence, the loss of family and the long lonely nights in the cell was always persuasive.

Something that always caused great arguments was the contrast between conditions in the men's prison and the Dóchas Centre. Generally students felt that the Dóchas Centre was too easy for the women. I met the groups occasionally and they would always say that it wasn't fair. I used to say, 'Well, the men's prison was built in 1850 and the Dóchas Centre was only opened in 1999, so naturally the facilities for the women are much better.'

I found it amazing that almost irrespective of background, whether socially disadvantaged or affluent, they were out and out hardliners. For example, they could never fully understand why prisoners had small televisions in their cells. I used to try to reason with them by saying that for any human being spending seventeen hours a day locked in a cell was a real punishment and the television helped to break the boredom and to keep them sane. 'If you lock up a human being for years you must stimulate and motivate them, otherwise they will be a bigger burden on society when they get out.'

But they wouldn't have any of it. 'It's too good for them. If you do the crime, you do the time. They should be on bread and water.'

Mind you, these teenagers weren't the only ones to come out with this kind of eye-watering stuff. When she was a law professor in Trinity, Mary McAleese brought a group of students in on a tour. Afterwards they came to my office to ask questions. I remember one very tall red-haired guy with a very posh accent saying, 'I take it that you compulsorily test all the prisoners for Aids in here.'

I said, 'God no. Why? Are you all tested for Aids in Trinity?'

'Of course not,' he said. 'We're not prisoners.'

'Ah, but you're a law student. Is it not the case that prisoners have the same human rights as every other citizen?'

He just muttered.

Sadly, in the last couple of months of my term as governor the school tours ended. They got caught up in an industrial dispute with the Prison Officers' Association over the public service cutbacks, and as part of a work to rule the school tours were stopped. It now appears they have gone for ever.

An unusual story about prisoners and the outside world encountering each other defies all categorization and was one of the most amazing experiences of my time in Mountjoy. In May 2001, the relics of St Thérèse of Lisieux were brought into the prison as part of the first Irish tour of the casket containing the saint's remains. A few months before the tour, one of the prison chaplains, Father Declan Blake, came to my office and told me he'd had a 'rather strange' request. He showed me a letter from the organizers asking for permission to bring the relics into Mountjoy.

I had heard of the Little Flower, as the saint is known, but I could only vaguely remember who she was. And I had never heard about the relics touring around the world. I said to Father Declan, 'Well, we take them dead or alive in here, so why not? Bring her in.' Broadcaster Donncha Ó Dúlaing was accompanying the tour, and he was delighted they were to be allowed into Mountjoy and felt they would get a great reaction from the prisoners. I honestly believed that there would be no interest in them whatsoever, and was sure that the prisoners would just laugh at the whole thing.

On a Friday at lunchtime the relics arrived. There was great difficulty getting the casket into the church in the prison because it was far too big to go up the narrow, twisty stairs leading from the main hall to the church. So they had to hoist the casket up and through a window.

I was absolutely astonished when I went into the church later that afternoon. There was a long line of prisoners moving past the casket slowly and in total silence. Most of them placed their hands on it and blessed themselves as they passed it. I think every single prisoner in Mountjoy went up to the church that afternoon and queued to walk past the relics.

The relics were taken over to the Dóchas Centre in the late afternoon, where they were to remain overnight. Because the regime in the Dóchas Centre was open and relaxed, we were able to allow relatives of staff and our neighbours from around Phibsboro to visit. The staff and some of the female prisoners stayed up on a type of vigil and spent the whole night making tea for the people calling. One of the prisoners was a young Donegal woman, Sharon, who had coped with major struggles throughout her life. The vigil that night brought the very best out of her, and she was extremely generous and caring. It highlighted once again that if you make a connection with another human being, or touch them in some way, it makes such a difference to their behaviour. She was touched that night and her response was to show kindness, hospitality and good nature. Sharon died a few years ago, in her twenties, in tragic circumstances.

The relics had the most profound effect. There was a peace and tranquillity throughout the prison while they were there. I could never fully understand why they made such an impression on the prisoners and why they got so much out of the whole occasion. In my twenty-seven years of association with Mountjoy, I never saw anything remotely like it before or after.

People often misinterpreted my motivation for having a public profile. They said that I was setting myself up for a life in politics or was going to run for this, that or the other thing. Even senior politicians sometimes said with a kind of a nod and a wink, 'I know what you're up to.'

The truth is that I had absolutely no interest in or intention of entering politics. My only motivation was to tell the truth and let the public know the factual situation in their prisons, to give them another perspective on the prison service and above all to represent a group of people who were voiceless, the prisoners. For years my great idol John Hume said that Ireland wasn't a country that was divided, but a people, and that the first step in reconciliation is listening to people, even if they are the enemy. Prisoners are the enemy of mainstream society, but that doesn't mean they don't have a story that should be listened to.

So over the years I have used the media to get the message across that prisons are complex institutions, that they belong to the public and that the public has ultimate responsibility for them. I decided early on that I would tell the truth as I knew it and that was all. No spinning, no lies. There is an expectation in the system that whatever the circumstances, you will show loyalty to it and defend it. For example, I sometimes heard other governors deny that there were drugs in their prisons. Everybody in the system knew that wasn't true, but I'm sure management was happy with them for spouting the official line.

When I took over in Mountjoy, department officials resisted contact with the media. Gradually, because of the level of public criticism in the mid 1980s, they changed and began to use the media in a more positive way. I became part of that strategy, and sometimes appeared on current affairs programmes when Mountjoy or the prison service was in the news. When the going got tough this suited them: they knew I was cool under pressure. Other times I was invited to participate in things and they would not allow it. There was no consistency. I felt it was not sustainable that sometimes I was supposed to be the public face of the prison service and other times, when a journalist called about some story, I was supposed to say I wasn't in a position to comment. I told them they couldn't have it both ways. Either I was free to speak out, or I wasn't. For many years I then made up my own mind about interacting with the media.

In June 1993, a team from RTÉ's *Would You Believe* came to the prison to film. The producer had sought to make the programme when Pádraig Flynn was Minister for Justice and he had turned it down flat.

When Máire Geoghegan-Quinn took over, the producer asked again. When the minister received the submission, the words 'Not recommended' had been scribbled on it by a civil servant. She wrote on it, 'Please get the governor's views on this.' I wrote back saying, 'I think it's a wonderful idea, it's time the prisons of Ireland were opened up to the public.'

The *Would You Believe* crew filmed a one-hour special in both the men's and women's prisons. It was the first ever documentary filmed inside an Irish prison and it went down brilliantly, showing the prison in a completely different light than people expected. The following year came *The Gay Byrne Show*'s special from the prison, in which Joe Duffy brought together victims and offenders. It was fantastic radio and nothing but good came out of it; the reaction from the public was very positive, and it was very positive for Mountjoy too.

Donald Taylor Black, a film producer, wrote to me in late 1995 and said that he was interested in producing a 'fly on the wall' type of documentary in Mountjoy. He proposed coming into the prison over a number of weeks to record the day-to-day happenings. We had a meeting in my office and I said I was open to it, 'but there will be no interest in it; nobody will look at a programme based on a prison'. I can still see the big smile on his face and him saying, 'Oh no, that's where you are wrong.' I said, 'Well, if you are fool enough to believe that, and if you are mad enough to put your money into producing such a documentary, good luck to you.'

As it was in the aftermath of the *Would You Believe* special, the Department of Justice, amazingly and to its great credit, gave him permission to bring in the cameras and to have almost unrestricted access. Donald and his little team spent about eight weeks filming everything. Prisoners and staff spoke their minds and were often critical of the system. He eventually produced a four-part documentary series, *The Joy*. The viewership was extraordinary. Over 880,000 people viewed the part focusing mainly on women in prison. They got a remarkable insight into prison life, as it was very intelligently put together.

Twice – on Christmas Eve 1998 and again in 2002 – Midnight Mass was broadcast from Mountjoy. In 1998, shortly before the broadcast was due to start, the prisoners in the choir got so hot from the heat of the cameras that most of them took their shirts off. They were a picture in vests and a fantastic range of tattoos, but they sang their hearts out and their behaviour was exemplary. Afterwards kind-hearted people wrote in offering to buy them shirts.

The last time a TV crew filmed in Mountjoy – in late 2007 for chef Richard Corrigan's cookery programme *Corrigan's Challenge* – times were clearly changing. Richard Corrigan visited a few weeks before filming and everything was arranged; all prisoners participating in the programme were agreed, and an outline was sent to the IPS. Two days before filming was to start we received an email from the IPS instructing that any prisoners in the programme were to be filmed from the waist down only. The idea of the programme was that Richard Corrigan would work with prisoners in the kitchen and bakery in Mountjoy, sharing his expertise with them, and here we were being instructed to film the prisoners only from the waist down. We told them that it couldn't work and they relented. Once again the programme was a great success.

With this episode, I knew that after a relatively brief window of openness and official enthusiasm for showing the prisons in a positive light, everything was back to being closed and secret and controlled. We never had a bad experience with any of the radio or television projects we did; they were all excellent and nothing but good came out of them. It was similar with the print media. Several journalists came in. Some wrote positive things and some were very critical. Sometimes journalists seriously wronged prisoners or the prison service and incidents were misconstrued or misreported. But the media got it right most times and the key thing was that they gave the public an insight into their prisons.

A few years ago the IPS issued a circular to all prison governors instructing them that all contact with the media should be done through the press office at IPS headquarters. I referred a number of journalists to the press office when they contacted me and that was the last I heard. I know that journalists were refused interviews with certain governors, including myself, without us ever being contacted. During my last couple of years in the job I went along with the instructions, apart from participating in a few programmes about social justice issues.

There is no way *The Joy* would have been made in 2010. Donald Taylor Black wouldn't even get inside the gates of the prison for a meeting, never mind getting inside to film. Despite the IPS having a press office with a number of full-time staff, the official attitude to scrutiny and enquiry is negative, defensive, anti-media and anti-information. And the most depressing thing is that it's all coming from the belief that the prisoner must not be seen and must not be heard.

20. Drugs

During most of my time as governor of Mountjoy, the question I was most often asked was 'How do they get the drugs into the prison?' And the next most popular question was 'Why don't you stop the drugs getting into the prison?' Most people believed that it was a pretty simple thing to do. Even when I explained that it was impossible to stop drugs getting into Mountjoy, many still believed that I was either closing my eyes to the problem because it was too tough to take on, or deliberately allowing drugs in because they helped to keep the lid on tension in the prison.

Nothing could be further from the truth. Drugs ruined the prison service during my time in it, and undermined a lot of the best and most positive programmes in prisons. So much of the bullying and violence in prison is directly related to drugs, whether it is prisoners owing money for drugs or prisoners refusing to carry drugs. Most of the trustee jobs that prisoners had in the old days had to be eliminated because they were put under severe pressure to move drugs around the prison. Prisoners working on the prison grounds or in the officers' mess, going out to work every day or on temporary release to family events, are under extreme pressure to use their hard-earned extra privileges to carry drugs.

A young man going out on temporary release to attend his child's First Holy Communion, who has perhaps never used a drug in his life, will be approached in the prison before he gets out, and told that a supply of drugs will be dropped off at his house – and he will be left under no illusions what the consequences will be if he refuses to bring them back into the prison. Now he is in a dilemma: if he doesn't bring the drugs back he will be attacked and beaten up or, worse still, cut up; if he brings them back there is every possibility that he is going to get caught. If he gets caught he will be in trouble with two sides: he will be classified as a drug supplier by the prison authorities, and he will be regarded as a 'grass' by the drug users. He has to decide whether to bring back the drugs knowing these risks, or not to return at all, being unlawfully at large, being rearrested and having his sentence extended.

Parents, partners, other family and friends may be coerced into bringing in drugs because the addicted prisoner is threatening to commit suicide or to harm himself. If they succumb and are caught, they are brought to the gardaí and charged with possession of drugs with intent to supply. Families are often blackmailed by third parties to bring in drugs. They are blackmailed to pay money into accounts to pay for the drug debts of their imprisoned family member. A staff member who uses illicit drugs himself or herself is open to blackmail. And there is always the possibility that staff will bring in drugs for financial reward. It is impossible to assess how common this is as it is so difficult to get evidence, but during my time in the service two officers were charged and convicted of bringing in drugs and contraband. The whole drug scene is one horrible mess for everyone, with few winners, except for a small number of wealthy godfather figures who stay far away from the action on the ground.

A prison is not an underground dungeon where prisoners are isolated and secluded twenty-four hours a day, seven days a week. The Irish prison system operates on what is called a free association basis. Prisoners share recreation areas, workshops, classrooms and exercise yards with other prisoners. It's the only way a prison can work; otherwise, prisoners would have to be kept completely separate and isolated from each other, something many prisoners wouldn't be able to cope with and would make them crack up. Not only this, but such a system would be a logistical nightmare and prohibitively expensive to run.

Drugs are so minute that they're almost impossible to detect. People can swallow them and conceal them on their bodies. A tiny package, say something the size of a box of matches or a packet of chewing gum thrown over the boundary wall into a yard where 150 men were walking around, will disappear in seconds. By the time staff organize a search of all the prisoners – because that's what would have to be done – the drugs have gone, just vanished. Prison rules require that all searches are carried out in privacy, so they could not be done on the spot. Even if searching prisoners in the yards was permitted, the reality is that other prisoners would mill around and it would be logistically impossible to carry out searches thoroughly.

For years Mountjoy has been bedevilled with drugs and mobile phones being thrown in over the walls from the houses in Glengarriff Parade, off the North Circular Road. Young fellows climb onto the roofs of houses right across from D yard and throw the drugs over the wall. A mesh fence was erected to stop packages getting over, but even that didn't eliminate the problem. The owners of the houses on Glengarriff Parade have a legitimate grievance because their houses are often damaged as a result of this. Though the prison is under no obligation to do so, the trades staff at Mountjoy repair the damage as quickly as possible; however, it is still terribly disruptive and frightening for residents. It is an absolute scourge and the only solution is to have a full-time garda presence on the road. While the local gardaí do their best, they just don't have the resources to man a patrol full time. The Dóchas Centre has a similar problem, with drugs and phones coming over the wall and into the courtyards from the North Circular Road on a daily basis.

Over the years a lot of effort was made to counteract this by erecting high fencing and putting netting over the exercise yards, but nothing was 100 per cent successful. Placing netting over the yards created a claustrophobic feeling and reduced natural light, and prisoners often climbed onto the netting or damaged it. In early 2010 the IPS agreed to erect netting over D yard. However, it's still not straightforward. The exercise yards are relatively big and accommodate up to 150 prisoners on outdoor recreation; they are also used by the prisoners to play football. If pillars are erected in the centre of the yards to support netting, they will prevent football from being played. In addition, they will have to be climb-proof, otherwise the prisoners will climb up and drag the netting down. The netting itself will have to be so high that the prisoners are not able to form themselves into a human pyramid to get up onto it or to pull it down or seriously damage it. And not surprisingly it's very expensive to erect: estimates as high as €200,000 were being mentioned as the cost of erecting netting over D yard.

★

So it was an ongoing battle to try to prevent drugs getting into the prison, and it's very difficult if not impossible when there is such a high number of seriously addicted people in prison. In 1996, the Trinity College psychologist and criminologist Dr Paul O'Mahony, who had done research on addiction levels in Mountjoy when he was with the Department of Justice in 1986, repeated his research. The proportion of heroin-addicted prisoners had increased from 31 per cent in 1986 to 67 per cent in 1996. I believe the figure for 2010 would be close to 80 per cent.

At times as many as 250 prisoners were on methadone maintenance. Methadone is a prescribed drug heroin addicts take to alleviate the worst symptoms of withdrawal and to stabilize them. Dispensing methadone every day was a massive undertaking and took about three hours. In recent years in Mountjoy, starting at 9 a.m., the methadone was dispensed by nurse officers (qualified nurses employed by the prison service) and medical orderlies (prison officers trained as paramedics). Prisoners lined up outside two dispensing stations, one on A wing and one on C wing, and were given the amount of methadone prescribed by the doctor in each case. Towards the end of my time as governor, a private company had taken over this function on contract, and qualified pharmacists came to the prison every day and dispensed the methadone. The involvement of qualified pharmacists was a major step forward and long overdue.

But just because a prisoner was on methadone was no guarantee that he didn't top up with something else. Apart from other illegal drugs like cannabis and cocaine, huge amounts of prescription tablets were found in Mountjoy every day. They were often found in the grounds of the prison, having been thrown over the walls; indeed, at times there were far more of these than any other drug. It didn't seem to matter what the tablets were for: the prisoners were prepared to take whatever was going. They would gulp them down not knowing where they came from or what the effects would be. In recent times, the emergence and spread of head shops has had an impact. The mind-altering substances available in these shops can be bought very cheaply, and they too make their way into the prison, again with devastating consequences.

Of course the best way of resolving drug addiction is prevention. Many prisoners come from drug-infested areas, where much of the local culture is built around and dependent on drugs, where the physiological and emotional pain is so strong that they have to get drugs to get away from their reality. The objective must be to prevent young people from as young as ten and eleven years old getting involved in drugs in the first place, because once they become addicted, it's an uphill task and in all too many cases an almost impossible one.

To stick with the remit of the prison service, I believe that the best way of resolving the problem at Mountjoy is tackling the demand for drugs – doing everything possible to help addicts get on top of their addiction. Addicts will do almost anything to get a buzz or a kick. They get clean not because they're forced into it but because they make up their minds to kick the habit and then get every support and encouragement to succeed. I remember one prisoner writing once, 'I alone must do it, but I cannot do it alone.' Relapsing is a reality of addiction, and many people have a number of relapses before kicking the habit completely. But it can be done.

At a meeting of Narcotics Anonymous in Mountjoy, a former prisoner shared how he eventually dealt with his addiction in prison. He went up to the front of the hall and said, 'Hello, I am an addict and I was also a scumbag a few years ago.' There was total shock at this statement, and from that second on he had the full attention of everyone in the hall. He went on, 'I was a scumbag because I robbed me ma and only a scumbag would rob his ma. I was here in this prison a few years ago serving four years and I was using heroin, and an officer used to say to me every time I met him, "You need help" and I used to say to myself, "Yeah, I do, get me some heroin and that will help me." But I got worse and worse and then one day I went to him and said, "I need help" and he said, "Right, I'll get help for you." And he got me over to the Medical Unit and I went on a detox course and the drug-treatment programme, and then I went to the Training Unit, and I'm drug-free now for almost four years. I have my girlfriend and two children back living with me, and I'm working every day, and it's all down to the officer being there when I was ready for help.'

Many prisoners use prison to get their heads together, as they say themselves, but most of them don't tackle their addiction. So while they might not take drugs for a long period, they are not cured of their addiction and it can surface again, and nearly always does. I've always said that drug addiction is usually a symptom of something much deeper inside the person. Many people use drugs to kill the pain within them, and that is why I actually believe that drug treatment cannot be enforced on people. People need to want to do it, they must consent and they must be committed to becoming drug-free, otherwise it's just a cosmetic exercise. I'm afraid that type of personal commitment is not always forthcoming from prisoners. The addicted person must reach the point when he himself says, 'I want help.'

I believe that when a prisoner arrives at that stage, then help should be available in Mountjoy for him. During my time in Mountjoy we were not always able to do that, and while over the years drug-treatment services improved massively – with the appointments of a consultant psychiatrist to head up the treatment programme and a part-time doctor specializing in drug addiction; the provision of methadone maintenance; the recruitment of addiction nurses, drug counsellors and a team of psychologists; and the routine referral of prisoners in treatment to outside clinics when they were being released – they were still totally inadequate to cope with the demand that arose out of having as many as 500 prisoners with some form of addiction.

Occupation and activities are an integral part of the solution. A psychologist in Mountjoy once pointed out to me that their work was often frustrated because when they would try to motivate prisoners to take up some activity, there were no such things in place. It's hard to talk to drug-addicted people about overcoming their addiction when the only activity available to them is walking aimlessly around exercise yards day in, day out.

21. Guiding Prisoners to a Better Life

I was on an interview board in Hawkins House in Dublin one day, when a young man from West Cork came for a job as a prison officer. A nice young man, but like many of us coming from the country for the first time, a bit shy and innocent. I asked him, 'If you were successful today, and you were working in Mountjoy next week, what do you think you would be doing every day? What sort of work would you be doing?'

'I'd be rehabilitating prisoners,' he said.

'Very good,' I said. 'Fantastic. And if you were working as a prison officer tomorrow morning up in Mountjoy, what sort of things would you do to rehabilitate prisoners?'

He looked at the floor and there was a long silence. I allowed the silence to continue for almost a minute – a long time in an interview. Little beads of sweat began to form on his forehead and the silence continued. Eventually, he looked up at me and said, 'Be Jaysus, you have me there.'

Though he didn't have a concrete grasp of what it would involve, at least that young man had a sense that working in the prison service was about doing something positive for prisoners. That represents an important turnaround in thinking over four decades.

Professional educational services were first introduced in the early 1970s, and they are now well established in all prisons. Indeed, this was one of the real success stories within the prison service during my time. Most of the credit for this must go to a wonderful coordinator of education for the prison service, Kevin Warner, who spent almost thirty years developing education in prisons. Kevin was a former teacher. Since he retired in 2009, his role has been filled by a general grade civil servant. This is a backward step. The role of the coordinator of education in the prison service is a specialized one, and it's essential that a professional education practitioner is appointed to this post.

When Mountjoy was built in 1850 there was no education in prisons and no purpose-built facilities have been provided for it since. The only space for classes was out of the way and inadequate. It was up two flights of stairs over the Catholic church, and for many years it had no toilets. A wide range of classes were available, including basic numeracy and literacy, English, Maths, History, Geography, Art, Home Economics, Crafts, Computers and Music. One of the issues with education in prison, however, is that prisoners who are educated are likely to be motivated to further educate themselves in prison, while those who are very poorly educated are often too embarrassed to attend and are very poorly motivated. Some years ago a survey of Ireland's prisons revealed that half of all prisoners were illiterate or semi-illiterate. Still, over the years, about 40 prisoners would attend classes in the Education Unit at any one time; and approximately 100 prisoners would attend on a weekly basis – some, like those taking the Junior or Leaving certificates, attending full-time while others would only attend one class a day.

There were no purpose-built workshops in Mountjoy either; most were just old cells converted into small workshops. The main activities in the workshops were woodwork, computer training, sewing – making towelling and jeans – building construction and baking: there was a modern bakery, where they made bread for all the Dublin prisons. While there was some excellent training – the courses in computers in particular were top class – the work mainly centred on producing items for various charities. Prisoners got great satisfaction out of doing it, and it was a great opportunity for them to pay something back to society. Perhaps the biggest achievement of this nature was when, over a two-month period, Mountjoy prisoners produced 82,000 different flags for the opening ceremony of the 2003 Special Olympics.

We had carried out a lot of other work for the Special Olympics before this, but still, when Mary Davis told me what she needed, I was in shock. I thought it would be too much of a stretch for us and was thinking of asking other prisons here and in Northern Ireland to help out – until I told the workshop staff and prisoners. 'No way,' they said. 'We will do them ourselves, even if we have to work day and night.' And that's more or less what they did. The prisoners were absolutely enthusiastic and for several weeks worked all through the day, taking no dinner or tea break. They made the flags by hand and sandpapered every single one to make sure there were no splinters.

Ever since, the staff and prisoners in the workshops in Mountjoy have continued to support charitable organizations, particularly before Christmas every year, when they are inundated with requests to make Santa hats and gowns for children in special homes, for the elderly in nursing homes, for sick children in hospitals and for many different groups and organizations.

Apart from the Dóchas Centre, where the women are up and out of their rooms at 8.15 every morning and stay out of them until 7.45 p.m., prisoners tend to spend around seventeen hours every day locked in the cells. When they are out of the cells, apart from the few that are involved in education programmes or those participating in activities in the kitchens, laundries or production workshops, there is little or nothing to do. There are activities for fewer than half the prisoners. The rest either stay in their cells or walk around the yards aimlessly.

Sadly, in the new prisons things are no better. When the new staff rosters were being discussed with the Prison Officers' Association over five years ago, governors were promised by the IPS that the regime for prisoners would improve with the flexibility that the new system would bring. Unfortunately the new system has made everything far more rigid. With no overtime available now, there is less flexibility than ever before.

Good though it is, there is a limit to what work training can do for long-term prisoners. What is needed is a number of production units or factories where prisoners can be trained to produce goods and then sell them on the open market and be paid a gratuity for such work.

In 1978 a small number of prisoners, under the supervision of prison officer Niall McGrory, left Mountjoy Prison every morning to go out to work in the community. This was then an innovative idea, and was an effort by the authorities in Mountjoy to give prisoners the opportunity of making a positive contribution to communities on the outside.

The purpose of the work party was to help groups or communities to build or refurbish facilities that they couldn't afford to pay contractors to do. The first job they took on was the refurbishment of the Holly-lands Community Centre in Churchtown, Dublin. This was a great success, and everyone agreed that the whole idea of a community work party from Mountjoy Prison worked very well and should continue.

Over the next four years they worked in centres and hostels in Glencree, Rathfarnham, Coolock, Walkinstown, Donnycarney and Ballymun. All the jobs were completed to a very high standard, and the work party got a great reputation and was in huge demand by communities all over Dublin. In 1982 Paddy Moloney joined Niall McGrory in running the work party, and they became a formidable twosome for over twenty-five years.

In 1983 the work party was invited to build a community centre in a newly formed parish in Hartstown, West Dublin. The main driving forces behind this development were the parish priest, Father Liam Hickey, and Martin Moran, a Clare man who worked in the Department of Justice's Prisons Division and was a very active parishioner in Hartstown. It was Martin's idea that the Mountjoy work party should build the community centre. One morning he invited me out to see the site just after the foundations were dug. I was shocked when I saw the size of what was being built. I said, 'It's John Sisk you need out here, not the Mountjoy work party. This is too big a job for our crowd; they'd never be able to do it.'

Martin was having none of it, however, and dismissed my reservations, saying, 'Yarra, of course they'll be able to do it. It's straightforward. It's only throwing a few blocks together.'

He was right. It was the biggest project that the work party took on up to then, and when it was completed it was a magnificent centre with excellent facilities, finished to the highest standards. It was a credit to all the prisoners involved; one of them, a plumber, designed and installed the central heating system, and an engineer later told me that the system was unique and as good as ever he saw. The centre continues to be a monument to the work of Father Hickey, Martin Moran, the Hartstown community itself and, above all, the Mountjoy Prison community work party.

As a result of the success of the Hartstown Centre, many other communities in West Dublin lined up to have community centres built in their area, and over the next ten years or so, new community and youth centres were built in Quarryvale, Bawnogue, Deansrath and Huntstown – all mighty jobs and providing badly needed facilities for all four areas.

In 2001 the work party moved to Ballinascorney, on the side of the mountains overlooking Tallaght in Dublin, to refurbish a workshop and family centre for the Matt Talbot Community Trust. The trust was the brainchild of Sister Caoimhín, a most wonderful woman who was a great friend to prisoners and their families, those from Dublin's Ballyfermot in particular. The trust had a few acres and a small building in Ballinascorney which it was using as a workshop for ex-prisoners on a FÁS training programme and also as a place where the families of the imprisoned could go for a few days' break in the summer each year. The project was to build a new workshop and refurbish the accommodation for families.

Once again the work party delivered, and in October 2002 the new facilities were officially opened by the Minister for Justice, Michael McDowell, who did a great job, praising the outstanding work of Sister Caoimhín and acknowledging the valuable work of the work party. Ballinascorney is something very special and a lovely monument to Sister Caoimhín's work and her unconditional love for prisoners.

The work party took on its biggest ever project when Father Dermot Laycock, a former chaplain in St Patrick's Institution, invited it to build a new parish resource centre in St Bridget's, Killester, where he had become parish priest. The budget for the project was over €1 million. Once again I was concerned about the capacity of the work party to take on such a big project, but I needn't have worried – Niall McGrory and Paddy Moloney were confident that they could do it and once again they were right. The centre opened in September 2004 and it's a beautiful building, with great facilities catering for the whole community.

The work party moved from St Bridget's to build a scouts' den in Larkhill in Whitehall, and then went to work in Albert College in

Dublin, renovating an old building. During this job, Dublin City Council raised an issue about insurance cover and asked to have the work party removed until the matter was checked out. So the Mountjoy Prison community work party was made redundant in 2009, and Niall McGrory retired. Paddy had retired in the summer of 2004.

The work party completed over twenty separate projects over the years, saving communities millions of euro. It also gave prisoners a meaningful way to repay society and was a positive public relations story for Mountjoy Prison. Its track record with prisoners was brilliant: over 3,000 prisoners worked on the various projects and only a handful ever absconded. They learned new skills, and many of them developed a work ethic for the first time. For example, during the work in Killester, two prisoners, qualified bricklayers, had been building a long wall around the grounds of the church, but were released before it was completed. Father Dermot said, 'That's great news for you, but it's a pity you haven't finished the wall.' They said, 'No problem, we'll come back and finish it off for you, Father.' He thought that they were joking, but the following Saturday morning they turned up in their truck and finished the work.

Better still, only a tiny number of those in the working party ever returned to prison after their release. In any other organization this would be regarded as a great record and achievement, but not in the IPS. A branch officer of the Prison Officers' Association told me that at a POA meeting with the IPS they were told that if the service had its way there would be no work parties going out of Mountjoy.

A separate work party concentrated on gardening under the excellent leadership of officers Sam Kelly and Michael Purtell. In 1999, Mountjoy entered a garden in the National Garden Exhibition and won a commendation. A number of organizations asked if we would consider giving the garden to charity, and it was subsequently recreated in a special school in Bray. We entered the exhibition again the following year.

Arising out of this we were asked to develop a garden at Beaumont Hospital for the Kidney Foundation. They had living accommodation close to the hospital for patients coming in for dialysis or for their families staying overnight. The garden work party did a beautiful job, and nearly ten years on, the garden is still growing and developing. Once again we were inundated with requests, this time to develop gardens in hospitals and nursing homes. The garden work party designed and created a beautiful sensory garden in the grounds of a residential unit for elderly patients at James Connolly Memorial Hospital in Blanchardstown. The work party didn't just develop the garden but developed strong relationships with the staff, the patients and their families, and actually became an integral feature of the unit for many months until the garden opened in September 2002. Indeed, some work party members still keep in touch with people they got to know at the hospital back then.

After that job the garden work party developed half a dozen further gardens, as well as doing extensive work in preparation for the Special Olympics in 2003. However, after the review of staffing levels took place in the mid 2000s, our garden work party was eventually disbanded and, despite my pleas with the IPS, I lost the battle and it stayed disbanded.

Both work parties did magnificent work and proved themselves over and over again. It is hard to understand then why the IPS is not in favour of such projects, which achieve so much good. It has no problem spending huge sums of money training sniffer dogs to search for drugs, but it appears never to strike the administrators that if prisoners were trained and doing meaningful work they might not need illicit drugs.

While educational and work activity is invaluable for prisoners, what is really required is a comprehensive programme that addresses each prisoner's needs and helps them to develop in such a way that they have a decent chance of integrating into normal society on their release. The Connect Project was just such an initiative, and it was potentially the best programme for prisoners I came across during my time working in the prison service.

In 1998 Martin Hickey, the coordinator of work and training in the Irish prison service, came to Mountjoy with a suggestion that we should apply for funding under the European Funded Integra Project. Martin had been doing mighty work since the mid 1970s and was always an innovative thinker. Integra's purpose was to help people make the transition from unemployment back into the workplace, with a special focus on those who came from socially disadvantaged areas. We applied and were approved.

A condition of the funding was that the prison would work in collaboration with an outside agency. The National Training and Development Institute, part of Rehab, tendered and was successful. Its researchers came into Mountjoy and conducted intensive research among prisoners and staff. The Options programme was set up to respond to the needs identified in the research.

Options was a fourteen-week programme during which a dozen prisoners looked both at themselves and at the options they had when they left prison. Various services inside and outside the prison attended the programme and explained their function to the participants. The prisoners worked towards drawing up Individual Planned Programmes (IPPs), where they set short-term goals for themselves. Goals might cover things like education – say tackling numeracy or literary problems – or addiction, or violence or behavioural problems, or family issues, or the need for counselling. All the participants also worked with the probation service towards their transition from prison to the outside community. By the end of the course, participants had a thorough understanding of themselves, what was available to them when they left prison, how to go about getting it and a sense of purpose about what they could do. The NTDI team monitored the courses and the prisoners as they progressed through them, so there was continuous feedback on how well it was working and how it could be adapted and grow.

The Options programme developed over the years, and its work on parenting was particularly extraordinary. Parenting organizations helped to develop a strand of the course, and one Saturday during every fourteen-week run prisoners' children were brought in for the day and left with their parents, under the supervision of the parenting organization. The mothers or grandmothers, who normally had responsibility for the children, got the day off. The prisoners found the whole thing an amazing, educational and fulfilling experience.

At the end of Options programme the prisoners were presented with a certificate to mark their successful completion of the course. It might well have been the first bit of recognition they'd had in their lives. (I recall Sister Mary Mullins, the chaplain of the Dóchas Centre, telling us about going to the funeral of a young woman who had spent much of her life in and out of prison. The only thing on her coffin to symbolize her achievements was a certificate that she had received for attending the summer school while she was in the centre.) Families were invited in for the presentation of the certificates. For them it was a significant day – to see the person who had often caused them great pain now achieving something positive made them proud and gave them hope.

The main strength of the Options programme was that the prisoner was central. Heretofore, the prisoner had no active role in discussions about his release. The prisoner would be interviewed by a probation and welfare officer, and then all decisions – about the date of his temporary release, where he would live, what he might do after prison – were made behind closed doors and without his input. It was crazy, but that was how it worked and still does to a large degree. At best they would be told what was decided for them a few days before it was due to happen. The plan was doomed to fail almost from day one, and it nearly always did. Most prisoners simply don't know what options they have or what they have to do. However, the Connect Project put the prisoner at the heart of the decision-making about his or her future. It was a genuine attempt to help prisoners get out of and stay out of lives of crime.

The prison officers working on the Connect Project were selected by interview and trained, first of all to be facilitators in the Options programme or mentors in the IPP process. Every one of them excelled: they were brilliant. They broke down many of the barriers between officers and prisoners and they became very skilled facilitators and mentors. They helped, supported, encouraged and monitored the prisoner in achieving the targets he had set in his IPP. If, say, the prisoner undertook to attend remedial education three times a week, the mentor checked and would confront him about it if he hadn't attended. The targets were reviewed on a regular basis, often weekly, to see if they were being achieved or whether a prisoner could improve or raise the bar a bit – or even if he needed to lower it, which was sometimes what was needed. Officers developed links with outside services and agencies, and this made a huge contribution to prisoners on release. For example, they would arrange accommodation for prisoners who were homeless, or go with a prisoner to get a copy of his birth certificate if he needed it. All this support helped to keep former prisoners from slipping back into living in a way that would see them landing back in prison. The officers worked way beyond what was expected of them and what they were paid to do. They made themselves available to prisoners at almost any time of the day or night, especially if a prisoner was finding it difficult to cope inside or outside the prison.

The great thing about all this effort by prisoners and staff was that the Connect Project worked. In the first two years, 174 prisoners participated in Options. Between May 1999 and November 2000, when the pilot scheme ended, 76 of them had been released. One quarter of those released went straight into jobs, several more went on to work-training programmes and four entered residential drug-treatment programmes. Almost half of the prisoners who were released went out to do something constructive with their lives, and by the end of November 2000 only a handful had returned to prison. While this was short term, and no real indication of the long-term benefits of the Connect Project, it was very encouraging.

In November 2000, owing to its initial success, the Connect Project was included in the first National Development Plan and around €58 million was committed to the programme over the six-year period of the NDP – 47 million for the prison side of the project and the other 11 million for the probation service to fund extra probation officers who would support it. Connect was to be rolled out to all the prisons in Ireland, starting at Wheatfield and Limerick.

However, the project soon ran into problems. Shockingly, the problems came from the inside, from those whose focus was supposed to be helping prisoners. Connect had a national coordination group made up of the heads of various parts of the prison service – probation, education, psychology and work training – alongside representatives of the Department of Justice; the head of the NTDI, Dorothy Gunne; and Padraic White, former managing director of the Industrial

Development Authority. Then at local prison level there were management groups of similar composition – all the services, Department of Justice officials and NTDI representatives. That prison officers were at the very hub of the programme caused resentment by some of the professional services, mainly at the most senior levels. As they saw it, prison officers were taking over some of their work. They also strongly objected to the research element of Connect, in which the effectiveness of various services was assessed on an ongoing basis. Eventually the heads of the education, psychology, probation and welfare services began to raise questions about the Connect Project's role.

An example of the lunacy of what happened was that a dispute arose over the title 'Individual Planned Programmes'. Some of the professionals argued that it should change to 'Individual Planned Vocational Programmes' and that the Connect Project should be confined to vocational training and stay away from broader concerns and personal development. A number of efforts were made to iron out the problems, but Martin Hickey and I would not agree to water down the project's core principles. We insisted that the Individual Planned Programmes would have to be based on a totally holistic approach, and refused to limit it to vocational development only.

Over time the project began to struggle. Though in Mountjoy all the services couldn't have been more helpful, in the end they had to do what their bosses decided, which was to cease cooperating with Connect.

What the project needed when things were really coming to a head in the early 2000s was strong decisive leadership from the IPS. All the services should have been told that the project was the project, and to just get on with it. But instead what happened was all sorts of pandering and messing around. I knew then that it was doomed.

A senior official was brought in from the Department of Justice to try to broker agreements and compromises. The prison governors were excluded from the process; as ever, the bureaucrats believed it was something to sort out with the professionals before informing their functionaries on the ground. Martin Hickey came under further huge pressure to move away from the original concept of the Connect Project, to dilute it and separate it from other programmes, but he stuck to his guns. He argued that unless proper holistic programmes were developed for prisoners, no real progress would be made and the prison system would continue to fail prisoners. As far as I'm concerned, Martin did everything right from day one. Martin is now retired, but in his long career he was one of the most outstanding officials in the prison service.

The clash of visions for the future of the Connect Project was never resolved, and from the mid 2000s it slowly disappeared. What happened with the €58 million provided for in the National Development Plan, I have no idea. The funding was probably drawn down by the Department of Justice and the IPS and used for other purposes. The National Training and Development Institute was forced to withdraw because it was unable to get the funding it needed to extend the programme to other prisons as intended and it couldn't get a long-term commitment from the IPS. And so a potentially wonderful programme died.

Given that the probation and welfare service is now solely a probation service, with no welfare remit, there is now a major gap in providing prisoners with the kind of hands-on support they need when they are about to leave prison and for the first few weeks following their release. Most prisoners have little choice but to return to the unfortunate situations they came out of. I am convinced that if good aftercare supports were available in the community, many prisoners would not reoffend. Lack of aftercare is costing us a fortune.

When I look back at it, I still find it hard to believe that a programme that clearly made a huge difference to the person who should count most of all in the prison service – the prisoner – was sabotaged by all sorts of vested interests. And the biggest let-down of all was the failure of strong leadership by the people in charge in the prison service. Why the project was allowed to die by the IPS only they can answer, but I believe it was a huge opportunity missed and a huge waste of public money. As for the politicians – who used the Connect Project time and again for political purposes, launching this and that report – they were nowhere to be seen.

Recently the IPS has introduced a new scheme – Integrated Sentence

Management. It is bound to fail because the prisoner is not directly
involved in the process. Once structures are in place, prisoners will
respond. But at the very start it is essential that staff get to know the
prisoner, and that won't happen unless the prisoner is involved in the
whole process – and certainly not if he is walking around a yard all
day.

22. Thornton Hall

When I joined the prison service in 1968, it was a small service with just three prisons – Limerick, Mountjoy and Portlaoise – and one detention centre, St Patrick's Institution. There were 420 adult prisoners and 196 boys serving detention, giving a total of 616 prisoners in the whole country. And there were only 330 staff working in the service. In 2010 there were thirteen prisons and one detention centre, well over 4,000 prisoners in custody and several hundred out on temporary release, and 3,600 prison staff, not including specialists like teachers, probation officers, doctors, psychologists, chaplains, counsellors and psychiatrists.

The massive increase in prisoner numbers is something that few are monitoring, analysing and questioning. Indeed, in recent years Ministers for Justice have boasted about how many extra prison places they have created. Every extra prison space created over the last twenty years has been swallowed up, and as new cell blocks become available, all single cells are doubled up even before the blocks are opened and officially called prison places.

In my early days, putting two prisoners into a cell was seen as undesirable and was never allowed. Currently there are hundreds of prisoners doubled up in single cells. Doubling-up prisoners on a wide scale is fundamentally wrong and is putting vulnerable prisoners at serious risk of sexual abuse, physical abuse, bullying and mental illness. The IPS simply ignores all the advice and evidence, and drives on regardless. The spin is that prisoners who are doubled up do it by agreement; however, nothing could be further from the truth. Most prisoners hate doubling up. The system is in such a chaotic state because of overcrowding that in places like Mountjoy, Cork and Cloverhill, there is no way that staff can carefully select which prisoners to double up; it's done very much on a hit-and-miss basis. We now know how scandalously children in state care were treated and neglected from the 1930s onwards and the terrible damage it did. If the present policy of doubling up isn't stopped, the same type of scandal may well re-occur in future decades and people will again be asking, 'How did it happen?'

In my last decade in Mountjoy, five prisoners died because of inju-ries received in attacks in the prison. In two of these cases, overcrowding was a significant factor. On 23 April 2000, Thomas Brady was stabbed in his sleep by his cellmate. They were good friends and appeared to get on well together, but one night the other prisoner claimed that he heard voices and he ended up stabbing Thomas when he was asleep. It was a deeply traumatic event which highlighted one of the real dangers of doubling up prisoners in single cells. Thomas's cellmate was found guilty in the courts and sentenced to life imprison-ment.

The incident highlights a particular danger with overcrowding – its effect on prisoners who are mentally ill and the dangers that poses. Dr Paul O'Mahony's research in 1996 found that one in four prisoners had an inpatient history in a psychiatric hospital and that 40 per cent had some contact with psychiatric services. The biggest problem towards the end of my time as governor of Mountjoy was not with the services in the prison – we had a very good in-house psychiatric service – but that there weren't enough beds to cater for the needs of the mentally ill in prison.

At the start of my service it was unknown for a prisoner who was certified insane not to be transferred immediately to the local psychi-atric hospital or to the Central Mental Hospital. But local psychiatric hospitals have withdrawn from almost any involvement with prison-ers – their attitude seems to be that they have no responsibility for prisoners, even if they are from their catchment area. That leaves a massively increased prison population totally dependent on the Central Mental Hospital for all inpatient services. However, the Central Mental Hospital has not had a corresponding increase in beds – the clinical director there, Professor Harry Kennedy, says that twenty extra beds are required for this purpose – and therefore cannot provide inpatient services on demand. As a result, a regular feature of prison during my service was that a prisoner would spend two, three and – on occasions – four weeks in a padded cell in Mountjoy awaiting a bed in the CMH.

On 31 July 2006, Gary Douche was attacked and beaten to death in the cell he was sharing with six other prisoners. It was a holding cell that was being used to accommodate prisoners, again because of over-crowding. There has been a court case regarding the attack, the court has made a decision and the man responsible has been dealt with by the law, but as Minister Michael McDowell ordered an independent enquiry into this case which is still going on, I will not make any further comment except to say that there is no doubt in my mind that the fundamental reason why that incident happened, like the Thomas Brady case, was overcrowding. If there were an adequate number of single cells available in Mountjoy to deal with the number of prisoners in custody, neither incident would have happened.

To complicate matters further, there is the relatively new phenomenon of prisoners on protection. During my time in Mount-joy, the number of prisoners on protection went from zero to well over 100. Protection prisoners are usually feuding gang members, sex offenders, and those who owe money for drugs, who have to be sep-arated from the main prisoner population. In addition, some of those on protection have to be kept separated from each other. At times in Mountjoy there were up to a dozen factions who all had to be kept separate, a logistical nightmare. If members of two feuding gangs somehow met – say if a prisoner was coming back from a family visit and another prisoner on protection was making a telephone call on the landing, or if through human error an officer let a prisoner out of his cell at the wrong time – the level of violence among them was shocking and savage. A prisoner could be grabbed in the exercise yard by three or four other prisoners and within a few seconds his face would be ripped apart from ear to mouth.

Keeping prisoners under protection meant that they spent between twenty-three and twenty-four hours every day locked up in their cells, mostly doubled up. How they didn't crack up I don't know. Prisons were never intended for this type of prisoner. The days of the big cell blocks of fifty or sixty prisoners are coming to an end. The prisons of the future will need to have much smaller cell blocks to provide not only safe and secure accommodation for protection prisoners but also work and recreational facilities for them.

At the other extreme of the prison population are those committed for non-payment of fines. In 2009, 1,500 people committed to Mountjoy – over 40 per cent of all committals –were imprisoned for their failure to pay fines. Some days up to twenty of them turned up, sentenced from anything from a few days to three months. Though the government is enacting legislation to prevent people being jailed for non-payment of fines, there is a need for an amnesty for all warrants already issued or these prisoners will continue to haunt prisons for many years to come. Once we decide that no one will be imprisoned for non-payment of a fine, we might also consider ways and means of punishing people who have offended in other relatively minor ways – deductions from social welfare, community service and charity work.

Overcrowding is not just about beds, as the IPS seems to think. The daily regime in prisons is seriously impoverished as a direct result of overcrowding, and prisons are now just warehousing offenders. If current trends continue, prisons will be little more than centres of human degradation and stand no chance of ever becoming places where prisoners can be set on a better path.

In December 1999, a Mountjoy redevelopment group was set up by the director general of the IPS, Seán Aylward, and he asked me to chair the group. I was told that I could appoint whoever I wished. The terms of reference were to look at the whole Mountjoy complex, which included Mountjoy Prison, St Patrick's Institution, the Training Unit and the Dóchas Centre, to assess its suitability or otherwise for re-development, outline a philosophy that should underpin any future redevelopment, and identify the principles of the prison regime that should operate in the new prison. We were asked to report by early summer 2000.

I assembled a group with a wide experience of the prison service. Included were a number of prison governors; officials from the IPS and the Department of Justice; the coordinators of work and training and education; the psychology and probation services; City of Dublin VEC and teachers; PACE (Prisoners' Aid through Community Effort), an organization that provides accommodation for prisoners leaving prison; two architects from the Office of Public Works; and representatives from the IPS Training and Development Centre and the Prison Officers' Association. An official from the IPS acted as secretary to the group.

We produced our first report in May 2000. The main conclusion was that the complex had the potential to be developed in a cohesive way and could provide approximately 800 places. We said that while the current site had its disadvantages, it also had a lot going for it: it was owned by the state; it was already a working prison and there were no major difficulties with the local community; the location was ideal for visitors; emergency services such as a hospital and gardaí were close by; and great savings could be made by integrating the existing four facilities on the site into one large one, so that, for example, there was one large kitchen instead of four.

Minister John O'Donoghue had appointed a Prison Authority Interim Board the previous year and the board accepted the report at its meeting in June. Seán Aylward told us to draw up a more detailed report including an outline development plan for the complex. In February 2001 we presented a comprehensive document with an outline design and development plan. The proposed design was very innovative and a total change from the old prison. It included an induction facility, accommodation for young people, two secure blocks for adult prisoners and a pre-release facility to replace the Training Unit. All the services would be located in a central hub, giving easy access to all the prisoners no matter where they were located in the complex. The cell blocks would provide most of the boundary wall, leaving a good amount of open space and providing much more natural light.

As chairman of the redevelopment group I was invited to present the report to the interim board's meeting in March 2001. The board accepted the report in full and recommended it to the minister. Seán Aylward told me a few weeks later that the minister had accepted the contents of the report, that we should now get on with it and start the work, and that the minister didn't want any more reports, only action. In early July, I had a meeting with three architects from the Office of Public Works (OPW) and officials from the IPS, and I had the impression that it was all guns blazing now towards the tendering stage.

Then, totally out of the blue, at a meeting with department officials on 16 August, they said that some part of the project needed to get going straight away as the minister wanted the work to be underway before he left office. They asked if there were any plans advanced enough to go to tender immediately – meaning any plans that were knocking around from before this process started, plans that, by definition, should now be redundant.

A number of years previously, plans had been drawn up to build a new main entrance into Mountjoy to create more room for lorries and heavy vehicles to enter the prison. To build the new gate, the old Governor's House, where the general office for the prison was located, would have to be partly demolished. But these plans were drawn up years earlier, and the new plans had the main gate leading into the proposed central hub. The officials mentioned revisiting the former proposal. Naturally, I totally opposed this and said so. I said it was disgraceful to even think of doing such a thing in the middle of the plans to redevelop the whole complex.

In a meeting with department officials in September, I was told that the minister had decided to go ahead with building the new gate, but they wanted to build it at the very front of the old prison, facing out towards the North Circular Road. This would require the main staff locker room to be demolished and a new one built.

After I got over the shock, I pointed out that if the gate was located in the front of the prison, traffic would be coming in straight towards the area where all prison visits are held. For noise, safety and security reasons it would be impossible to continue to hold these visits. We had a heated debate, to put it mildly, and I asked that my reservations, and indeed the reservations of the development group, be conveyed to the minister.

I heard nothing further until January 2002. At a meeting about other matters, Seán Aylward told me that there was another change of plan: the two front wings of the prison facing the North Circular Road – A and D wings – would not now be included in any refurbishment; they were going to be retained for historical reasons. The rest of the redevelopment was to go ahead on the remainder of the grounds.

I pointed out that there was no way this could be done if the front of the old prison was excluded, as the A and D wings accounted for over half of the entire site. I feared the worst at that stage and felt that the redevelopment of Mountjoy was dead in the water.

On 4 February an official from the IPS told me that the replacement of the main gate was going ahead at an estimated cost of €8 million. Once again I strongly opposed it and pointed out that it bore no relationship to the new plans and would have no real function because of the prison's layout at that time. Three weeks later I got a phone call from an IPS official who said that at the official opening of the new IPS headquarters in Clondalkin on 8 April, Minister O'Donoghue was going to announce that the Mountjoy development was going ahead and that he had given approval for the first phase, this first phase now being the building of the new gate which had nothing to do with the original plan. As far as I could see, the development that was going to be announced was not the one that was originally submitted or agreed, and there were no new plans to take on board the decision to retain the A and D wings of the old building nor the building of the gate.

It had all the signs of a cock-up and a shambles. A few days after that phone call – on 29 February – I attended another meeting with a number of officials, including an OPW architect. I said the new strategy was a waste of public money and that unless the final decision was made about the Mountjoy redevelopment plan, and unless it was part of an overall plan, there was no way that a new main gate should go ahead. I said it would be madness to demolish the main locker room to make way for it.

My opposition and my vehemence were not appreciated. On 8 April, Minister O'Donoghue made his speech in Clondalkin detailing all his department had done and would continue to do to improve the prison service. It included the plan to rebuild the gate at Mountjoy. The general election was less than six weeks away.

On 8 May there was another meeting, this time to prepare for the commencement of the building of the new gate. Once again I said I could not and would not be associated with the process and I wanted my opposition recorded. It was a disaster and would make a total farce of the proposed redevelopment of the complex, as well as being a total waste of public money.

In June, Michael McDowell took over as Minister for Justice and he obviously had a different approach as there was no more talk about the plan to rebuild the gate for the rest of 2002.

The following 24 January, an official from the IPS phoned me to say that an engineer, Paul Forde, had been appointed to carry out an assessment regarding the refurbishment of the prison. I knew Paul, and I assumed he would come to the prison to discuss the pros and cons of the whole thing with me and other senior staff. When I hadn't heard from him by early February, I rang him. 'Paul, when you're in the prison the next time will you call up and see me? I would like to talk to you about the refurbishment. I've major reservations about refurbishing the A and D wings as it would ruin the whole concept of the redevelopment plan.'

His response was not what I expected and made me feel that I was now being left out of the loop. He said he was having a meeting with the IPS the following week, and would mention to them that I wanted to meet him, and call in to see me after that.

On 1 April the chief trades officer in Mountjoy called to my office and told me that he had received a phone call from an IPS official saying that the next day he would be visiting the prison with two guests and he wanted access to all areas. The chief trades officer asked, 'Does the governor know about this visit?' He replied, 'No, you tell him.' When the chief trades officer asked the purpose of their visit, the official said that he was not free to say.

The three men came in, walked around the prison and never came near my office or spoke with me. Later I heard that they were in to value the site. Sometime later again, I discovered from a source in the IPS that the Minister for Justice had asked the Prison Authority Interim Board to examine the feasibility or otherwise of developing Mountjoy, St Patrick's Institution, the Training Unit and the Dóchas Centre as a complex and that the board had formed a subcommittee to look at the whole thing. It was the exact same brief as the group set up by Seán Aylward in December 1999 and chaired by me. The subcommitee never visited the prison and never spoke to me or any of the staff at Mount-joy.

Towards the end of April 2003 I got a letter from the IPS enclosing a copy of Paul Forde's report for my information. I didn't read it. I just readdressed the envelope and sent it straight back to the official who had sent it to me. I wrote on the envelope that it was outrageous to send me a report into which I had had no input.

A few weeks later I heard – again, on the grapevine – that the Prison Authority Interim Board had made a decision: Mountjoy and the Training Unit should be demolished; St Patrick's Institution and the Dóchas Centre should be retained; part of the site should be sold off; and a new 'greenfield' site should be purchased to accommodate a new prison. By the time I heard about it the report had been approved by the Prison Authority Interim Board, accepted by the minister and was on its way to government for approval.

I wrote to the director general of the IPS protesting at my exclusion from the whole process. I said that as governor of Mountjoy Prison I believed I had a right to be involved and that I was being deliberately excluded. I said that as far as I was concerned this was a case of bully-ing, as under the civil service guidelines excluding a person from a process that they had a right to be involved in was an act of bullying. Seán Aylward spoke to me about it during a meeting at IPS headquar-ters, and he subsequently wrote to me. The gist of his response was that there was no question of being deliberately excluded and it was just an oversight.

A few days later I got a copy of the subcommittee's report in the post. It was as crazy as I had heard: they proposed to demolish the Training Unit – a relatively recent (1975), purpose-built facility with great educational and training amenities and excellent workshops – while retaining St Patrick's Institution, a Victorian building that was nothing more than a prison for juveniles. In my response I said that asking for my views at that stage was a charade and I believed the decision to relocate was already made. I was right.

In August 2003 Michael McDowell visited Mountjoy. He walked around some of the prison and in particular the B division. He turned to me at one stage and said, 'I haven't decided yet whether Mountjoy is staying or going, but if it stays I intend to put toilets in all the cells and that will be it. I don't go along with this idea that if you're putting in toilets you have to put in new windows and doors and all sorts of other refurbishments.' As he walked on I said to myself, *You'll put no toilets into Mountjoy on their own, because if you bore holes in the walls to put in sewerage pipes, the whole prison will collapse, especially the walls of the cells – they're built with old-fashioned bricks and mortar.* Prisoners could bore holes from one cell to the other with a spoon, so you could imagine what it would be like if big holes for piping had to be bored through the whole prison: it would just fall apart. I didn't share this with him because he did not invite my opinion. I'm sure he felt that he knew what was best.

In the summer of 2004 Minister McDowell appointed an expert group to select a suitable site for the new prison. I was not asked to be a member. Indeed, I only became aware of its existence by accident a few months later.

The Department of Justice placed advertisements looking for a 100-acre site within ten to fifteen kilometres of Mountjoy. Thirty-one offers were received. The expert group examined them and for one reason or another they were all found to be unsuitable: too big, too small, too costly, in the wrong location, and so on. Then, at a meeting of the expert group on 18 January 2005, a new site was put forward, a farm called Thornton Hall, which had been offered to the IPS shortly before Christmas – less than a month earlier. This site was 150 acres, one and a half times the size of what was originally advertised. The IPS had an offer on the table for €199,000 per acre – almost €30 million in total. At the meeting, without some members of the expert group ever seeing the site, the decision was made to recommend the purchase of Thornton Hall.

On 26 January 2005 I was out driving when I heard a report on the one o'clock radio news that a site had been purchased for the replacement of Mountjoy Prison. Two minutes later I got a telephone call from an official at the IPS. He said the Minister for Justice was about to announce that he had approved the purchase of a site to replace Mountjoy.

'I know,' I said.

'How do you know? Who told you?' he said. 'It's not being announced until three o'clock.'

'I've just heard it on the news,' I said.

Questions continue to be asked – rightly – about the process through which Thornton Hall was acquired. Why the rush in doing the deal? The land was zoned for agricultural use, but the price paid was more in line with prices paid for development land. No investigations so far have come up with satisfactory explanations for the peculiar sequence of events. On top of everything else, quite late in the day the property advisor the IPS had retained to help it find the site discovered he had a distant family relationship to the farmer who owned Thornton Hall, and while he offered to withdraw from the process, his offer was turned down. At a Dáil Public Accounts Committee meeting held in October 2006, when the Controller and Auditor General's report on Thornton Hall was under discussion, Fianna Fáil TD Seán Fleming said, 'I must publicly congratulate Mr Aylward and everyone on his side of the table on achieving outstanding value for money in obtaining a prison site at €200,000 per acre in the Dublin area. One would not obtain sites for Government purposes in Portlaoise, Mountrath or any provincial town at that price. In the long term this will be considered an outstanding achievement.' That more or less sums up the logic behind the deal.

My understanding is that over €41 million has been spent on the site so far; that is, until the summer of 2010. On 27 July 2010 the Minister for Justice, Dermot Ahern, announced that the building of the prison would be phased in over a number of years, targeting 2014 as the most likely date to have the first phase of 400 security cells ready for use. He indicated that a further 1,000 cells would be provided in later phases.

In announcing that the 400 new cells would accommodate 700 prisoners, the minister clearly signalled that the doubling up of prisoners is now official policy. This is one of the most backward steps ever taken in the Irish prison service. In the nineteenth century, prison managements established as best practice that prisons would be based on single cell occupancy. They knew then that having more than one prisoner to a cell placed individuals at risk of physical and sexual abuse. In addition, they accepted that for many reasons, not least their sanity, prisoners need their own space. I hope that human rights organizations – including the Council of Europe's Committee for the Prevention of Torture – will oppose this regressive move.

A number of other important issues were raised by the minister's announcement. He indicated that even when phase one of Thornton is completed, Mountjoy will continue to operate. For years the official position has been that when Thornton Hall is up and running the Mountjoy complex will be phased out, so this represents a fundamental shift in policy. It is depressing to think that Mountjoy will continue in its present condition indefinitely.

Moreover, it appears that nobody is alarmed at the explosion in prison numbers. The official position seems to be onwards and upwards, with no indication of any concern about the increase in cost – both financial and human. And finally, when the minister says that 400 cells will be ready for occupation in 2014, does this mean that all the other vital infrastructure will also be provided, like kitchens, workshops, education facilities, medical services and so on? Will it be sufficient to service 2,200 prisoners in the long term, or will this be another case of inadequate piecemeal development? And how much of the land will be enclosed by the perimeter wall? Just imagine 150 acres of land surrounded by a high wall.

To cap it all, after the acquisition of Thornton Hall, the Office of Public Works got the chequebook out again to acquire a premises next door to Mountjoy, Egan's Cash and Carry. The idea was to augment the Mountjoy site and increase its appeal for possible purchasers. Rumour had it that it cost something in the order of €28.4 million. Now that the property market has collapsed, its value has also collapsed. So the taxpayer has once again lost out and the chances of ever getting back the cost of this land are very slim.

The tragedy is that the Mountjoy complex could have been re-developed to a very high standard and completed many years ago, providing excellent secure accommodation for 800 to 900 prisoners.

As for my exclusion from the process that led to the purchase of

Thornton Hall, the only explanation I can come up with is that because I had so strongly opposed the building of the new main gate at Mountjoy, officials believed that I would also have strongly opposed closing down Mountjoy and moving to a greenfield site. In fact, I was quite neutral on it. There were good arguments for and against.

The main argument for moving to a greenfield site was that it creates more options. I agree with that. And the space is a big plus, though there is absolutely no need for 150 acres. Also, building at Thornton Hall will be able to proceed without the complications of doing it alongside a busy working prison. On the other hand, the word is that to access the site they're going to have to build a new road, which will be costly.

As for the 'against' arguments, first there is location. Losing the proximity to services like hospitals, the fire brigade and the gardaí is a big drawback. It will also be very inconvenient for the families going to visit. Most visitors will have to take at least three separate bus trips to reach the new location — that's assuming that when it opens there is a public transport link in place. For those bringing young children on visits and having to negotiate public transport, going to the prison will be a day's work.

Another concern that I have is the 'out of sight, out of mind' attitude that is evident in the approach to locating and developing Thornton Hall. One of the first things the IPS did after buying the site was to plant hundreds of trees all around it so that in a few years, when the trees mature, the prison won't even be seen from the road.

One of the most shameful aspects of how the relocation decision was made was the total lack of communication with the staff in Mountjoy. Not one person working in the Mountjoy complex, regardless of grade or role, received any communication from the minister or any official in the Department of Justice or the IPS informing them what was to happen regarding something that was of vital interest and importance to them.

There is no way that a project of the magnitude of Thornton Hall should be handed over to the Department of Justice or the IPS to design and build. I say this because of their spendthrift and unimaginative track record. With the exception of the Training Unit and the Dóchas Centre, there has been no innovation in the design of any of the other prison buildings constructed over the last thirty years. The prison service continues to build the same type of prisons, making no allowances for the changing profile of the prison population. For instance, it is mad to be building high-security cell blocks when 80 per cent of prisoners are serving sentences of two years or less. Mountjoy is a concrete jungle, Wheatfield and Cloverhill are now in a similar situation, and Portlaoise and the Midlands prisons are getting there. There appears to be no appreciation that open space is crucial in any prison.

I think few prison practitioners over the last thirty years or so will disagree with me when I say that overall the prison building programme has been most frustrating and, in many instances, a disaster. Buildings have had to be redesigned, often two or three times. By far the biggest scourge is changing direction in midstream: a building is designed for one purpose, but midway through construction there's a change of plan. Another scandal is when contractors are brought into a prison to do a job, usually refurbishment, without detailed plans or specifications being in place. This is always a contractor's delight: once the job starts, the contractor is in total control and the sky is the limit. Over the years the prison service was, and still is, the goose that lays the golden egg to the building industry. Some prison governors must also shoulder the blame for much of this waste, as individual governors often demand changes to buildings when they are close to completion. This is most likely to happen when there is a change of governor: the new governor immediately disagrees with his predecessor and demands changes to the whole building. Building designs should be agreed at national level and not be subject to the whims of individual governors or officials. God only knows how much all of this bungling has cost the taxpayer over the years, but I'm certain that it runs into many millions.

23. The Politicians

During my time as a prison governor, eleven politicians held the office of Minister for Justice. I was always amused when people asked, 'What's the minister like?' or, when the prison service was in the news, 'Why don't you tell the minister what you have told us?' or 'What does the minister say about this when you meet with him?' From the frequency of such questions I can only assume that people will be surprised to learn that, despite being the most senior prison governor in the country for twenty-six years, I never met any Minister for Justice for a formal one-to-one briefing or a private discussion. There were of course meetings with other officials present, and occasional casual conversations, but nothing more structured and focused ever happened.

Civil servants see it as exclusively their role to deal directly with ministers, and they do everything in their power to maintain this situation. It gives them power, influence and control. This situation also suits the politicians because they know their best interests are being looked after and their civil servants are doing their utmost to protect them from controversy and problems. Key to this is controlling the flow of information to ministers.

In my experience only one Minister for Justice ever broke free of his civil servants and that was one occasion when he was in the early stages of his ministry and hadn't been fully indoctrinated. After an incident in Mountjoy in 1997, John O'Donoghue phoned me to ask for a briefing. I was delighted at this extraordinary development and thought, *Things are going to change at last*. Around the same time he called the governor of Portlaoise over an issue there. However, it didn't last. John O'Donoghue was reined in very quickly and the status quo resumed.

During his predecessor Nora Owen's term she set up an advisory group to review drug treatment in the prison service. It was chaired by a senior civil servant. The group recommended that the probation and welfare service should be given the lead role in delivering drug-treatment programmes. I totally disagreed and wrote a four-page submission putting forward my arguments against the group's conclusions and making a number of recommendations. A few weeks later at a meeting of the group, the chairman announced that the minister had accepted the recommendations of the advisory group. 'Did the minister read my submission?' I asked.

'It was in the file,' the chairman said.

'I don't care about where it was,' I said. 'What I want to know is did the minister actually read it?'

'It was in the file,' he repeated.

Of course it was in the file, buried at the bottom of it. I knew there and then that making submissions to ministers was a waste of energy. There was no way that somebody outside the fold would be allowed to get to the minister.

Being known as a safe pair of hands is a huge advantage if you have any ambition in the civil service. And the top priority for the ambitious senior civil servant is to ensure the minister is seen in a positive light. One senior civil servant used to say to me, 'I want to pull together a little package for the minister soon.' The little package was always the opening or launching of something – anything where the minister was at the centre of the action, taking all the credit. In the prison service they sometimes opened the same facility a second or third time, especially if an election was coming up.

My experience with the drug-treatment advisory group revealed to me just how self-interested the whole system was. The probation and welfare service made a submission that it would be able to deliver a comprehensive drug-treatment programme for Mountjoy without additional expenditure. I knew there and then that its programme would not be worth a spit. My suspicions turned out to be well founded: it was nothing other than a mishmash. Three separate treatment services, all excellent operations in their own ways, were to be involved. The trouble was that they had entirely different addiction and treatment philosophies. I argued that any credible programme for Mountjoy had to have a single clear philosophy and strategy underpinning it; otherwise prisoners would be confused. At the meeting no one backed me up, but on the way out those representing one of the treatment services pulled me aside to say they agreed with me but as they were so dependent on funding from the probation and welfare system, they didn't dare stand up to the consensus of the group.

In due course, and with great fanfare, there was an official opening by Minister Owen of the new drug-treatment programme in the Training Unit, the first ever in the Irish prison service. It was that thing of wonder – a programme that cost nothing. Well, almost nothing: a new urinal was installed to assist urine testing. Far more was spent on the official opening. For years afterwards there wasn't even one drug counsellor available to the drug-addicted prisoners in the Training Unit.

My obvious lack of interest in playing along with these kinds of charades meant that I was written off by many civil servants. The system operates on the basis that political expediency is the first thing to be considered when any idea or proposal is put forward; the idea's usefulness to those actually in the service – prisoners and staff – comes a poor second at best. And often what's in the best interest of the political system or the minister is not in the best interest of the prison service. The senior civil servant is expert in managing this and ensuring that the minister's political interests are looked after first. With all of that at the top of their agenda, they saw me as nothing more than a maverick and they actually said as much on a number of occasions. 'Lonergan wouldn't understand the political dimensions to these types of decisions; he only sees the prison side.'

Though in latter years it was perfectly obvious that key officials had little time for my input and no respect for my approach to things, there was never any attempt to get rid of me. I knew, though, that I was on thin ice and that if anything serious went wrong in Mountjoy it would have been the end of the road for me.

Having said all that about the limitations of my relationship with ministers, I can also say that I saw enough of them – or, tellingly, didn't – to form opinions about their level of engagement with their role and their priorities.

Michael Noonan appointed me to the job in Mountjoy. Whenever

I met him, which was seldom, I always found him to be a friendly and decent man. As I have described earlier, I saw his steely side when we had a series of suicides in the prison in 1985. In a few words he made it very clear that my neck was on the line. As I had deployed extra night guards, had talked to staff about how vital it was for them to be on full alert for unusual behaviour and had got the Samaritans in to provide staff training on suicide prevention – and as, short of confining every prisoner to a padded cell, suicides cannot be completely prevented in prisons – I felt I was responding as proactively as I could, and had a sense of urgency about the problem that was at least as great as the minister's, and probably far greater.

Michael Noonan's successor, Alan Dukes, was a true statesman in the office. For the year or so that he was there he worked exclusively in an independent and objective way. He didn't care whether a prisoner was from his own area, from his constituency in County Kildare or from Timbuktu: he read the files himself, he evaluated the various observations and recommendations and then he made his decision, totally impartially. At one meeting with governors he said, 'I can't understand the contradictions between garda reports and a prison governor's report; they are usually the complete opposite to each other.' We explained that the gardaí were dealing with the offender in the community, often in the immediate aftermath of the crime, whereas governors were dealing with him or her in a completely different environment, often years later. He said, 'I understand', and from that day on he balanced these opposing perspectives.

My only regret about Alan Dukes is that he wasn't in the Department of Justice long enough. I say that although I strongly disagreed with him when he was in office. He was an establishment man and completely opposed the Whitaker Commission's recommendation to separate the management of the prison service from the Department of Justice. He believed strongly that the Department of Justice should continue to hold total control over the day-to-day operation of the prison service. At that time, in 1986, a year after the Whitaker Report was published, I was a strong advocate for its recommendations and indeed lobbied for their implementation. Nearly twenty-five years on – with the benefit of hindsight and having experienced eleven years of working in the new but fundamentally flawed independent IPS – I have no hesitation in saying that Alan Dukes was right.

Gerry Collins took over from Alan Dukes. He had at least one eye on the political consequences or benefits of everything he did. During the strike in 1988 when he visited Mountjoy, he spent more time talking with the striking officers than he did with the staff on duty. And in the aftermath of the strike, when a number of officers who had worked through the strike and were expelled from the POA as a consequence asked to meet him to talk about their difficulties in work, he refused – on the grounds that he could only meet the official representative body of prison officers, the POA.

Two things about Ray Burke's spell as minister have remained with me. In an address to staff in the aftermath of the 1991 riot at Mountjoy, he referred to the prisoners as 'thugs and scumbags'. I was in Portlaoise at the time, but I heard about it afterwards and I was astounded that the minister would use such crude language about the prisoners. It was a terrible example to set his staff.

Second, he set up the first ever sentence-review group, chaired by Dr Ken Whitaker, to review the sentences of long-term prisoners. This was a progressive step because over the years of the Northern troubles a big backlog of long-term prisoners had built up and there was an urgent need to move them on. This was particularly true in Portlaoise. At the end of the meeting in which he briefed the governors about the new initiative, he invited us to raise any other issues we had. I said we believed it was time to build a new independent women's prison. He turned to an official and said, 'Take a note of that, and when we are refurbishing St Patrick's do something in the women's prison.'

I said, 'Minister, we are not talking about refurbishing a wing of St Patrick's Institution; we are talking about building a completely new modern prison.'

His expression darkened and I knew he was annoyed. He turned to the governor of Arbour Hill Prison and said, 'How are things in Arbour Hill?'

Ray Burke was replaced by Pádraig Flynn in 1992. I never met Pádraig Flynn. I never spoke with him and he never visited Mountjoy.

Máire Geoghegan-Quinn took over from Pádraig Flynn in 1993.

She was the first female Minister for Justice, and on her second day in office she came straight to Mountjoy to visit the women's prison. I was impressed that she prioritized female prisoners so early in her office. To this day I admire her for the compassion she showed towards female prisoners and for her decisiveness in making the right decision to build decent facilities for them. On a personal basis I found her very friendly. She used to tell me off for calling women 'girls'.

Nora Owen carried on where Máire Geoghegan-Quinn left off. The building of the women's prison was deferred on a number of occasions, but she steered it through and eventually got government approval to go ahead and build it. Though she had moved on from the Department of Justice by the time it opened, she remained supportive of the new prison and continued to support it even after she left politics.

As a minister she was conscious of her image as a politician. I asked her to open the new kitchen in Mountjoy in 1995, but she turned me down saying that it would only attract negative publicity and accusations that hotel-style catering was going on in the prison. It might well have got that kind of coverage. My view was that it was up to the minister to give leadership, and events like this were an opportunity to challenge the public in its views about what prisoners should and shouldn't get, and to say that it was official policy that prisoners get decent and well-cooked basic food and that this was the civilized thing to do. Mountjoy was constantly being criticized for poor facilities, and this was a lost opportunity to counteract this image. She also missed an opportunity to do something fundamentally right around drug treatment, accepting a Mickey Mouse proposal from the probation and welfare service, supporting it and implementing it. Perhaps she didn't recognize quite how woefully inadequate that proposal was. On a personal level Nora Owen was a nice, kind, approachable and good-natured woman, however, and a good Minister for Justice.

When Nora Owen was the minister her opposite number, John O'Donoghue, came up with the spurious notion of a 'zero tolerance' to crime, and it went down a treat with the general public. He gave Nora Owen a tough time all through her period as Minister for Justice and then took over the office himself in June 1997 and spent five years in the Department. For all his bluster, on all occasions I met him I found John O'Donoghue to be very different from his public image – an image, of course, created mainly by himself. He attended a number of our annual plays in Mountjoy, took a genuine interest in the prisoners and in his contact with them showed a humanity, a kindness and a compassion that was as impressive as it was unexpected.

My first ever encounter with Michael McDowell took place in Blackhall Place many years before he became Minister for Justice. We were both taking part in a debate about crime. He was a backbench TD at the time and during the debate he said, 'I believe that prison should be a place of punishment and that prisoners should be punished while in prison. I don't go along with the view that going to prison is in itself sufficient punishment.'

In response I said, 'I totally disagree with you', and explained why. I ended my remarks by saying, 'For that reason alone I hope Michael McDowell will never be Minister for Justice.'

A few minutes later he slipped me a note that read, 'I might be some day.'

I wrote on the back of it, 'And if you are I will serve you loyally.'

He became Minister for Justice in June 2002 and, of course, I went on to serve him loyally.

In a *Sunday Independent* interview in March 2010 Michael McDowell said that before he became attorney general and then Minister for Justice, he was 'prejudiced against' the public service. He certainly was. I heard him criticize it myself in that Blackhall Place debate. But he said that after he became attorney general and then Minister for Justice he changed his mind. Indeed he did.

No one ever fitted into the system like Michael McDowell; he just became the system. During his term, prison governors asked to meet with him once to discuss a difficulty they were having about their pay. But when we told the director general of the IPS that we intended to seek a meeting with the minister, he told us that he was totally opposed to the minister seeing us on the issue. Sure enough, when the Association of Higher, Civil and Public Servants wrote to the minister's office requesting a meeting, the reply came back that he was refusing to meet us and we should deal directly with the director general of the IPS. It was the first time I could recall a Minister for Justice refusing to meet prison governors.

In my view, Michael McDowell changed his position on the civil service because civil servants changed their position on him. That night in Blackhall Place he told us a story about being left sitting in a waiting room for ages when he visited the Department of Justice on business one day. When he was no longer a backbencher, but their boss, that all changed. No wonder he had an epiphany about the virtues of the public service and could see how hard-working his officials were.

Brian Lenihan never visited Mountjoy while he was Minister for Justice, and I never met with him or spoke with him during his term as minister. While I had no dealings with him, the vibes coming from the Department were good. A number of important decisions in the cases of a few long-term and high-profile prisoners were long overdue when Brian Lenihan took up office, and he dealt with them speedily and decisively within days. He let it be known that the facts should be presented to him in all cases and that he would make up his mind based on the facts, and that he wasn't interested in precedent. I honestly believe that if he had been in the Department for longer he would have left his mark.

In May 2008, Brian Lenihan was replaced by Dermot Ahern. Up to the time of my retirement in June 2010, Dermot Ahern did not visit Mountjoy. I never met him or spoke to him. I think that summarizes Dermot Ahern's interest in and commitment to prisons.

When we were drawing up the invitation list for the Dóchas Centre's tenth anniversary celebration in November 2009, naturally we included Máire Geoghegan-Quinn and Nora Owen. An IPS official told us that the Minister for Justice could not attend the event. He also said that the minister did not want either Máire Geoghegan-Quinn or Nora Owen to be invited, especially when he himself wouldn't be there. We decided to ignore the official and we invited them both. I was delighted to see Nora Owen in attendance.

24. A Service Going Backwards

The natural dynamic in a prison is one of mistrust. In prison nobody really trusts anybody: prisoners don't trust one another, they don't trust the system and they don't trust the prison staff. Equally, members of prison staff don't trust the prisoners and often they don't trust one another. Finally, prison management doesn't trust the prisoners and it doesn't trust staff. And currently, prison management itself isn't trusted by the IPS.

An absence of trust creates an environment of fear and insecurity, and human beings simply don't thrive in such an environment. There is no personal growth or development and little relaxation or enjoyment. When people feel trusted, they respond positively. Trying to create trust – in an environment where it might least be expected or fostered – was what guided my career in the prison service and what I tried to bring into my professional relationships, whether with staff, management, prisoners or their families.

However, this was always a struggle and at the end of my career I have to conclude that the day of prison governors working in healthy, positive environments, where they are trusted to do their jobs, is further away than ever. In fact, the job is all responsibility but with no real power, and it's very difficult to do the job when that's the case. The Irish prison governor has no control over the number of prisoners being committed to his prison; no control over the number of prisoners accommodated in his prison on any day or night; no power to release or transfer prisoners out of his prison; no power to refuse to take prisoners, irrespective of how overcrowded the prison is or whether he has suitable accommodation or indeed any accommodation at all for them; no control over the number of staff assigned to his prison, their recruitment and selection, and that goes from the most junior to the most senior – the governor must take what he gets; no control over the staff assigned to search staff and visitors at the main gate of his prison; no control over staff rosters; no power to discipline staff, except to record a warning, which can be appealed against to the minister; no control over the trades staff responsible for the maintenance of his prison; and no real control over any of the agencies providing services in his prison. He cannot allow anyone into the prison without approval; he cannot speak to the media about an internal issue without approval; he cannot change a telephone line without approval; he cannot buy a few tins of paint without approval; he cannot buy a desk or pocket diary without approval. I could go on.

This centralized, bureaucratic approach to management leads to ridiculous situations. For example, if a cooker in a prison kitchen breaks down, the prison must get approval from headquarters to have it fixed. On one occasion the Mountjoy trades officer was asked, 'Could you not wait until you have a couple more breakdowns before you call in the maintenance contractor?' The area of prison maintenance is in tatters, with qualified tradesmen on the prison staff now supervising contractors coming in to do the jobs that five years ago they used to do themselves. Stores staff in Mountjoy told me that diaries ended up costing much more after the instruction not to purchase them locally was issued.

The change in rostering arrangements back in 2005 was a massive propaganda victory for the Department of Justice and the IPS. All involved – but chiefly Minister McDowell – claimed huge kudos for eliminating overtime and driving down staffing costs. The reality was that though there was a small minority of staff who were almost obsessed with overtime, by the mid 2000s there was no huge interest in overtime at all and the prison service was almost unworkable because staff refused to do overtime. To resolve this sham issue, overtime was eliminated completely and many hundreds of new officers were recruited to plug the gaps in the system. There was little or no cost saving – indeed the cost of salaries and benefits likely outstripped the cost of overtime – but rigid new staff rosters removed all flexibility from local management in their staffing arrangements.

Unless a governor has financial control, or some real influence over financial resources, he cannot do the job properly. A governor should not have to beg for necessary resources to run his prison effectively, but that was the situation at times, certainly in latter years. If you weren't amenable and agreeable, you didn't get what you needed and then the changes and improvements you wanted to introduce could not happen. The official position in recent times was that despite serious cutbacks and a huge increase in prisoner numbers, it was the governor's responsibility to deliver results – regardless of whether, say, the prison was short of ten, twenty or fifty staff. From a control and accountability perspective it is very frustrating to have the responsibility for everything and power over nothing.

To add insult to injury, all the time governors' powers were being diminished there was a concerted effort to undermine the practice of delegation within prisons and to go back to a time when the governor was expected to do everything himself. An example was in August 2008, when for six months all governors of closed prisons were directed to stand at the main gates at 8 a.m. and 2 p.m. every day to oversee the introduction of staff searches. Officials seemed to have little appreciation of the purpose of delegation, and much of their thinking ran along the lines of, *You must nail somebody for everything and the higher up you go the more you nail them to the cross.*

A prison like Mountjoy, or indeed any organization, cannot work on that basis. It can only work when people are given responsibility and a clear brief, and the governor's job is to coordinate that brief and make sure that it is being done, but not to do it all himself. Though everything won't be perfect, it's the best way to develop people and to get the best out of them.

This brings me to the nub of the issue, the IPS. Right through this book I have been extremely critical of the IPS. Perhaps my level of criticism is commensurate with my level of disillusionment: the hopes I had that taking operational control of prisons out of the Department of Justice would mean huge improvements in the service have been bitterly disappointed. Instead, as I have outlined, the service has gone backwards.

The IPS came out of a 1996 government decision to take day-to-day operations of the courts and the prisons out of the Department of Justice and to set up two independent agencies to manage them. The government brought together an expert group to identify what was needed to establish an independent prisons agency. Prison governors were not invited to participate, and when we objected we were told we couldn't be included because the Prison Officers' Association wasn't invited to participate either.

Right through the 1980s and '90s I was a strong advocate for an independent prisons board with a chief executive reporting to it. The idea was that the Minister for Justice would continue to be responsible for policy, the board would be responsible to the minister for implementing the policy, and the chief executive would be responsible to the board for the day-to-day running of prisons.

In 1999 Minister John O'Donoghue appointed an interim prisons board with twelve members. He also announced the creation of a new post, director general of the prison service, to be filled by open competition. Seán Aylward, an assistant secretary in the Department of Justice, became the first director general of the IPS. Brian Purcell, director of operations of the IPS, took over as director general in 2004.

The board that was set up in 1999 was the worst of every world. As it was set up – and continues to operate – on an interim basis, it has no power, no authority and no direct role in the management of the prison service. Its role is solely advisory. The director general of the IPS is required to brief the board on his or her activities, but the board has no authority over the office. Instead, the director general reports to the Department of Justice. The de facto situation is that the IPS is an integral part of the Department, but at the same time is superficially independent of it. Yet another Irish solution to an Irish problem.

The main impetus for separating the prisons from the Department of Justice came from a key recommendation of the 1985 Whitaker Report that decision-making should be moved out of the Department of Justice and delegated to local prison management. If the Whitaker committee came back today it would get a major shock, because if anything decision-making has become more centralized.

To add to the frustration, there is no channel to raise issues. In the old system, if I had a problem as a governor, I could talk directly to a senior official in the Department and, depending on its seriousness, he would bring it to the notice of the minister and get a decision.

Within the current system I always felt alienated and isolated, as did many other governors. I was between a rock and a hard place: as governor of Mountjoy Prison I had no option but to accept what the IPS decided, irrespective of whether I agreed or disagreed. For instance, the IPS increased the official capacity of Mountjoy several times over the years without consultation or agreement. I had no structure to express concerns or grievances. If there was a statutory prisons board in place, it would change this situation and governors would have a forum to work out differences of opinion about issues in their prisons. A board would be a safety valve not just to governors but to all staff, prisoners and their families.

It was common for most of the governors I worked with over the years to be absolutely terrified of senior officials in the Department of Justice. The reasons are obvious: officials always got in first with their spin on things, and often this was – and still is – the only side that the minister heard. So if a governor had a run-in with a department official the consequences could be fairly serious.

In my early years as a prison governor we stood shoulder to shoulder with one another and insisted on at least being listened to. We had some great battles with officials, but I always knew that we would stand together no matter what. Not surprisingly, as the status of the prison governor was gradually eroded, that solidarity also eroded. Understandably people read the lie of the land and realized that they had to look after their own patches. By virtue of its management culture, the IPS had divided and conquered. One of my big disappointments on leaving the prison service is the lack of unity, loyalty and camaraderie among prison governors.

Staff, on the other hand, are lucky to have a strong union, the Prison Officers' Association, to protect them. Were it not for the POA, a number of Ministers for Justice and a larger number of officials in the Department of Justice and the IPS would have enjoyed dismantling and destroying the working conditions for prison staff at all grades, including prison governors.

The POA had been in existence for over twenty years before it began to have some influence in the late 1960s. Before that, officers were treated appallingly. The association had some rocky times, particularly in the late 1970s and '80s when there seemed to be a lot of belligerence and strife for its own sake. The POA today is a far more professional, better trained and more responsible organization, and for almost the last twenty years in Mountjoy I had excellent working relations with the branch officers.

Prison officers must be at the heart of everything that happens in the prison service. Prison officers deal with some very difficult prisoners, some of whom are aggressive, mentally disturbed, physically sick, chronically addicted or violent, and many of whom lack normal coping and survival skills. Add to that the horrible conditions prison officers are forced to work in, in prisons like Mountjoy, and it takes an exceptionally able, committed and talented person to be really good at the job. And the very good prison officer's work seldom comes to light because the good officer prevents things from happening by early and skilful intervention rather than by responding to trouble.

Unfortunately, one or two bad apples can discredit the whole service and people often only remember the disgruntled or abrupt officer. But over the years I received many letters from visitors praising the sensitivity and kindness of prison staff, and that's the way it should be. I met many caring and sensitive prison officers during my service – again, contrary to public perception. Many officers did wonderful work behind the scenes – low-profile stuff such as relating to prisoners, talking to them, encouraging them and being kind to them and their families. They formed relationships that went on for years and across generations. One evening a prisoner arrived at the main gate of the Dóchas Centre with a garda for committal. Two officers – one, Catherine, who had been in the job for nearly thirty years, and the other, just learning the ropes – went to get her. Catherine went straight over to the prisoner, threw her arms around her and gave her a big hug. The young officer was taken aback but said nothing. They went through the reception procedure with her: she was twenty, and it was her first time in prison. When she was finally put into her room for the night, the young officer asked Catherine why she had hugged her. Catherine said, 'I nursed her when she was a baby in the old prison.'

★

The IPS needs to look at the training of prison officers. Recruits still do their training working on the ground in prisons. However, now that their two-year training period is a course accredited by the Institute of Technology in Sligo, they also spend a few weeks a year in the classroom. This is a move in the right direction. Young men and women, recruited into the service in their early twenties and going straight on to the landings in prisons, are still, in many ways, totally unprepared for the type of atmosphere and the conditions they find themselves working in. They need educating about building up relationships with prisoners, understanding human behaviour, coping with violent and aggressive prisoners, preventing difficult situations rather than being forced to react to them, and how human rights apply to prisons and prisoners. It is very unfair that young people working in such a complex environment receive no follow-up training or development. They need ongoing training and support to ensure that they grow, mature and reach their potential.

There is also a need for ongoing training and developing at supervisory and management grades. Many staff members are put into responsible positions with little or no training and no preparation, and if they fail they are heavily criticized, which is grossly unfair. I am convinced that with better training and a greater emphasis on personal development, we would have a far more settled and peaceful prison service, with less aggression and less violence.

Officers need ongoing training, too, to cope in an increasingly challenging environment. Despite my years of experience I still found myself shocked and disturbed by events in the prison, particularly deaths of prisoners. One of the main functions of a prison is to provide safe and secure custody for all prisoners, and the death of a prisoner in custody was always very upsetting and challenging. It didn't really matter whether the death was accidental, from natural causes, or the result of a drug overdose, suicide, misadventure or stabbing.

Psychologists working in prisons have made a major difference to the lives of many vulnerable prisoners and helped them to develop the skills to cope with imprisonment. As a result there has been a big reduction in self-harm, suicides and self-mutilation. On the other hand, however, there has been a rise in the level of violent attacks between prisoners, and of the five violent deaths that occurred during my years running Mountjoy, all happened in the last decade. These were among the blackest and most devastating experiences of my career. Thomas Brady and Gary Douche I have already mentioned. On 27 January 2004 I was just leaving Glasnevin cemetery after a funeral when I got a call from Mountjoy to say that two prisoners had got into a fight on one of the landings in B wing and that one had been stabbed and taken to the Mater. A few minutes later there was another call to say that the man, Alan Greene, had died from his injuries. When I returned to the prison, the entire place seemed to be in a state of shock. And when it had sunk in, it became clear that this kind of incident – a knife attack on a landing – had terrifying implications.

As one of the cornerstones of the prison system is that prisoners are held in safe and secure custody, on this occasion I felt that the prison had failed and that I had failed the Greene family. I apologized publicly to the family for this failure. Some people in the IPS thought that it was not a wise decision to apologize, but I felt that it was the right thing to do. The then Inspector of Prisons, Mr Justice Kinlen, said that it was the first time that he ever saw a public servant accepting responsibility for such a thing, and he commended me for doing so.

On 26 July 2007 there was another fatal stabbing. Derek Glennon and a companion were walking up and down a yard, chatting away, apparently friendly, when the companion pulled a knife out of his pocket and stabbed Derek in the chest. Derek collapsed and died almost instantly. The prisoner responsible was charged and later convicted and sentenced for the offence. The attack on Derek Glennon was totally unpredictable and almost impossible to prevent: staff were close by, but they noticed nothing unusual until the actual stabbing occurred. The CCTV footage showed that the incident had apparently come out of nowhere.

A death like Derek Glennon's, combined with the massive increase in violence in the prison in recent years, presents real challenges for the new generation of prison officers. What was most frightening was the savagery of the stabbings and cuttings, and how little time it could take to do serious physical damage to a prisoner. One of the nastiest weapons was made by taking two small blades from a disposable safety razor and sticking one on each side of a toothbrush handle. The blades were usually welded into the handle by melting the handle with a cigarette lighter, leaving two parallel blades about a quarter of an inch apart. When this weapon was dragged across a face, the blades made a double cut that could not be stitched because the incisions were so close together.

On 9 June 2009, just before 7.30 p.m., David Byrne was struck on the side of the head with a sock with batteries in it. He walked away and appeared to be all right. Later that night he felt weak and was taken to the outpatients clinic at the Mater Hospital. He returned to the prison in the early hours of the following morning and went to bed. Before 8 a.m. he was found to have serious breathing difficulties and was transferred back to the Mater. He was sent to Beaumont Hospital, where he had an operation, and was transferred back to the Mater. He died in the Mater on 3 July without ever regaining consciousness.

A crucial aspect of the running of our prisons is a robust system of external oversight through the visiting committee system and the inspectorate of prisons. I regret to say that the latter is in considerably better shape than the former.

Most visiting committees have between nine and twelve members. They attend a monthly meeting in the prison where they discuss any issues that have arisen during the previous month, and they meet with any prisoner wishing to see them. All prisoners have the right to put their names down to be seen by the visiting committee. Sometimes they appeal to them against decisions made by the governor, even though the visiting committee doesn't have any real power in that field. The committee often hears grievances and complaints and makes representations on behalf of the prisoner. These might be about things like temporary release or family issues.

When I took over as governor of Mountjoy in 1984, the practice was that the governor always attended the visiting committee meetings and sat next to the chairman. The chairman ran the meeting, but when the prisoners came into the meeting to highlight their problems it was usually the governor who dealt with them, not the committee members. Indeed, the members were often very uncomfortable dealing directly with prisoners.

On my appointment as governor I told the visiting committee that I would not be attending their meetings, but I would be available to deal with any problems or issues that they wished to raise with me after their meetings. I explained that I believed visiting committees should be totally independent of local management, and that prisoners should be able to see them on their own to discuss whatever issues they wanted to in private. That would give the visiting committee a sense of independence and distance from the prison establishment, and it would also give the prisoner more confidence that the visiting committee was genuinely independent. This could never happen if the governor was sitting at the table when the prisoner entered the room to talk to the committee. Of course, this forced the visiting committee members themselves to stand up and be counted, because many of them actually hid behind the governor. Some members were opposed to my decision, while others strongly welcomed it. After a short time it became the norm.

When I went to Portlaoise in 1988 I did the very same thing; however, the visiting committee there at that time, dealing with subversives, was taken aback at this policy and asked me not to implement it. Nevertheless, I went ahead and never sat in on visiting committee meetings in Portlaoise. Very quickly it became much more independent and I think was a far stronger committee as a result.

In the old days, visiting committees were appointed, generally speaking, in a non-political way. The original philosophy of the 1925 Act establishing the visiting committee system was that they would be made up of people from the local communities where prisons were situated, to be a sort of watchdog on their prisons, making sure that prisoners were not abused or neglected. When Loughan House was opened in 1972, the governor was asked to nominate a number of local people who would be suitable for appointment to the visiting committee there, and I recall that when they were appointed their political affiliations were not raised at all. That was the case in all prisons then: people were chosen for membership of visiting committees as responsible members of society, and they accepted their appointments in voluntary fulfilment of a civic duty.

In the 1990s, however, this changed. Members of visiting committees were appointed from all over the country. So you had the situation of visiting committee members travelling from North Donegal to Cork Prison or from South Kerry to Loughan House in County Cavan. In Mountjoy, one or two members were from Dublin and the rest were from all over the country, which meant they travelled hundreds of miles to and from meetings. Some people were on two or three different visiting committees, so that it was almost a full-time activity for them. Because of the generous expenses paid for all this travel, the system was open to abuse by politicians wanting to give supporters nice little earners. All political parties were guilty of this: when one party gained control, they dumped all the people that had an allegiance to the opposition and replaced them with their own.

Over the years a number of people who served on visiting committees – including some of the political activists – were genuinely interested in the welfare of prisoners and their families and really took their appointments seriously; however, they were always contaminated by those political activists who were only in it for the glory and the expenses. Members who took their appointments seriously and asked difficult questions or wrote honest reports were quickly isolated, badmouthed and removed from committees at the first opportunity. That visiting committees became the plaything of politicians brought the whole system into disrepute.

When Michael McDowell was Minister for Justice, he put a cap on expenses. It is less lucrative nowadays than it used to be, but governments still appoint people to visiting committees generally on the basis of their political affiliations. Indeed, the vast numbers of people on visiting committees now are appointed on this basis.

A further deficiency in the system is that very seldom, if ever, is anybody appointed to a visiting committee from the areas from which prisoners originate. Most members are from affluent areas from which few prisoners come. So there are rarely people on the visiting committees with in-depth understanding of prisoners' backgrounds, representing the interests of their families and communities.

Unlike the visiting committee system, the independent prison inspectorate is operating in the way it was designed to. Mr Justice Dermot Kinlen was appointed the first Inspector of Prisons in April 2002, and after his death in 2007 Judge Michael Reilly took his place. The inspector has the power to make unannounced visits to prisons to inspect conditions at any time of the day or night, and he reports directly to the Minister for Justice. The inspector often challenges the whole system, and he certainly challenged me while I was governor of Mountjoy Prison. However, we all have to see the bigger picture, and the bigger picture is that it's in the best interests of everyone to have an independent inspectorate. Provided it's given the resources, it will continue to make an important contribution to the prison service.

Many years ago I had a conversation with a young official in the Prisons Division of the Department of Justice in which he said, with great glee, 'Do you know that I am one of the few people who have the power to move a person from one part of the country to another?' He was referring to his role in transferring prisoners from prison to prison. He went on to talk about how much he enjoyed the power he had.

I was horrified at this attitude. Such a mindset has no place in the prison service, but I met many people both in the system and outside of it who seriously abused the power they had. I always believed that power was a responsibility, and unless it was treated as such it was a very dangerous thing to give to anyone.

Prison staff who swaggered around demanding respect because of their position were generally despised by prisoners and colleagues. The big secret in prison – and indeed in life – is to earn respect, not to expect it or demand it. Once you have earned people's respect – in the case of prisons, from the prisoners and the staff – then you are on a winner.

I believe that leadership is about getting the best out of others, and you definitely don't do that by humiliating or terrorizing them. Something I found to be very helpful, and was always appreciated by staff, prisoners and members of the public, was to take time to explain my decisions. It was amazing how often a prisoner would say 'Thank you, governor' after I had punished him for a breach of the rules. He was thanking me for the time I had taken to explain the reasons for my decision.

I believe that there's good in every human being, and my job was to find it and nurture it. I accepted from day one that I couldn't force people, including prisoners, to change, but I could sow the seeds by being kind and understanding to them and by listening to their stories. It's no accident that the most used phrase spoken by prisoners was 'Are you listening?'

Another rule I have is never to wrong anyone, and that very much included the prisoners. I believe that it is far better to let a guilty person off than to convict an innocent one. That was often tested in the prison, but I always stuck to that principle. I believe that people in authority should never put the boot in, even when they are in the right. That's often the best time to show a bit of compassion and mercy.

Another important principle is to be honest and truthful at all times. Again, once the prisoners knew and believed that I was upfront with them, they accepted my decisions. When I gave an undertaking to them I always honoured it, and it was the same with staff.

I tried to treat everyone the same, irrespective of who they were. I believe that you can't have one style or approach for one group of people and a different set of values for another group. I applied these basic values in my dealings with everyone, because I believe you can never go wrong by being kind and respecting other people's dignity.

25. My Last Day in Mountjoy

I retired as governor of Mountjoy on Friday, 4 June 2010. I started thinking about retiring late in 2009 and decided I would wait until I had completed my twenty-sixth year of service as the most senior governor in the prison service. I was already the longest serving officer in the prison service, having completed forty-two years on 7 March 2010. I could have continued serving until my sixty-fifth birthday.

One of the main reasons for my longevity in the job was the gift of extraordinary good health; I was never out sick for a day during my forty-two years of service. Another reason was that from day one I made a point of leaving the job behind at the end of each day. Once I came out the gate of Mountjoy in the evening, that was it: I never talked about Mountjoy at home or anywhere else, I never thought about it and I never worried about it. I realize I was very lucky to be able to do so. Over the years I have known several people in positions of authority where the pressure of the job was a killer and they constantly worried about what might go wrong and even woke up during the night thinking about work. However, my modus operandi and my survival strategy was to do my best while I was in Mountjoy and then to forget it afterwards. I got on with family life and enjoyed my daughters growing up. I was very interested in all sports and was very involved with Kilmacud Crokes, my local GAA club in Stillorgan, for many years. I loved gardening, and found that very therapeutic. I served on the boards of many charities and accepted invitations from community groups and parent associations around the country to talk on topics such as parenting, the scourge of drugs, the role of community and the importance of volunteerism. I read a little. I caught up with family and friends. I always kept physically fit, and still do. I go for a run at least three times a week, getting in between fifteen and twenty miles in total, which I find both physically and mentally helpful and a wonderful means of relaxation. Nothing beats running through the countryside, connecting with nature. I had a very full life outside of work.

The other thing that helped me over the years was the unshakeable grounding I got in how to treat people in my childhood in Tipperary. When I look back, it's clear that many of the values I grew up with were central to my conduct as a prison governor. My mother was very strong on honesty and the importance of never wronging another person. Respecting the old and the vulnerable was something that we took for granted; we knew no other way. Canon Hayes was a great influence too: caring and sharing was his priority, and even as children we were aware of his philosophy. Above all, his belief that all people were equal was a powerful message that stayed with me for life, and I still believe that every human being is special and deserves the same respect as the next. The fact that there was an active community spirit in our parish was another major influence: we learned the importance of helping others and got real enjoyment from it and valued it. I believe that there was something of Bansha in what we developed in the Dóchas Centre in Mountjoy.

Coming up to retirement, I knew that I had given it my best shot for twenty-six years: I had few regrets; I had all sorts of wonderful memories and some very sad and terrible ones too. I had worked with many great people and a few who were by far the best human beings I ever met. For all the uncaring, unimaginative and bureaucratic officials I had to deal with over the years, I also met some incredibly helpful and supportive people in the Department of Justice: Dick Crowe, a great visionary; Frank Dunne, a man of the highest integrity and decency and a person who really cared about the prisoner; the late Martin Moran, who did more good in one hour than most of us did in a lifetime; Tom Quigley, personnel officer in the Prisons Division for a number of years, who was a genuine friend to the prison service and to prison governors; Tommy Maguire, a true gentleman; accountant Gay Harris, who modernized the financial system in the service and was a sound man to boot; Michael O'Neill, who was always prepared to listen and was a man of great humanity; Tony Cotter, Frank Lyons, Denis O'Neill, Henry Mitchell and Dave Tyndall, all wise and decent men; Michael Mellett, a good-natured man and decent in all his dealings with me; Bernice O'Neill, an honourable woman who always acted professionally; and Tim Dalton, secretary general of the Department for many years and a good friend to prison governors, always open and approachable.

But since the prison service moved out of the Department of Justice, my relationship with it gradually deteriorated and for the last few years I was out in the wilderness. I stuck to my principles and values and never compromised myself, and despite being in Siberia, I still got great job satisfaction working with the staff in Mountjoy, helping the prisoners and their families in whatever way I could.

Working in the prison service was my life for over forty-two years. I enjoyed every single day of it. I never woke up in the morning and thought, *Oh no, do I have to go in today?* I got insights into areas of life that I would never have got in any other job, doors opened for me that I never even knew existed, and I met some extraordinary people in prison and outside of it. I said on a few occasions over the years that I wouldn't change my life for the world and that if I was starting all over again I would do exactly the same thing again.

Years earlier I had made up my mind that when the time came I would go very quietly, with no farewell functions or 'surprise parties'. So I decided that I would take a week's annual leave starting on Monday, 10 May 2010, and that during that week I would notify the IPS of my intention to retire on 5 June. At that stage I took all the remaining leave due to me, which covered me up to and including Friday, 4 June.

I drove into the prison on the evening of 11 May, getting there shortly after 6 p.m. I parked outside the prison on the avenue and went in the main gates up to my office. Over the previous few weeks I had cleared out my desk and was ready for the off. I gathered up a few personal letters that were under my office door, signed off my governor's journal for the last time, writing that I was retiring on 5 June. I put the zapper for the prison car park on the desk, pulled the door of my office closed and locked it, and put the key into an envelope and under the door of the deputy governor, who was in charge during my absence. I wrote on the envelope that it contained the keys of my office and that I wouldn't be back. Then I went down the two flights of stairs and into the prison grounds, and walked the short distance to the main hall of the prison, calling into the keys' office of the prison to get the numbers of prisoners in custody for the very last time. The numbers in custody completely dominated my time in Mountjoy. First thing every morning it was, 'How many have we today?' And last thing every evening it was, 'How many have we now?'

When I got to the keys' office, a young officer called Gráinne Hyland was sitting behind the old wooden counter with the big numbers book in front of her. I knew Gráinne very well as she had filled in as my secretary many times and was excellent. She was surprised to see me and said, 'I thought you were on leave, governor.'

'I am, but I had to call into my office for a minute,' I said. 'How many have you this evening, Gráinne?'

'Six hundred and seventy-seven,' she said.

'Brutal as usual,' I said.

As I turned to leave I said, 'I'll see you, Gráinne', and walked out the main hall for the last time.

I went out the main gate, took one final look back at the prison, and as I said good evening to the gate officer, I knew that this was indeed the final curtain for me and my link with Mountjoy was over. I drove out the prison avenue and home for the last time. I felt no emotion and there were no tears: I just knew that it was time to go.

Acknowledgements

Throughout my life, and during my career in the prison service, I have been fortunate to meet and work with many outstanding people. I have had to omit many of these from the main part of this book, but I would like to mention and describe here some of those people who made an important contribution to my life and to making the prison service better.

First, going back to my youth in Bansha, I'd like to mention again the late John Moloney, a fine example of the best the GAA has to offer. John's greatest achievement was nurturing the youth of his native parish for generation after generation. For most of my contemporaries he was our role model. Indeed, the amount of voluntary work people put into the GAA in my youth was unbelievable. In the late 1960s Galtee Rovers/St Pecaun's club bought a piece of land close to the village for use as a GAA pitch, and all the work in developing it was done on a voluntary basis – Saturdays, Sundays and every evening for months people came and worked hard for the sake of their parish.

You cannot separate the GAA from the parish or the parish from the GAA: they are one and the same thing. The GAA has a huge responsibility to promote community living and community activities, and I'd say the challenge for the organization now is to connect to the up-and-coming generations, especially at a time of great doom and gloom. It is one of the few organizations that has the capacity to inspire young people and to give them a sense of purpose and identity and a will to live.

When I first moved from Bansha to Dublin, a young neighbour called Bernie Keating came with me and we got digs with Nora Phelan in Windsor Avenue in Fairview. She looked after us as if we were her own children and I'm still in contact with her to this day.

Patrick Looram and Michael Fitzpatrick were the two assistant chief officers during my time in Limerick Prison. Paddy Looram was a lovely man and he was very good to prisoners. Even though he didn't smoke himself, he would always have a cigarette for the most misfortunate prisoners and they all liked him. He was very good to staff too. We used to love to see him on duty on the Sunday we had a match or when there was a big hurling match in the Gaelic Grounds. He would wink and nod at you to go off. Cork man Michael Fitzpatrick was one of the most conscientious men I ever met. I always found him sound and easy to work with, and he was also kind to prisoners and would never wrong them.

Michael Hayes was the chief artisan officer, and he was a great worker and most knowledgeable in the area of prison maintenance. He could turn his hand to anything. He was assisted by a lovely quiet man called Tom Lenihan, another great worker.

As I mentioned in the main text, P. M. Kelly was the clerk in Limerick when I started, and Denis Kelleher and Michael O'Neill were his very able assistant clerks. All three became governors during their careers.

Bill O'Keeffe was the reception officer and greatly admired by all the staff in Limerick. He was a bit older than many of us, but we still saw him as one of us. None of us was the least surprised that he became governor of Limerick Prison for many years. He was very capable and smart and really nice to boot. One little story sums him up. He was up in Dublin one day attending a legal briefing in connection with an action a prison officer was bringing against the Department of Justice. A senior official representing the Department was also there, and when Bill was giving his views on the case to a senior counsel, the official interrupted and said, 'Hey, who's side are you on anyway?' Bill said, 'I'm on the side of the truth.'

The basic grade prison officers could be broken up into two groups: one was a small group of what I felt at that time were elderly people, although they were probably only in their fifties – men like J. J. O'Malley, who looked after the mat shop, where prisoners made floor mats by hand; John Burke, who normally looked after the grounds; Jim Healy, who was a supervising officer; and Paddy Walsh, who was usually in charge of the wood yard. The other was a group of younger, single officers, who I hung around with when I had free time: Pat

Carroll, Frank McCarthy, Jim Madigan, Jim Buckley and Willie Kenny. I joined some of the lads who had a flat – it was actually a small room – in a house in Upper Gerald Griffith Street, about 300 yards from the prison. Pat Carroll had one room and Morgan Downey had another one, so there was a bit of competition for new lodgers. It was mad but the craic was mighty and we seldom slept for long anyway.

Many left the job over the years and the others have all retired now. They include: Jerry Forde, Pat, Mick and Tom Lynch, Joe Costello, Vincent Foley, Richie O'Donnell, Frank McCarthy, Gerry Hoey, Paddy Dowling, Eamon Kavanagh, Jim Madigan, Jim Buckley, Charlie Grogan, John O'Dwyer, John O'Shaughnessy, Tony Cleary and the late Brendan Moore. A few, including Paddy McInerney, Jim Lavin, John Lyons and Willie Kenny, joined shortly after me.

When living in Limerick I played hurling and football with Eire Óg/Commercials, one of the oldest clubs in Limerick. Sadly, it's no longer in existence. The club's downfall was that it never had its own field, a huge disadvantage for any club. The late Con McGrath was the main driving force behind the club in my time.

The late Michael O'Neill and his wife Bridget had a shop across the road from the prison, and they were both good friends to me. I still keep in touch with Bridget and call for a cup of tea when I'm in Limerick.

During my early years I was an active member of the Prison Officers' Association, and I worked with a few people at national level. Jim Wardick, a Tipperary man and the POA's first full-time secretary, was a wonderful negotiator and a man of the highest integrity; I learned a lot from him. I subsequently worked with him when he was governor of staff training in 1980. Roscommon man Michael P. Mulhern was general treasurer at the time, and a fearless activist. The association's president, Tim Nealon, was then the diplomatic face of the POA. He was quiet, refined and gentlemanly, and spoke with a low soft voice, but he was also very able. I found all three to be very committed trade unionists, and they brought about great improvements in pay and working conditions that prison staff still benefit from.

★

I already knew a few prison officers in Shanganagh as I had worked with them in Limerick: Joe Costello, a Limerick man; Michael Lynch and John O'Shaughnessy, both from Portlaoise; and Eamon Kavanagh, who was from Stradbally in County Laois. And, of course, Chief Officer Tim Nealon, who I knew from the POA. The two supervising officers in Shanganagh were John Cotter, who later became governor of Limerick Prison and eventually governor of Cork Prison, and the late Matt Mannix. Matt was a big man, well over six foot and at least seventeen or eighteen stone, and a real character and an extrovert. He had the ability to communicate with the boys and always spoke their language. They respected him and he had great influence with them. But he was also one of the kindest and most good-natured guys that one could meet.

I shared a room in Shanganagh with a young officer called Myles McFadden from County Donegal. Another young man who became a good friend over the years was fellow Tipperary man Martin Corrigan. We went on many trips to see Tipperary play hurling – 'pilgrimages' we called them. His wife Marian used to make us salad sandwiches, which I always called 'cabbage sandwiches'.

During my stint in the Training Unit at Mountjoy in the mid 1970s, Bob Farrelly was in charge of the workshops for the prisoners. He was a decent man and did a marvellous job. Des Mulhare was the chief officer, and he too was a kind and good-natured man.

I found all the staff in Loughan House in 1972 to be decent people and easy to get on with – people like Jerry Forde, who I knew from my days in Limerick, Andrew Lang, Patsy McCorry, Francis McManus, Pat Lindsay, Paddy Martin, Gerry Coggins, Liam McGirl, Tommy Keaney, Pete Fitzpatrick, Jerry McMorrow, Mick O'Donnell, Tom Dormer, Ciaran Kennedy, Tony Gilbane and the chaplain, Father Eoin Collins, were very reliable fellows. And I must mention Tommy McGourty. Although he joined as a prison officer he was a carpenter by trade, and so he was put on maintenance work from day one. He was a great worker and kept the place going almost single-handedly for years.

I lived in Loughan House during my first posting there, and the staff cook, Mrs Margaret McGlynn, was like a second mother to me.

She couldn't do enough for me, and even after I left, every year without fail she used to send me a big home-made Christmas cake in Mountjoy. She was a real lady and I will never forget her kindness.

We had great neighbours in Loughan House. I think of people like the late Brian Dolan, Vincent McGovern of the Bush Bar, the Greens and, above all, our neighbour Martin McSharry. Martin lived just over the road and he was a top-class farmer. He used to call in regularly and was a great friend to Loughan House. He would always give jobs to prisoners when he could. Reverend and Mrs Ritchie were neighbours on the other side of the house, and they too were very supportive. Mrs Ritchie was a member of the Loughan House Visiting Committee for many years.

After P. M. Kelly was transferred from Loughan House to Portlaoise in 1974, Michael Barry took over as governor. Mick was a native of County Leitrim, so in many ways he was coming home, with Loughan House only a few yards from the Leitrim border. Mick was a character and an extrovert. Barney Travers, the chief officer at the time, summarized it perfectly on the day Mick arrived when he said, 'Well, you could hardly get a word out of P.M. he was so quiet, and it looks like we won't be able to stop this man talking.'

Mick and his family lived in the Governor's House when they moved to Loughan House. I really enjoyed my time working with Mick Barry. He was very kind, generous and good-natured, and so was his wife May and all their family. Mick was a man who got stuck into everything that was going on, and he was much more likely to be in his overalls fixing a leaking tap or out saving the hay than sitting in his office. He was a country man at heart, and he was totally at home in Loughan House.

Barney Travers was from County Roscommon, and he had worked most of his time in Portlaoise Prison until he was promoted to chief officer and transferred to Loughan House in 1973. He was a very quiet, easy-going man and an absolute gentleman. One day I got talking to a young prisoner who was being released and was waiting for the bus. I asked him about his time in Loughan House and I happened to say to him, 'If you had a personal problem here, who would you go to?' Without hesitation he said, 'The chief. I'd go to the chief.' I was taken aback a bit, not only because Barney was elderly and I thought that the younger prisoners wouldn't have much in common with him, but also because he was so easy-going I thought they might say, 'Sure, he wouldn't do anything about it anyway.' I said, 'God, that's a surprise. Why would you go to the chief?' And he replied, 'Ah, he is an old man, he would understand.'

The second time I worked in Loughan House in 1977–9, Father Eamon Lynch was a full-time Catholic chaplain there. He was a native of County Cavan and did tremendous work with the boys, not only on religious matters, but also on a human, caring basis. He was very supportive of them in all activities – sport, recreation – but mostly he talked and listened to them, and he was personally very supportive of me as well. Many of the old staff were still there, but new people had also come in, including John Delorey, Eamon Goonan, Chris McCaffrey, John McDermott, Jimmy Waters, Bridget McKenna, Sheila Higgins, the late Ann McMorrow Brady, Ann Greevy and Lillian Byrne. Andrew Lang was still in the general office, and he worked day and night to keep the administration of the house in order and was also a great support and friend to me. Denis Kelleher was then the director (governor), and he and his wife Anne could not have been more supportive to me and my family.

During my first brief stint in the general office in Mountjoy in 1976, while I was training as an assistant governor, I worked with Christy Murray, who could do as much work as ten men when he put his mind to it. Bertie O'Brien, Pat Dunne and Bill Keaty were also very supportive. Bill was a native of Tipperary too, and we worked together for many years and he is still a great friend.

In the two years I spent in staff training I worked very closely with Eamon Kavanagh, the chief training officer. In 1980 there was a huge recruitment drive in the prison service, and that year we trained 360 recruit prison officers, which was a massive undertaking considering the very limited facilities we had and the tiny number of staff involved in training – only four were full-time and one part-time. In addition to Eamon and myself, there was Eugene McNamara, who looked after physical fitness and the drill, and Ambrose Maloney, who looked after self-defence, subsequently called control and restraint training. Training 360 recruits in one year was difficult work, and at times close to slavery, but Eamon in particular worked very hard to get the job done.

During the strike in Mountjoy in 1983, Superintendent Bill O'Herlihy from the Bridewell Garda Station was the officer in charge of the gardaí during the dispute. He couldn't have been more helpful to us, and he ran a great show. The gardaí brought in a big catering van that we called 'Wanderly Wagon', and my namesake Christy Lonergan really looked after us for the two weeks. He fed us like kings.

Two key figures in the production of the first Mountjoy information booklet in 1986 were Damien O'Meara, a basic grade prison officer who was studying for a BL and took on the job of pulling it together; and a member of the visiting committee, Colm Brangan, who worked in the publishing business and offered his services on a voluntary basis, designing the layouts and proofreading.

During the suicide crisis at Mountjoy in the mid 1980s, the Department of Justice official who came to our crisis meeting in the prison was Tom Stokes. He was an absolute gentleman, a man of the highest integrity, and he was very supportive of me both during the meeting and afterwards.

When I went to Portlaoise Prison in 1988, it was my first time working closely with the other two security services, the gardaí and the army. It was a pleasure to work with them, and I found that the senior management of both services were all decent and honourable men and a credit to their organizations. Garda Inspector Noel McCarthy had daily contact with the prison, and no man could have been more cooperative or professional.

The singer Christy Moore is one of the most generous people I have ever met. I wasn't long in Portlaoise when I got a telephone call from him wanting to know if he could come and perform for 'the lads'. I said, 'No problem, but we have five factions here, and they can't or won't mix. You can come, but you must sing for all five groups.' 'When can I come?' he replied. Christy came down to Portlaoise on five separate evenings and sang for each group. He often came into Mountjoy to sing for the prisoners. One evening he was leaving the Separation Unit after singing for the prisoners there when he noticed a locked cell. He asked John Dooley, the prison officer escorting him out, 'Who's in there and why wasn't he at the concert?' John replied, 'That's a man called Anthony Cawley. He's on protection and couldn't go.' Christy said, 'Open that door and I'll sing a few songs for him.' John opened the cell door and Christy sang three songs. Anthony was so thrilled. Unfortunately Anthony died tragically in prison a number of years ago.

An unsung hero of the Mountjoy hostage siege is Chief Officer Vincent Duffy. He was one of the first people on the scene and tried to get the prisoners to give up at the very beginning. They were very abusive to him. Some of them blamed him for their confinement in the Separation Unit. Vincent decided on Saturday evening that he was more of a hindrance than a help, and so he withdrew, saying, 'I'm only making things worse. I'd be better off out of here.' He went back to work in the main prison. If he had had any ego he would have insisted on staying, but he saw the bigger picture. He showed outstanding leadership in a very tense and stressful situation.

As part of our efforts to reform the old women's prison in the mid 1980s, we brought in a hairdresser, Carol Lamont. Carol did an exceptional job, not just as a professional hairdresser, but in creating a sense of normalization in the women's lives. She had a wonderful relationship with them.

Finbarr Wall, principal architect at the Office of Public Works, provided excellent leadership to the team building the Dóchas Centre in the late 1990s.

During my time as governor of Mountjoy, Marcie Barron was the supervising teacher in the Education Unit in the old prison and in the Dóchas Centre. She gave great leadership and commitment to the women at a time when education wasn't really a priority in prisons. She managed the transition seamlessly from the Portakabin in the old prison to the far more modern facilities in the Dóchas Centre. Louise Condon, the home economics teacher in the Dóchas Centre, also worked up in the old prison in a tiny classroom in the old Portakabin, and hers was the most popular room in the place. Every Christmas she had a little party and it was the highlight of Christmas for many prisoners. Louise transferred to Dóchas and her classroom is still a homely and warm place. She continues to prove that there's no substitute for treating people with kindness.

Eddie O'Brien was both the industrial manager and formerly the chef in the Dóchas Centre. As the chef, he made an enormous contribution to Dóchas. Through his efforts the kitchen received many awards for its high standard of food and catering. In addition, the women spent many happy days working in the kitchen under his stewardship, and they learned a lot of skills.

Edel Hibbits served as a prison officer for a number of years in the Dóchas Centre. She was an exceptionally caring woman and was very well liked and respected by all the prisoners. She was involved in the Connect Project and did a super job helping the women to build up their confidence. Subsequently she transferred to Portlaoise Prison, as she intended to get married and live in County Laois. Unfortunately, while driving to work one morning in August 2002, she was killed in a road accident. Sadly, she was at an advanced stage of pregnancy at the time. Even though she had left the Dóchas Centre almost two years before her death, many of the women had not forgotten her and when they heard about her tragic death they were deeply upset.

Two former members of staff who transferred out of the Dóchas Centre on promotion in the recent past, Frances Daly and Mary O'Connor, also made lasting contributions. They were exceptional people, the complete opposite in terms of personality, but an ideal combination as chief officers. I couldn't measure their contribution, except to note that they are still remembered by the women.

James Daly has been in the Dóchas Centre since it opened, and is probably the most popular member of staff. Very early on he was christened 'Arthur Daley' after the character from the TV show *Minder*. Many of the women found in James Daly great humanity and compassion, integrity, decency, maturity and kindness, and they went to him regularly in a crisis, knowing that he cared about them. He made a big contribution to their lives and epitomized all that was best in Dóchas.

Among the many others who gave great service in Dóchas were Julie O'Donoghue, Breda Shasby, Denise McAuley, Aileen Grealy, Martin Butler, Paddy Nolan and Tara O'Connell. Catherine Haugh, now retired, worked in reception for years and was a bit of a legend – a great woman, very kind and very good-natured.

Father Eamon Crossan was the first full-time Catholic chaplain in Dóchas. He was a very quiet and reserved man, but he had a wonderful presence. When he was leaving to take up a post in a parish in 2002 we had a little going-away function, and I think every single woman brought a gift or made some contribution, whether it was a poem or a bit of handcraft. Many of them said the same thing about him: 'He was always here for us. He never interfered, but he was always here for us.' His quiet presence was his strength.

Sister Mary Mullins replaced Father Eamon, and she has spent the last eight years or so as the full-time Catholic chaplain in Dóchas. She is caring, compassionate, a great listener, and a very kind and generous woman. Every minute of every day while I was there somebody was looking for Sister Mary. It's a tough calling to be there for everyone the minute they need you, but she did it with style, generosity and a great sense of basic Christianity.

Dr Catherine Hayes made a huge difference when she took up duty as the first female doctor in the women's prison. She set very high standards and left her mark there. She was succeeded by two doctors who shared the practice, Dr Patricia Carmody and Dr Mel McEvoy, and they continued this high standard of care. Currently there's a wonderful doctor in the Dóchas Centre, Dr Therese Boyle, who has done exceptional work in a most professional and caring way. Dr Helen O'Neill, consultant psychiatrist, is also a most compassionate person. All of these doctors, supported by round-the-clock nursing staff, under the management of Breeda Doyle, have provided a very high standard of medical care that would stand shoulder to shoulder with any institution in the world. Jeanette Campbell was a medical orderly in the old women's prison for years and transferred to Dóchas in 1999. She is a legend and has made a huge contribution over the last thirty years.

The psychological service in Mountjoy has continued to grow and develop over the years, and people like Colm Regan, Ann O'Rourke, Gemma Anslow and Stephen Harper were all very helpful and committed people.

Overall I would say that one of the few areas to make significant progress in Mountjoy for many years was the medical and psychiatric service. The recruitment of full-time nurses, nurse supervisors and managers, along with extra doctors, made a massive difference, however, and the first nurse supervisor in Mountjoy, Nurse Ann Collins, and the complex nurse manager, Nurse Enda Kelly, did great work in restructuring the medical services there. Dr Damian Mohan, consultant forensic psychiatrist, and his team of doctors provided excellent in-house psychiatric services. Professor Harry Kennedy, clinical director at the Central Mental Hospital, also greatly improved in-house psychiatric services in all the prisons, and the only shortcoming now is a lack of beds for prisoners in need of inpatient care, something that is completely down to funding.

From the very beginning of the drama project in 1986, three prison officers did great work: Paul Woods, J. D. Corcoran and Paul Roche got totally immersed in the project and put a huge effort into it. Frances Daly, Jackie Hurley, Ashling Dunne and Tara O'Connell were equally supportive in the Dóchas Centre, and put their hearts and soul into it. But one man stood out above all others and that was John Dooley. From day one he was Mr Drama, and he broke down every barrier that ever existed between prisoners and between prisoners and staff. To say that he broke the mould is an understatement: he was outstanding, and he deserves great credit for the work he put into the plays over the years. But it was not just the plays that he got off the ground: all through my years as governor he organized entertainment for both the men's prison and the Dóchas Centre at Christmas, including bingo sessions, which the prisoners loved. He also played Santa Claus at the children's party at Dóchas and the visitors' waiting room every year. He was the best man to ask if you wanted to arrange anything official or otherwise in the prison, and he was so natural and humane with the prisoners. For me he's a legend and he always will be.

In the early drama productions in the mid 1980s Mick Ferris made a wonderful contribution to stage-building. He was a skilled craftsman and a lovely fellow to work with, always willing to do whatever he could to help. He transferred to Wheatfield Prison when it opened in 1989, and died a number of years ago. Richard (Dick) Keane took over the stage-building from Mick, and he too made a huge contribution over the years. He was also a very skilled stage builder-cum-designer, and he and Alison Doyle designed and built some fabulous, top-quality sets.

In mounting the plays we got tremendous voluntary support from the outside community, especially from people in RTÉ and the Abbey Theatre. I'll never forget the efforts of John Comiskey, who came in from RTÉ to help with the lighting; he was such a generous man, and when our backs were to the wall on the Sunday before an opening night he worked all day and into the night to get the lighting right.

Two outstanding drama performances were staged in Dóchas in the early 2000s, one by Australian Karen Martin, who came to us with her own play, which had been staged successfully in Australia. The play came out of her research about the lives of Irish women transported there in the early part of the nineteenth century. She discovered that many of them were put into refractories, or mental homes, and kept there until they died. Her play was based on the lives of three such women. Three of the four main parts were played by women in the Dóchas Centre, and they were just great. Mary Louise O'Donnell came in from DCU and produced *Factory Girls*, and again it was a fabulous production.

The plays, as well as the tours of Mountjoy by schools and other groups, took a lot of organizing. Eithne Mulhern set up the tours originally and got them well established, and in later years Fiona Moran did mighty work ensuring that they always ran smoothly; the staff in the detail office were also very supportive. And of course the officers who conducted the tours, who worked their lunch hour, week after week, deserve special mention and thanks. Mountjoy's involvement in the Special Olympics was one of our greatest and most rewarding experiences, and once again I have to say that Martin Hickey, the coordinator of work and training, was fantastic and couldn't do enough to support the project.

All four officers who led the Mountjoy work parties over the years – Neill McGrory, Paddy Moloney, Sam Kelly and Mick Purtell – were exceptional and a great credit to the prison service. We were blessed to have them. They left a mark that will last for a long time to come.

The National Training and Development Institute was more than enthusiastic in its commitment to the Connect Project, and their two main workers in the prison, Paula Lawlor and Emma McDonald, were super people. Dorothy Gunne was then the director of the National Training and Development Institute. She was very committed to Connect and couldn't have done more. She was flexible but also very determined that the principles of Connect wouldn't be compromised. She generously shared her wisdom and experience with us. While all the officers who worked on Connect were great, Paddy Kavanagh took to it like a duck to water and the initial success of Connect was very much down to him.

In September 1996 Helen Haughton, the woman who helped bring about a proper visitors' waiting room, suggested introducing a course for prisoners called the Alternative to Violence Programme. It was a personal development programme but really focused on the individual taking personal responsibility for his or her actions. It was presented by trained volunteers from the outside. Prisoners could train as facilitators, but they had to have an outside person with them at all times. The AVP course has been a fantastic success and hundreds of prisoners have participated in it over the years; the feedback has always been very positive.

Ciaran Leonard was the supervising teacher in the male prison during all my time there, and he and a wonderful team of teachers provided excellent educational opportunities for the prisoners.

Over the years hundreds of probation officers worked in Mountjoy and the Dóchas Centre, and they were always helpful and cooperative in all my dealings with them.

All those who have worked or work as chaplains in Ireland's prisons deserve great credit. In the bad old days the sole source of nurturance and support for prisoners were the prison chaplains. The main work of prison chaplains is just to be present in the prison and to be seen by the prisoners as individuals who are not part of the establishment. That symbol of independence is vital, and prison chaplains are often the only connection prisoners have with the wider community. Without doubt the most popular and respected people in Mountjoy were the sisters who worked as chaplains. I recall a piece of research that was done: 'Who would you go to in the prison if you had a personal problem?' An overwhelming number responded, 'One of the nuns.' During my latter years as governor a number of lay people were appointed as chaplains and they are already making a positive contribution.

In the 1960s, civil servants in the Prisons Division of the Department of Justice were ultra-conservative and very autocratic. The first person to break that mould was a man called Tom Woulfe, a gentleman famous in GAA circles for his activities with the Civil Service Hurling and Football Club and for his great efforts and determination to get rid of the GAA ban on foreign games. He was one of the main driving forces against the ban in Dublin for many years before he eventually succeeded in having it removed. He spent a number of years as superintendent officer of prisons (the most senior post in the Prisons Division) in the Department of Justice in the 1960s, and he was the first man to recognize the need to bring a bit of humanity into the whole prison system. He was very friendly, good-humoured and approachable, and was anything but an autocrat. When he visited prisons he spoke to staff, something that was unheard of at a time when even their governors didn't speak to them.

Tom Woulfe left his mark on the prison service, and the changes that he brought about simply by being friendly, approachable and humane set a new trend that underpinned the service for many years. Immediately following Tom Woulfe, Dick Crowe became very prominent in the Prisons Division of the Department of Justice. I have mentioned Dick in the main text, but I'd like to add here that he was one of the first officials to recognize the importance of the role of the prison officer and their great untapped potential. He really did try to develop a service in which prison officers had an important and integral role to play. He also actively promoted a more positive and caring regime in prisons and was totally opposed to any brutality in the treatment of prisoners. He was a man of great intelligence and wisdom, and he once told us as young prison officers in Shanganagh Castle, 'Remember the truth never goes away.'

In the 1980s and '90s I was secretary of the governors' branch of the Association of Higher Civil Servants, now the Association of Higher

Civil and Public Servants, and during that time I got wonderful support from my good friend and colleague Vincent McPherson. There was no better man to be with when going to a difficult meeting with department officials. He was a tough negotiator and never sold out on any issue. He retired over ten years ago, but we continue to be great friends. John Dowling, Sean O'Riordan and Dave Thomas were the three full-time general secretaries in the AHCPS during my time as a governor, and they were all exceptionally supportive.

In Mountjoy I had the great support of Eithne Mulhern as my secretary for almost sixteen years, and she was outstandingly loyal and conscientious during that time. She played a central role in Mountjoy's restructuring in the 1980s, and I couldn't have asked for a more honest or supportive person. Following Eithne's promotion a few years ago, Fiona Moran took over, and she was also a most cooperative, efficient and loyal person. I am greatly indebted to both of them.

Jim Petherbridge was the chief officer in Mountjoy for most of my service, and he was unique: a very cool and capable man, and a very decent one too. We enjoyed a great working relationship and we continue to be good friends. During his last few years of service he was promoted to the rank of deputy governor and continued to serve in Mountjoy until his retirement a few years ago.

Liam Davis, who died in 2010, was the senior chief officer for my first few months as governor of Mountjoy. I could not have asked for a more capable or loyal man, and I greatly admired him. Jim Woods also worked with me in Mountjoy for many years, and he became a very good friend too.

I want to record my thanks and appreciation to all the hundreds of staff of every rank who worked with me in Mountjoy over the years, too many to mention by name but who all made their own contribution. Most of the time it was a tough place to work, but my great consolation was that I could always depend on the staff and they never let me down.

Few people not directly connected to the prison system or prisoners take any interest in prisoners, but a small number of people have done

wonderful work for them and their families. One of the most significant of these is a Dominican sister, Sister Caoimhín Ní Uallacháin, a
former teacher who, in retirement, started the Matt Talbot Trust in
Ballyfermot to support prisoners, ex-prisoners and their families. One
of my best ever decisions in Mountjoy was allowing her into the prison
to visit prisoners from Ballyfermot. She was – and is – a most extraordinary woman. Irrespective of who the prisoner was or what crimes
he had committed, she could see the good in him and was prepared to
give everyone a chance. But she was no fool or soft touch either, and
they couldn't hoodwink or con her. Although she retired officially
about ten years ago, to this day, without fail, once a week she comes
into Mountjoy to visit the prisoners.

Up there too is Father Peter McVerry. I have known Father Peter
for many years. He is a man of great compassion and commitment
who questions our failure as a society to look after the most vulnerable, and his special concern is the youth. Father Peter has been their
friend and advocate for decades, many years before he had a public
profile. Having a public profile is his way of getting attention for
issues of injustice, and his main purpose is doing the sort of work on
the ground that he has been doing for so many years. He regularly
made representations for young people he knew who ended up in
prison. He kept in touch with them during their imprisonment and,
like Sister Caoimhín, he was always there to help them when they
were released.

Alice Leahy, from Fethard, County Tipperary, has spent most of
her adult life looking after the poor, the homeless and the disenfran-
chised through the drop-in centre Trust near Christ Church in Dublin.
Our paths often crossed because prisoners often have no proper accommodation to go to when they leave prison. Day in, day out, Alice
Leahy and her small team offer the hand of friendship to the margin-
alized, treat their wounds, wash their bodies, give them clean clothes
and above all show them acceptance by taking the time to have a chat
and share a cup of tea.

I want to pay tribute as well to the Merchants Quay Project, a drop-
in and drug-treatment centre started and supported by the Franciscans
and staffed nowadays mostly by lay people. Its open-door policy is

unique in the modern world, and I can't overemphasize the importance of that policy: anybody who is in difficulty is welcome and there are not many open-door facilities in Ireland today. It's very important that their work and truly Christian approach is recognized, appreciated and supported.

I thank all the communities, organizations, parishes, schools and colleges who opened their doors to me over the years. It was always a great privilege to be invited and I am very grateful to all of them for their kindness and generosity and the welcome they extended.

I thank all the prisoners that I met over the years, the vast numbers of whom were respectful and cooperative and in many cases more sinned against than sinful.

I want in particular to thank Marsha Hunt for encouraging me over many years to write a book about prisons. She did marvellous work in Mountjoy helping the prisoners to write, and edited a book of their life stories, *Junk Yard*.

I thank Ann Lehane for all her hard work typing this script – without her help and expertise I would have been lost.

I thank the management and staff at Penguin Ireland for all their support and for their belief that I had a book in me. In particular, I thank Patricia Deevy for her patience, skill and support. She has been superb.

Finally, I thank my wife Breda and my daughters Sinéad and Marie for their help, support and encouragement at all times, especially during the many days and nights that I spent writing this book; and my sister Cait, for jogging my memory around my childhood in Toureen. A special thanks goes to my daughter Marie for helping me to conquer the computer – without her help I would have been banjaxed.

Index

He just wanted a decent book to read ...

Not too much to ask, is it? It was in 1935 when Allen Lane, Managing Director of Bodley Head Publishers, stood on a platform at Exeter railway station looking for something good to read on his journey back to London. His choice was limited to popular magazines and poor-quality paperbacks – the same choice faced every day by the vast majority of readers, few of whom could afford hardbacks. Lane's disappointment and subsequent anger at the range of books generally available led him to found a company – and change the world.

'We believed in the existence in this country of a vast reading public for intelligent books at a low price, and staked everything on it'
Sir Allen Lane, 1902–1970, founder of Penguin Books

The quality paperback had arrived – and not just in bookshops. Lane was adamant that his Penguins should appear in chain stores and tobacconists, and should cost no more than a packet of cigarettes.

Reading habits (and cigarette prices) have changed since 1935, but Penguin still believes in publishing the best books for everybody to enjoy. We still believe that good design costs no more than bad design, and we still believe that quality books published passionately and responsibly make the world a better place.

So wherever you see the little bird – whether it's on a piece of prize-winning literary fiction or a celebrity autobiography, political tour de force or historical masterpiece, a serial-killer thriller, reference book, world classic or a piece of pure escapism – you can bet that it represents the very best that the genre has to offer.

Whatever you like to read – trust Penguin.